Don't Take a Joke as a Job

Scott Redington

Copyright © 2012 Scott Redington

ISBN: 9781973118947

The right of Scott Redington to be recognised as the author of this work has been asserted by him in accordance with the Copyright, Designs and Patents Act 1988. All rights. reserved. No part of this publication may be reproduced, stored in a retrieval system, or transmitted in any form or by any means, electronic, mechanical, photocopying, recording or otherwise, without the prior permission of the copyright owner

Disclaimer

This is a work of fiction. Names, characters, authorities, businesses, places, events and incidents are either the products of the author's imagination or used in a fictitious manner. Any resemblance to actual persons, living or dead, or actual events is purely coincidental. Any words or actions attributed to historical figures are used in a fictitious manner in order to progress the storyline of this novel.

For my family, those I lived with and those I worked with.

In the Beginning

The last few days at Hendon were a bit of a blur, my whole intake had received their final exam results and all of us bar one had passed. I suppose this would be the time to say that I felt sorry for him but I didn't, he was a twat and it was small wonder he had got that far.

That's not to say that I breezed through my training, on the contrary it was very hard going and I sometimes found myself being given an extra parade during the evening for kit inspection due to my poor classroom results and the dubious state of my uniform. The first one I couldn't really do much about, I hadn't been the world's best scholar when I had attended school and had left as soon as I could at the age of fifteen with the bare minimum in CSE passes. That had been over nine years before and having to immerse myself back into the classroom environment once again had filled me full of dread. The problem with my uniform was solely down to the lack of shine on my boots. I couldn't get the hang of 'bulling' them; getting the toecaps to shine like a mirror was alien to me. My previous jobs had been on building sites or working in chicken huts, in fact the only time my footwear had shone in the sunlight was the few minutes it had taken to get them out of the box and slip them on before treading in something unsavoury. I never cleaned them, it was pointless, and in fact I would actively avoid touching the bloody things, putting as much distance as possible between us once I had the opportunity to take them off. I dread to think how many hours I wasted in my room at training school with cotton wool, kiwi parade shine and a fair amount of spit, endlessly applying coats of polish before buffing them up. I had my books and prompt cards close at hand so that I could rote learn while I carried out my inane bulling. It wasn't as though I had anything better to do but the bulling and studying made the evenings long, boring and lonely.

***

Hendon Police Training School was a long way from my wife and daughter who were still living in Suffolk; it was also a long way from the world I was leaving. Prior to joining I had been a self-employed builder; well that's what it said on my application form. On reflection I think I might have been 'gilding the lily' (as I would come to know these exaggerations to be called in my new profession) as I had been a labourer and some way short of being able to call myself a builder.

The building game hadn't been my first choice for a career; I had left school wanting to travel and see the world. At that time this was only the domain of the rich and famous and as I didn't fit in to either camp I settled for a job in the merchant navy. Because I was only small in frame and stature it was decided by the recruiters that I would be a catering boy which is ship talk for 'dog's body'. It was a hard life for a sixteen year old, especially one that had led a bit of a sheltered life in the backwaters of a small Suffolk village. However I soon realised that if I was to survive I would have to get street smart pretty damn quick and I set about adjusting to the life of a mariner.

I had signed a contract with a company that hauled liquid cargos around the world. They explained that there would be no passengers to worry about upsetting and plenty of chances to see places that were off the tourist trail. They forgot to mention that the cargo we hauled was so bloody dangerous that most decent places in the world wouldn't let us within ten miles of their shores. Consequently we either docked at some run down god forsaken port or were anchored so far offshore that the only chance of seeing any exotic places were through very powerful binoculars.

One 'exotic' place we did get to visit I could have easily done without. The conflict between the USA and Vietcong had just about reached its conclusion, the Americans still had 'advisors' in the country but everyone else with any modicum of sense had hightailed as far away as they could. The country was about to implode in the vacuum they had left behind and the only daft sods willing to head that way were all on board my ship. I had grown up watching the reports on the TV regarding Vietnam, seen the demonstrations and all the propaganda both for and against the US intervention. When I had visualised seeing far flung countries this had not been on my bucket list. So when we had a company agent brief the ship's crew regarding the dos and don'ts whilst in a war zone I have to admit to being somewhat apprehensive. Most of the agent's advice consisted of doing nothing more than keeping as much of the ships steel hull between us and the outside world.

On our way down the Mekong Delta a burnt out hulk of a large ship was pointed out to us, a BP tanker not too dissimilar to our own, the gaping hole in her bow evidence of the effects a magnetic mine attached to the hull could inflict. Suddenly the sanctuary of our solid, bullet proof hull lost all its attraction. The shrapnel from the blast had shredded most of the tanker's crew and the fire and confusion had just about accounted for the rest. Suddenly sleepy village life seemed very attractive.

To prevent us from being on the receiving end of similar treatment we had small gun boats escorting us, the crews of which would randomly drop sonic grenades that would detonate underwater and ring through the entire length of the ship. The first twenty or so made my nerves jangle but eventually I just learned to adapt and faze them out of my consciousness. In fact I became so unconcerned I managed to ignore all the instructions about keeping within the confines of the ship and wangled myself and my mate an invitation to join the crew of the gun boat to fire off some of their weapons. Working in the kitchen had its upside; we always got the best food and could eat whenever and whatever we liked. Cooking up some steaks for the guys in the boat didn't really fall into that category but I didn't think anyone would mind. My friend brought a crate of beer with him and we lowered our plunder down onto the gunboat before following after it. At school I could never get the hang of climbing up the gym ropes, shinning down one was much better, it turned out I was a natural and I reached the deck with only a few scorch marks on my palms.

On the small craft one of the crew showed me how to load and fire his M16 rifle and my mate was given a Colt pistol. The soldiers had spent the day blasting away at the foliage and forest debris that floated down the dirty river. The trick was to aim just underneath the waterline so that if anyone was using it to screen their approach the bullet would hit them.

The M16 is a very easy weapon to fire and extremely accurate even in the hands of a complete novice like myself. Our new soldier friends had quickly consumed the food I had brought and were making short work of the beer. The empty cans were tossed into the river and after a few seconds I would be instructed to shoot them. Every time I hit one or got close to it they would open another can to celebrate and so the saga continued late into the afternoon.

Bolted to the front of the boat was a large calibre machine gun with a heavy protective plate for the operator to hide behind. I wanted to fire that gun more than anything in the world and was over the moon when the sergeant said that he would take the boat down the river and I could let rip.

However, before we could cast off the Chief Mate on my ship suddenly got wind of where two of his charges were and his call to us to get back on board was neither polite nor friendly. Unfortunately getting back onto the ship necessitated climbing up the rope I had so easily shinnied down earlier and I soon found that my lack of skill in that department was going to be a real problem. Not able to form a step with my trailing foot I was forced to haul myself hand over hand up the rope which was fine until the rope touched the ships side and left me nowhere to hold on to. I hung there perilously close to falling the backbreaking distance back onto the deck of the gunboat until I was unceremoniously hauled over the railings and back on deck. The bollocking I got from the Chief Mate was on reflection far worse than anything I would have endured had I been left to fall.

We left 'Nam' a day later and I never did get to fire that big gun, which was probably just as well as knowing my luck I would have ended up sinking the bloody ship.

***

I worked on the ships for a couple of years until I met the girl that was later to become my wife. Leaving the navy I extended my exulted CV to being able to boast of jobs such as chicken catcher and vaccinator (this being a promotion from having to scrape chicken shit off their cages once they had been moved on to the processing factory). I also worked in a factory that made glass fibre leisure craft, sawing up offcuts of wood that were used to reinforce the hulls. The job was tedious but at least I didn't permanently stink of chicken shit and ammonia. When my wife became pregnant I had to go to work with my father as a builder's labourer to make up the deficit in income. I was not built to be doing this type of work; other labourers were stocky muscly blokes able to lift twice as much as I could. I also had to contend with my father forgetting that I was no longer twelve years old and now had my own family to look after. However it was good of him to take me on as he must have had his doubts that I could perform.

All these unglamorous jobs helped to pay for our mortgage and gave my wife and me a quasi-comfortable lifestyle. We lived hand to mouth without any savings or being able to take any holidays but we were happy and making a life for ourselves. The arrival of our daughter made me feel the need to 'better myself'; being self-employed in the building game was fraught with danger as a couple of weeks of bad weather or work drying up would have spelt disaster for us financially. It was always a constant worry that would keep me awake late into the night.

When I left the navy I had thought about applying for the police cadets but some tearful pleading from my future wife prevented me from doing so, she knew that this would mean I would have to go away from home again. We had been going out with each other on and off during my time in the navy; the six month postings overseas weren't conducive to a stable loving relationship and she foresaw problems if I had to go away again.

***

I still had the desire to join the police, a pipe dream that would see me able to have a stable and fulfilling career and regain a bit of self-respect for myself. Once we had the extra mouth to feed I saw an advert inviting recruitment for the Suffolk police force but I didn't think I had much to offer. I had barely scraped through school and had managed to get minimum grades in my final exams; none of the jobs I had done previously showed any form of police officer potential (apart from my ability to deal with shit from my chicken cleaning days). I threw caution to the wind and applied and was pleasantly surprised when a Sergeant came to my house to visit and have a chat. I was even more amazed when I got through to the next stage and attended their headquarters to take an aptitude test which I passed. I would have gone on to be invited in for an interview had they not stopped their recruiting within months of me passing the competency test.

I was left in limbo until Suffolk let me know that Cambridgeshire Police were actively enlisting and that they would pass my details on to them, so I was ecstatic when I was invited for an interview with the Chief Constable. Three of us turned up at Head-quarters; a lad from the army who had been a sergeant in the Redcaps (military police), another lad who swanned in and was greeted like a minor celebrity by the recruitment staff, and me. It turned out that this minor celebrity's father was already a high ranking officer within the Cambridgeshire force. We were all informed that we had been shortlisted from over a hundred applicants and that this final interview was for the one vacancy that they had open.

My ex-army colleague looked at me and said "We are just here to make up the numbers mate. Foregone conclusion this, it's all about nepotism".

I nodded in agreement, the truth is I didn't know what nepotism was, it sounded something similar to sleeping with dead bodies and once we entered the interview I wished that it had been just that.

I was asked to sit on a small wooden chair in the middle of a vast office whilst the Chief Constable sat behind a desk the size of an aircraft carrier. It was quite demeaning, like being called in to see the headmaster at school only a hundred times worse, this wasn't some open toed sandal wearing liberal who was 'disappointed' in me.   This bloke was some hard arsed copper who had the power to change my life, which he did…but not for the better.

Having established that I didn't get much chance to watch the news or keep abreast of public affairs other than reading the Sun newspaper and then only if someone in the works hut had one, he asked me what I thought was the most important story of the week. I hadn't a clue but suddenly recalled that John Lennon had been shot and killed on the street outside his apartment in America.

"John Lennon being shot on his doorstep sir" I said confidently.

He erupted. "You think that was important?" he bellowed across the vast wasteland that was his office.

"Would have been pretty important to him sir" I replied.

I learnt two very important lessons that day; firstly some people ask questions that don't have a right answer. The question and subsequent grilling afterwards is to establish if you have the moral fibre and ability to be able to argue your corner. The second was that being a smart arse to a Chief Constable will produce a look that could kill and will result in you getting a very, very rough ride in an interview! He ripped me a new arsehole and I staggered out of his office and drove home totally unaware as to how I got there. Needless to say I didn't get the job…it went to the young lad whose dad was in the force; must have been a bloody big surprise for both of them!

A year later I was sat in front of two Metropolitan Police Commanders going through the whole sorry process again. I had mentioned my earlier encounter with nepotism when I was chatting to the Met recruiting sergeant. He told me not to worry as all the officers in the Met were expected to be bastards and therefore they wouldn't have fathers!

I grilled him as to which departments my new interrogators were from and found out that one was from Traffic and the other from CID. During the interview, when they asked me what department I thought I would like to specialise in I told them that I was sure that after establishing my credentials as a patrol officer I would see where my natural bent would take me, I intimated that I was interested in the Traffic department and CID but didn't know enough yet about the skills required for either department. Even I could smell the bullshit in the air but they were obviously desperate so I got the job...I could have walked on fresh air I was so pleased.

The rigors of the medical were not as intrusive as the casual stares I had received in the showers from the resident old queen when I had been in the navy. Stripping naked and touching your toes in front of a couple of doctors sitting on the other side of a desk at the end of the room can't reveal much about your physical and medical condition, other than you have all your own limbs, can bend at the waist and your head doesn't topple from your shoulders when you do so. The medical, interview and my pathetic CV told me everything I needed to know about the Metropolitan Police...they were as desperate to give me a job as I was to take it. A marriage made in heaven...or Hendon whichever way you looked at it

***

When I finished my training at Hendon it was time to face the big bad world and put into practice everything I had learned, my freshly bulled shoes would stave off all evils, the razor sharp creases in my trousers and tunic were capable of scaring the most capable villain into confessing their crimes, I was now one of London's finest. I could march like a metronomic demon, spout chunks of law and recount numerous points to prove in criminal offences.

Armed with my newly learnt skills I met with my new shift hoping that I would inspire some confidence in them with my freshly pressed tunic, gleaming shoes and closely cropped haircut. It was unfortunate that despite being twenty four years old I still only looked sixteen; the uniform being that little bit too big for me made it look like I was on work experience and wearing a grownup's hand me downs.

There were two sizes in clothing at Hendon, too big or too small and the bastards at Hendon must have had a sweepstake to see who they could make look the most ridiculous. My 'outfitter' must have swept the board for my intake; the stuff he handed me gaped around my neck, waist and chest, the trousers having the ability to perform badly in all three areas. When I asked if he had anything smaller he shouted back "No I bleedin' haven't…try Mothercare"; this drew unsolicited laughter from my fellow recruits but only temporarily as they soon had to take their own turn with my tormentor. Some of us had trousers that had to be hoisted high up on to your chest so that the trouser leg hems didn't drag on the floor; your bollocks were forced to part company with each other at the beginning of the day and were only reunited once you could slip back into civvies at the end of the evening. Others had trouser hems so short that they became good friends with the top of the wearer's socks they were in such close proximity to each other.

My trouser belt had to have more notches' put into it as it wasn't tight enough to keep the waistband hoisted just below the edge of my ribcage. I had to remove and re-sew on the shirt cuff buttons in order to make them as tight as possible. When I marched and swung my arms my hands would disappear while the sleeves worked their way, gravity assisted, towards the floor and flapped like foppish flags from the end of my tunic sleeves.

However, without doubt the most absurd looking items were the helmets we had been issued. Some were cavernous, bucket like affairs that rested on the officers ears, the chin strap hanging down on the wearers tie knot. Others were like pimples balanced precariously on top of the head, defying both gravity and inertia. The drill sergeant obviously didn't have the same sense of humour or dress sense as the stores department and had a complete meltdown after we had marched around the parade square for our first lesson. Helmets toppled, trousers slipped down and baggy tunics remained facing frontwards even though the wearer had smartly turned to their right inside the uniform.

We were all marched back into the stores and a very verbal slanging match ensued behind closed doors which resulted in the 'tailors' reassessing our needs, this time with tape measures. Now I am not saying that I returned to my room with a perfectly tailored uniform but at least I didn't look like a scarecrow.

Hitting the Streets

For my first day on shift I was proud to show off my new found ability to look smart and had taken great care in ensuring that my debut appearance with my new work mates wouldn't let the side down.

It was a bit of a shock to see just how scruffy you could actually make the uniform look. White shirts that had been worn continuously for several days at a time developed a grey death like pallor becoming limp and stained, never returning to their former colour even when washed. The problem with serge is that it needs constant pressing in order to get the nap to lay flat and remain uncreased; most of my colleagues had either never run an iron over their strides or had forgotten to switch the bloody thing on when they did. Canteen medals and dried food stains decorated the tunics of a few and in time of great famine would have fed a family of four for a week.

I was introduced to my new shift by the sergeant, who I was pleased to see had paid the same attention to his uniform as I had. He didn't help my cause for popularity though when he pointed out my pristine attire, "This is how you shower of shit should be parading, half of you look like bags of shite tied up in the middle, the other half of you haven't even bothered to make *that* much effort". He shook his head, handed out the beats and jobs for the day before leaving us all to get on with it. One of the older 'sweats' turned to me and said "Let's see how shiny and smart you look after your first pub fight", another added "It'll be a different story once he has been covered in some drunks puke". I was stunned, I had already caused some upset and I had only been at work half an hour...still I only had another thirty years to do!

Probationers at that time spent their shift under the watchful eye and tutorship of an experienced officer. Or as it was in my case, an officer who continually skived off her area to go and meet up with her mates for a cup of tea and a natter. The sergeant had put me with her in order to slow her down a bit and she viewed me as an anchor around her neck.

Any chance to put me down, humiliate me or just leave me standing on the side of the road because I hadn't heard the radio was taken with glee. To make matters worse, nobody at Hendon had thought to mention the age old tradition of declaring to a senior officer when asked that your beat was secure. It was a simple thing and would have taken seconds to explain but this vital piece of information had been neglected in my training. My first encounter with the shift Inspector was at the end of my first shift, I walked into the packed report writing room to find him standing in the doorway. I acknowledged him and he asked me if 'all was correct'. Not being aware of the correct response I told him "Yes thanks, everything's fine". This of course was a huge cause of mirth amongst my colleagues and announced my first big fuck up on my first day.

The correct procedure would have been for me to announce to the inspector "All correct Sir". This term was a throwback to days when officers had specific beats and you were in fact declaring that there was no crime or disorder on your patch, so heaven help the officer if this wasn't the case. In older days when officers did their patrols on foot they would check every alley and pathway to ensure that all the premises were secure. Some would then tie a piece of black cotton across the entrance which would indicate to them when they returned that nobody had been down there since their last visit. That practice had stopped but the traditional declaration had remained.

After that encounter with the inspector on the first day I heard my crew partner telling everyone that I was never going to make it as I was 'bloody useless'. The fact that she had seemingly made a career out of being useless was an irony lost to her. The term given to those who take out probationers was that of 'puppy walker' and although not very Politically Correct by today's standards, adequately summed up the situation quite well. As a probie you knew bugger all and were in fact a liability to both your colleagues and yourself. A good puppy walker would teach their charge the tricks of the trade and try and keep them out of harm's way. My caring tutor had actually purposely put me in danger on a couple of occasions, once sending me to the top of an iron fire escape to cover a rear entrance of a premises we thought still had the suspects in and then neglecting to tell the dog handler that I was up there.

Police dogs you might think would be happy to see a fellow crime fighter when they are working. Unfortunately that's not the case, these evil beasts have only one thing on their mind when they are let off their lead and that is to bite whoever comes their way albeit bad guy or cop... it's all the same to them.

Not aware of this concept I heard the sound of claws on metal and in my innocence was pleased that someone had sent a dog to help me out. It wasn't until this bear like creature fixed its eyes on me that I began to worry something might be wrong. I started to encourage it to go further up the steps by yelling "Go on then get him", and I will never be sure if it was that attitude or the fact that my radio started squawking that made it dash past me and up to the door. The dog handler followed behind his pooch a moment or two later and was completely shocked to find me A) on the stairs and B) unharmed.

"You must be fucking mad being up here when the dog's loose" he remarked as he ran past.

"I got sent up here before you got here" I replied, it wasn't like I had tried to outsprint the hairy beast that had just shot past me.

"Well someone doesn't like you very much then do they?" he added malevolently.

He was right of course, someone didn't like me, and when the shift found out what had happened I could see that some of them had a few concerns.

A short time after this I had a stroke of luck when my mentor got warned for a crown court appearance and was to be away for a few days waiting to give evidence. I got shunted around with whoever wasn't quick enough to get out of the briefing room fast enough. One of these shifts was an early turn and I got posted on the prisoner van with a great character called Gaz. The van was used for picking up arrests that couldn't be placed in a car, shoplifters and dirty jobs such as drunks who had either shat themselves already or were quite likely to do so.

The first job of the day was to visit a section house that was miles off our area, Gaz explained that it didn't matter how far we went as that was what the blue light on the roof of the van was for…getting back to your beat quickly. We had a huge fry up breakfast before heading over to his place to collect his dirty bedding. This was then taken to a laundrette who accepted the cleaning tokens we were issued with each month to keep our uniforms clean. Gaz informed me this practice was a waste of time as some drunk would puke over you the first chance they got and having seen the state of his uniform I believed him; another set of stains would hardly make any difference. He informed me that when your uniform got tatty you went to the clothing van that visited the area every week and requisitioned new kit thereby making the cleaning tokens redundant. This he explained was a real problem for the local laundrettes as they relied on our tokens to make ends meet, so in the interests of keeping the local economy going he had all his domestic washing cleaned instead. It was really quite public spirited of him to be helping out the local economy so selflessly.

We ran his errands and kept ourselves busy all day doing everything but police work and were only a couple of miles away when we got a call to deal with a drunk who was causing a nuisance. I hadn't made an arrest yet and this was going to be my first. As Gaz hurled us through the heavy afternoon traffic with the blue light flashing on the roof and the electric gong sounding out its warning of our desire to get past, I ran through the questions we had been taught to ask at Hendon to ascertain if someone was drunk.

The guy was still causing problems when we arrived in a cloud of tyre rubber and brake dust, he was lurching in and out of the traffic, gesticulating whenever someone objected to his presence by sounding their horn. Gaz mounted the pavement next to the lumbering bloke as we both jumped out and I approached this wretched creature.

"Hello sir, are you ill or injured?" I enquired in text book style.

Both Gaz and the drunk looked at me as if I was insane.

"I'm drunk you twat" was the reply I received from the man once he managed to focus properly on what had been said.

Gaz opened the back doors of the van, "Get in the van Paddy, you're off to the nick". He looked over to me as if to say well go on then, nick him.

I hadn't even established if he was ill or injured, his voice was certainly slurred but that was partly due to the fact he had a thick Irish accent and virtually no teeth. I was also supposed to make sure that his eyes were glazed but due to them being so bloodshot it was hard to tell. He was certainly unsteady on his feet and his breath did smell strongly of alcohol, it also had more than a whiff of halitosis to it.

I eventually relented and said the magic words for the first time, "I'm arresting you for being drunk and disorderly". I started to give the caution but Gaz shook his head and called over to the drunk.

"Just get in the bloody van Paddy and we'll pop you down the nick".

My first arrest placed himself in the van and we headed off to see the custody officer.

After a quick process through custody Gaz checked my arrest book to ensure that I had covered all the points to prove; I had dealt with my first real customer and felt that a milestone in my new career had been passed.

"Scott, I know what they taught you at Hendon" Gaz counselled "but don't fuck about with drunks; they can turn real mean very quickly so it's best to get them banged up in the back of the van as quick as you can. Everything else gets sorted out back at the nick".

It was bloody good advice and has saved my skin on more than a few occasions. I learnt more in that day with Gaz than in the previous few weeks with my designated puppy walker; granted not all of it was police work but it was all related to how you did the Job. It was the first time that I had let myself believe that I just might be cut out for the police force after all.

***

My nemesis returned after three days and things slowly turned sour again. The sergeant, seeing that there was an atmosphere between us cut me some slack and let me go out on patrol on my own despite the accompaniment period not yet being over. As I walked out of the parade room my now redundant mentor was informing the shift that they should keep an eye on me as I would probably get lost.

Determined to prove myself I headed for the High Street; it had a dedicated bus lane which some drivers decided was a better proposition than queuing with the rest of the traffic. We would get no end of complaints from London Transport regarding their buses being impeded and from irate motorists who were playing by the rules and were fed up with these self-important idiots who thought they were above the law.

I didn't believe in reporting people for the sake of it, but certain things really got my back up and this was one of them as there was no need for it. It was nice to hear the bus drivers and commuters tooting and giving me the thumbs up whenever I stepped out and pulled over the errant motorists who had just undertaken everyone who had formed an orderly queue. If I was greeted by those magical words "Haven't you got anything better to do?" my life was complete as quite frankly I hadn't and if I had I would have willingly made time to do it later.

It was while I was waiting for such a victim that I heard the immortal words "Stop that man". Now even during our training that phrase was never uttered, it was something said in a bygone age, long ago when officers were known as Peelers and the city was a much more sinister place.

But I had heard it being shouted, and when I looked up could see a shopkeeper running after a fairly fit looking young man who was gaining distance from his pursuer with every step. I ducked back behind a lamp post unseen and grabbed the lad by his jacket as he shot past.

He had been trying to use a stolen credit card in one of the shops and it had been flagged at the tills; he had run away which had led to his arrest. Gaz brought the van and I loaded my man into it. I had turned out his pockets and found a bunch of keys on a ring, one of them denoting that it belonged to a Honda car.

"Where's your car?" I asked.

"Don't have one" he replied.

"You've got a car key in your pocket".

"That's from a while ago" he replied.

Now I've been lied to on many occasions, I can sometimes detect a lie straight away but more often than not I can't tell immediately. There are plenty of people out there who will tell you a bare faced lie straight to your face and not even flinch as they do it. In cases like that it's best to let them believe that you believe them as this will prompt them to embellish the lie or go on to create others, you are in their eyes a mug and a gullible one at that. Good liars have very good memories but they are in a league of their own. I love to play the affable fool, smiling and nodding as the bullshit tumbles from their lips. It actually encourages them to say more and the more they say the bigger the hole they dig for themselves. Now if someone is telling you a lie about something that seems insignificant to you at the time it's because you don't fully understand the extent of what they are trying to hide and this is your starter for ten.

On this occasion I decided to let my man think that I wasn't interested in the car key and dropped it and all his other possessions into a plastic bag so that they could be booked in at the station. Once he was safely ensconced in his cell I booked out his possessions and went through them with a fine tooth comb. He didn't want me to know about his car... why?

I went back to the shopping centre and walked the entire length and breadth of the carpark. The key on his key ring had a remote locking fob and I pushed the button every time I found a Honda. On the second floor I found it, a fairly new Civic parked in a corner. I opened the boot and found a selection of new items still unopened and in the store bags, they even had the receipts so I could see the order he had bought them in, no doubt all purchased on the stolen credit card.

The car was recovered back to the yard at the police station and I was told that as the arrest had been for a fraud and because I had found the other purchases, CID would deal with it; it was too big a job for someone like me who was still 'wet behind the ears'. I was allowed to help the detectives search the vehicle for further evidence and they gave it the once over happy that it was all in order. I continued to poke and pry and found that a plastic cap over a cubby hole could actually be removed if you pulled hard enough and once it came loose I was able to get my hand into the opening. Inside there was a cloth bag with another bunch of keys but this time all for Triumphs (they were still just about making cars then). I reported my findings to the detective assigned to the case and far from being angry that I had dared to go and re-check the car after he had said it was clean, he was quite encouraging.

I had also noted that there had been a shopping list tucked in the back of my man's wallet and on it he had listed, amongst other things, *set of Stag wheels*. Also on that list were all the items I had recovered from his car earlier in the day.

I was also a little uncertain about the fact that the Honda civic had undergone some welding work on the slam panel under the bonnet, the paint was a couple of shades lighter on the welded section that contained the vehicle identification number. I remembered at Hendon a short input from the Stolen Motor vehicle squad and this had been one of the places to check.

I rummaged through the internal phone directory and contacted them. They asked me a couple of questions then told me to describe the chassis plate that is situated under the bonnet by the radiator. The style of pop rivet used to secure it led them to believe that it had a false identity. I told them about the hidden keys I had found and was informed that Triumph Stags were being stolen by a particular individual on a regular basis. The perpetrator would steal the vehicles from the used car forecourts before changing their identity and selling them on. They suspected that the thief was from the Brands Hatch area and I knew that my man lived near there as we had spoken briefly about the race track.

I shot back upstairs to the CID office; at that time in my career there was still a 'them and us' attitude and the office could be a hostile place towards anyone in uniform. About to enter the lion's den I took a big gulp of air for courage and pushed open the door. The DC who was going to be dealing with the credit card thefts was sitting at the far end of the room. He had a desk next to the window so must have been fairly high up in the office pecking order. I stood in front of his desk and waited for him to finish his telephone call.

"Hi Scott, found anything else?" he joked.

"Well I'm not really sure" I said, "I've got a bit of a hunch". I could see his eyes start to glaze over; he had already given me the benefit of the doubt for double checking that he had searched the vehicle properly and now here I was about to do my very best Sherlock Holmes impersonation. I could tell he had no desire to play Watson.

"I think that the Honda in the back yard is a ringer and I've just been speaking to the guys at Chalk Farm about the keys I found". There was a spark of interest in his eyes which gave me the courage to continue. "They have had a load of Triumph Stags nicked from around the South London area and they have been liaising cross border with Kent who has had the same problem". There was now a definite interest and I explained about the Identification numbers on the Honda and the shopping list. I finished off by telling him that our guy lived in the area the Stolen Motor Vehicle squad thought the thief was operating from. When I had finished he sat there and doodled on the edge of his jotter. I had now committed my credibility and if I was wrong or if he thought I was wrong then I had pretty much confirmed that I was everything my tutor had said I was.

"He looked up and fixed me with his eyes, "Wait here" was all that he said as he rose from his chair and walked over to the detective sergeant's desk. I could see the two of them discussing the situation and weighing me up. I couldn't blame them; here I was just weeks out of training school with a theory based upon a bunch of keys, a shopping list and a conversation with Chalk Farm. The DS nodded several times before picking up his phone and making a call. When he had concluded his conversation he stood up and wandered over to where I was standing.

"John has just been explaining your theory to me" he said.

I assumed that John was the detective I had been speaking to as I only knew him as DC Davies. I nodded and waited for him to continue. "Seems like you may have stumbled onto something that's potentially quite tasty". He dragged a chair over and beckoned me to sit down. "I've just spoken to the guys at Chalk Farm and they are quite excited about the possibility of nabbing this joker". He sat on the edge of his desk and seemed to be weighing up something in his mind, eventually he asked "Have you got a civvy coat?"

I told him that I had and he told me to go and get it while he spoke to my sergeant and squared it with him for me to accompany them on a warrant. I grabbed the coat from my locker and as I left the changing area I could see my nemesis standing by the door.

"Chucking it in already?" she asked with a sneer.

I didn't reply, just gave her a smile and walked past.

"To be honest I didn't think you'd last this long" she called after me.

I sat around the CID office for what seemed an age, making cups of tea and coffee to keep myself occupied and feel a little bit useful. DC Davis returned to the office and waved a sheet of paper at me.

"Got it" he said triumphantly.

He held a search warrant in his hand that had been signed by a magistrate; it was the first of many that I was to see and execute over the next thirty years. Within twenty minutes we were four up in the CID's Vauxhall Cavalier and heading out into the sticks.

The address was in the middle of the countryside and had a sprawling shingle yard with several vehicles parked on it in various states of repair. A Honda Civic similar to the one I had found in the carpark sat in a corner, the rear end completely smashed in and evidence of some recent work evident in the area the vehicle identification numbers should have been. It was a good start but there wasn't any indication that the Stags had ever been there. The DS spoke to our suspect's wife and showed her the warrant; she was tearful but tight lipped. I sat with her in the kitchen while the detectives searched the house and outbuildings.

Donna, as I found her name to be, made me a cup of tea and we sat talking;

she was cagey and I could see that she knew a lot more than she was telling us. I couldn't blame her really, why would she want to shop her own partner? She asked about the reason for his arrest and I told her that he had been using a stolen credit card. Her face went white and she asked whose name had been on the card. I could see no reason for not telling her so I did. The sharp intake of breath and flushed cheeks indicated that I had hit a nerve. By the time I had teased it out of her we were starting on our second cup of tea, this time I was making it whilst she sat and talked.

Her partner and brother had been out the previous evening and had bought a takeaway, her brother had paid with his credit card and it had been the last time he could remember seeing it. He had discovered the loss that morning and phoned to see if he had left it at their house.

It was quite obvious that the man now sitting in the cells at Lewisham Police station had found the card and decided to go on a spending spree. I didn't fancy his chances in court but they would be a lot better than the ones of him having a happy family reunion if he got bail.

The detectives returned to the kitchen empty handed and the DS looked over and gave his head an almost unperceivable shake. I cornered him and explained the circumstances surrounding the card and that the woman was now angry and likely to be susceptible to a kind word or two. He winked "Make a detective out of you yet" he said encouragingly before telling me to have a poke about while he had a chat with the lady of the house.

I wandered through the house and tried to think like a villain; there were obviously not going to be any vehicles hidden behind the sofa but there might be paperwork or at least something to indicate that this was our thief.   My father had illegally owned a shot gun which he had used for poaching in order to supplement our cooking pot, he had built a secret cupboard in the lounge next to the chimney in which he had hidden the gun and the ammunition.

Having been a builder I also had a good idea when it came to structural proportions and when I saw that the built-in wardrobe floor didn't go as low as I would have expected I started to investigate. The DS came to find me only to see me lift out a false panel and reveal a compartment full of old number plates, documents and photographic memorabilia. We had found the evidence we needed and I was fully vindicated (if not a little lucky) in my suspicions.

Despite having been on duty for over sixteen hours I was running on pure adrenalin, the CID were going to interview my prisoner that evening and I was going home to bed as I was due back to work in less than eight hours' time and I doubted that I would be able to sleep.

Back on shift the next morning I was bleary eyed as my suspicions about not being able to sleep had been correct. I had lain awake running everything through my head over and over again and as a consequence I was late up, only just making it into the briefing room before the start of parade. My nemesis noticed me slip into the room.

"Thought you'd buggered off" she said out loud and a small group of officers laughed at her quip.

I hadn't been able to tell anyone about the previous day's job and thought that the sergeant should be my first port of call once I actually knew the outcome. At the end of briefing the sergeant informed me that the Detective Inspector wanted to see me in his office before I went out on patrol. The now familiar voice of doom snickered and called out "Must be a record, you've only been here a few weeks and you're already in the shit". I left the room with her laughter still ringing in my ears.

The DI was an amiable chap and jumped up and shook my hand when I walked nervously into his office. "Good morning Scott, I wanted to give you an update on the job last night. We have charged him with nicking motors to the tune of nearly a quarter of a million pounds. The guy has thrown his hands up and the DS and his team are singing your praises young man". He let go of my hand and sat on the corner of his desk. "That was a great bit of work you did and I know that the lads at Chalk Farm will want to add their thanks". He shook his head "Fuck me, straight out of training school and you chalk up a nick like this. I would have given my right nut for a job like that". He smiled, "Nicking fucking drunks and shoplifters was all I got in my first year!"

He then marched me down to the canteen where the unbelievable happened; he put his hand in his pocket and bought me a cup of tea. Which on the face of it doesn't sound that generous, but believe me when I say that when you are looking for recognition from your peers, that's the way to do it. The whole of my shift were there as the DI explained to my sergeant my involvement in the previous day's job and gave me full credit for the whole thing. When he left, my team got me to explain everything. Everyone seemed pleased for me, all except for one sour faced individual who sat in the corner trying to avoid catching anyone else's eye. It was the last time she ever openly slagged me off and with her no longer on my case I was able to get on and do the job I was paid to.

Snakes and Ladders

You'd think that it would be the people who make the job unusual or interesting but often animals of varying shapes and varieties manage to ruin your day as well.

Anyone who knows me well will tell you that I don't like snakes; and when I say don't like them I mean bum clenching, heart pounding hate them. It's an irrational fear I am told as we don't tend to come into contact with them very often in the UK. I know that there is a nest of adders not more than a mile from my house so I make sure that I never go there and to date they haven't felt the need to come and visit me. It's an arrangement that's suits us all fine. In certain rural parts of the country there might be the odd one or two knocking about but they are allegedly pretty timid and don't venture too far from their nests. So working in one of the busiest areas of London you'd think would be a fairly good chance of avoiding them altogether…

"Papa Kilo Four Five, Papa Kilo Four Five from MP please attend…" Our call sign blurted from the radio and gave us an address to attend in Brockley, the caller apparently having a problem with an unwanted visitor in his garden. The dispatcher hadn't really been able to get much more information other than the man would explain the whole problem when we got there. I was working with Pete Allen that day who had about twice as much experience of policing as I did; a four year veteran of seeing everything and doing everything, if he hadn't been so tight fisted he would have probably bought the t-shirt.

"Just what I need" he grumbled, "sounds like either a trespasser or a bloody tenant dispute. Why can't the bloody call centre filter out this crap and tell people it's a civil matter rather than send us to do it. Waste of bloody time".

Pete may have only completed four years on the street but he had accumulated the cynicism and negativity of a thirty year veteran.

"Well it's not like we had anything else to do is it?" I foolishly observed.

"We were prowling the streets looking for fucking villains, that's what we were fucking doing, now we are dealing with a steaming pile of shit we shouldn't be poking our bloody noses in".

I took the ice cream cone we had just purchased for him as he negotiated the heavy traffic out of Lewisham High Street towards our next call. We had in the past thirty minutes cruised up and down the High Street while Pete checked out all the young female shoppers in short skirts. The sun had made its annual short appearance and most of the female population of the area were celebrating by wearing next to nothing. The only police work we had done was to pull over an ice cream van so that Pete could check out his vendors licence.

"I take it you've got a licence to sell ice creams?" he asked the Cypriot male who was driving.

"I'm not selling, just driving" the man tried to bluff.

"Have you got ice cream in the freezers?" prompted Pete.

"Yes sir".

"Well you're not telling me that you suddenly thought; I know it's a lovely day so why don't I take all my ice creams for a jolly in the van, they'll really enjoy that. Is that what happened sir, sudden desire to take your tutti frutti for a jolly?"

If cynicism had been a currency Pete would have been a millionaire.

The poor driver sat dumbfounded, he had obviously woken up to some rare sunshine and chanced his arm hoping to flog some lollies. Unfortunately for him he had come across some jobsworth who was sizing up to spoil his day.

"Give the bloke a break" I had whispered, "poor sod probably only gets about four days of sunshine a year. I bet most of the time he doesn't even have to switch his freezers on its so bloody cold". I hadn't signed up for this sort of crap, our area had one of the biggest problems in the Met with street robberies and we were shaking down some poor soul who was trying to make an honest, albeit semi-honest, living.

Pete checked the tax disc and kicked the tyres, "I take it it's got an MOT?" he ventured.

At last the officer had asked for something the driver actually had and he rummaged about in the glove box until he found the tatty certificate and thrust it eagerly in Pete's direction. It had a couple of weeks to run before it expired and looking at the state of the van it was going to be a close run race to see which lasted the longest.

"Come on Pete, give the guy a break; at least he's not out there mugging people" I pleaded. I had hoped that my mention of muggers might actually motivate him to look for some. When he was of a mind to be he was a bloody good thief taker but his mood swings affected his performance and today we were at a low ebb.

"What about the poor sods who have got licences who will be put out of business by this fly by night?" he snapped back.

"Fuck 'em, they are all bloody villains around here" I retorted, "Last month they were setting fire to each other's vans and I don't recall you being that worried about them then". There had been a big falling out between two local families and a turf war had developed which had escalated into a spate of arsons and the only jingles to be heard in Lewisham at that time came from the fire engines who attended the smouldering ice cream vans.

Seeing that the officers who had stopped him had reached an impasse he enquired "Would you like a couple of ice creams officer's while we sort this out?"

"We will have two 99's with flakes, seeing as you're asking" replied Pete.

Mr Whippy went into the back of his van and selected two of the biggest cones he had in stock, filling them with ice cream and ramming home a couple of flakes before presenting them to us.

"How much?" enquired Pete.

"I can't sell them to you officer, I haven't got a vendors licence" was the drivers reply. He had obviously dealt with officers in his own country and if he could get away with the loss of a couple of ice creams as opposed to his days takings then he was going to come out on top.

"If I even so much as hear you sounding your hooter I am going nick you for trading without a licence" Pete muttered as he and his overloaded cone disappeared into the sanctuary of the beat car.

I slapped a couple of pound coins on the counter which was all the change I had, "If I was you I would piss off up to Blackheath, I bet you'll do a roaring trade there". I gave him a wink and followed Pete to the car with ice cream running down my wrist.

"Did you just give him some money?" Pete enquired.

"I paid him for the 99's" I said, a little annoyed that he had witnessed the act because now he was going to have a go at me for being soft.

"You're fucking soft you are" he said on cue.

"Blokes just grafting Pete, that's the difference between you and me; you see everything as black and white and I've lived in the real world where people take risks to put food on the table".

He rubbed his thumb and forefinger together "Hear that? World's smallest harp playing for you and your new best mate".

"Pete…you need to shut the fuck up and start licking…your ice cream's dripping into your lap".

He looked down at the puddle that had formed on his groin…"Bet he fucking planned that, the bastard", was all he could muster.

***

I threw the remnants or our soggy ice cream cones out of the car window as we pulled up outside the address we had been sent to. It was a house typical of the area, a semi-detached dwelling that had been sub divided into maisonettes. The garden was encased in a six foot high brick wall and a West Indian man in his late sixties opened the solid wooden gate that gave access to the houses as he beckoned for us to follow him into the garden.

Pete and I had decided that it was too bloody hot to be wearing our flat hats so we left them on the back seat alongside all our other paraphernalia. As we were in shirt sleeves due to the hot weather there was no opportunity to shove my truncheon up my sleeve just in case there were any nasty surprises coming our way. In view of this I eased the leather strap from out of the specially designed truncheon pocket in my trousers and slipped it under my belt, as this pulled my truncheon from its pocket and placed the hand grip where I could get to it quickly if necessary. Initially it went against the grain to suspect that everyone was out to get you but it soon became a pleasant surprise when you found someone who wasn't.

While I was doing this Pete was franticly trying to remove the ice cream stains from his trousers.

"Looks like your cock exploded" I observed, "I think you might need to empty it a bit more often". It was a cheap jibe, the whole relief were aware that Pete's wife didn't enjoy his bedroom advances and he seemed to be in a constant state of sexual tension which probably accounted for his mood swings.

"I bet the bastard knew it wasn't frozen properly, that's why he filled the bloody cone up so much. Probably get salmonella or legionnaires disease".

"How the fuck are you going to get legionnaires, you get that from air conditioning don't you?" I didn't know the full ins and outs of the disease but I was bloody sure that the Legionnaires didn't get it from eating ice cream cones from a dodgy vendor.

"Think about it...that's all air conditioning is, just a bloody big freezer unit that blows the cold air about. Legionnaires would be all I fucking need, another bleeding excuse for the missus to blank me at night".

"Make a nice change from her having a headache though" I offered before dodging into the garden to avoid Pete's angry glare.

Putting aside our petty differences we left the street and entered the garden that served both the maisonettes. There was a distinct dividing line between that which was the responsibility of the upstairs occupant and that which had been tendered to by the downstairs tenant. Half the garden had been lovingly looked after; a well-manicured lawn was surrounded by flower and shrub beds which showed no evidence of any weeds. Bees and butterfly's shared the air and manoeuvred around each other to reap the benefits of the hard work of the resident gardener. A small fish pond, complete with waterfall and fountain laid down the backdrop sound track befitting such serene surroundings. It was a veritable corner of Eden and the gentleman who had let us into the garden explained that it had been his labour of love. The other half of the walled space was overgrown to such an extent I expected to see prehistoric mammals circling the wild and dense fauna. Expeditions in search of previously undiscovered species had tackled far less exciting prospects than this.

The old boy could see our confusion and consternation at being confronted with such contradicting areas within such a small confine. "Mrs Jenkins is house bound" he offered by way of explanation, "she doesn't like me to interfere with her garden though" he added dejectedly.

Pete hissed "Probably tried to give her bush a trim, randy old sod".

Mr Robert's and I both tried to pretend we hadn't heard him.

Realising that his little joke had fallen flat on its face, Pete snapped into official mode. "Perhaps you can enlighten us as to why we are here?"

In his lilting Jamaican accent Mr Roberts explained that on two occasions recently he had seen a snake by his fish pond. The last time had been that morning when both he and the postman had witnessed it taking a dip. The postman had declared that he wouldn't be attending the address again until the situation had been rectified so Mr Roberts had called us.

Now over the past two years I had encountered many situations where my knowledge of the law and procedures had been a distinct advantage and I checked through the indexes' of my mind to see if anything had lodged itself there, dormant and just waiting for a situation like this to arise. There was nothing in there that remotely fitted the bill. I wasn't even sure it was a police responsibility to remove unwanted reptiles from the public's gardens. Pete came to the same conclusion just before I did.

"You need to contact London Zoo mate, get their reptile people out here. They will have all the proper equipment and such…nets and traps, that sort of thing. Not a police job I'm afraid" he said in an authoritive voice.

"I phoned them and the RSPA and they both said that as it's a matter of public safety then I should contact you first.

Wily old git I thought, he's one step ahead of us already and now we are going to be saddled with the job of catching the bloody thing.

"How long ago did you see it?" enquired Pete who was obviously thinking along the same lines as me, fucking RSPCA and London Zoo dumping their problem in our laps.

"It was about three and a half hours' ago" Mr Roberts advised us.

"Be long gone by now" I offered, "won't want to stick around if people have seen it. Stands to reason, snakes are shy timid creatures. It will have been under your gate and down the street as quick as it could".

"No officer, there is a long strip of rubber at the bottom of the gate to stop rats getting in". Mr Roberts pointed out the rubber and the drag lines on the concrete path that evidenced the tightness of the fit between the two. "He is still here...somewhere"

Pete and I inadvertently looked down at our feet to make sure that it hadn't broken cover and was waiting to strike us at the first opportunity it got. We still hadn't established what sort of snake it might be so we were both a little wary.

"How would you describe the snake sir?" I asked.

"It is about three feet long, thicker than a broom handle and has red markings on it" he offered.

"Could be a python. We had one escape when those lads stole that strippers car from the petrol station, don't think that's turned up yet" Pete volunteered.

"Hardly surprising bearing in mind where she was making it put its head every night" I joked.

A few weeks previously a young lady who earned her living by performing 'exotic dances' to the drunken rabble in a pub cellar had pulled up to get some petrol at a local garage in the early hours of the morning, she left the keys in the ignition when she went to pay and before she knew it a group of local tea leafs had jumped into the car, started the engine and driven off into the night. They probably couldn't believe their luck when they saw the aluminium camera case on the back seat and must have opened it to see what plunder they had managed to steal. It must have been quite a surprise when a six foot python emerged having been disturbed from its slumber. The car had been abandoned about a mile away from where it had been taken, the doors wide open, the engine still running and the empty case still on the back seat. A passing cabby had relayed the story in between fits of hysterical laughing, he had seen the car pull onto the pavement and three lads leap out and run like the very devil was chasing them. The guy who had exited from the rear door had been screaming as he had left the vehicle and his shrieks could be heard long after the boys had left the street and taken to a back alley. The cabby also witnessed what he described as 'a snake the size of a small fucking tree' exit from the open door of the car and disappear into the night. No mention of this had reached the ears of the press and the divisional supervisor had threatened everyone than none would. The last thing Lewisham needed was a story that would put it back in the spotlight.

Mr Roberts pondered for a moment, "No it wasn't a python, I seen plenty of them and it wasn't one of those".

I caught Pete's eye and could see him thinking the same thing...bet the old boy had been to one of the strippers 'exotic dance' shows.

"I'll get the nick to call the reptile house at the zoo and see if they can identify it from Mr Robert's description" I suggested. It was a bad move, a very bad move because the call was broadcast over every officer's personal radio and the response was deafening.

"Sounds like a one eyed trouser snake".

"Could be a pyjama python".

"If its head smells of fish it could be that strippers".

"I thought it might be a penis python but mines bigger than that".

The replies just kept coming but not one of them was of any use to us. Fortunately the controller had a modicum of sense and did actually phone the reptile house and describe what we were up against. They were extremely helpful and said that it might be poisonous or not and to give them a call when we had it captured. Fucking brilliant! You could see why they were the bloody experts and we were the idiots faced with the problem of finding it. I bet David Attenborough wouldn't get this sort of run around, not when he had the might of the BBC behind him!

In policing terms we were 'fucked', there were no other avenues available to enable us to 'cuff' this job and with heavy hearts and deep seated resentment we resigned ourselves to our fate.

"Do you have equipment to trap the snake with and transport it?" Mr Roberts asked.

I lifted my truncheon out of my pocket and Pete jangled the handcuffs that he had looped through his belt at the back of his trousers.

"You will need to have something long and stout" he remarked after eyeing our meagre tools of the trade. "I don't think your equipment will be up to the job. These things have fangs you know and if you are not careful you could get a nasty bite".

I heard Pete muttering "No shit Sherlock" under his breath.

"Have you got a broom or something like that we can borrow?" I asked just in case Pete decided to add to his comments. The actual equipment I had in mind would have been a shotgun or flame thrower but we would have needed to have been in Deptford to find a household with that sort of firepower. Brockley was still seen as a posh part of our area despite the murders and street robberies.

Mr Roberts beckoned us into his tidy kitchen and reached into a tall cupboard before bringing out a soft headed broom. Pete pushed past me and snatched it out of his hands. It was obviously going to be every man and snake for himself from now on.

"I don't suppose you've got another one of those?" I asked hopefully.

Pete smirked and said "There was a bamboo cane by the back door, you can use that".

I looked pleadingly at Mr Roberts in the vain hope that he was a two broom man; the house was certainly clean enough for him to be that pedantic. The old boy shook his head and apologised for his lack of forward planning. Just as I was about to despair and resign myself to going on a snake hunt with a bamboo switch he reached into the cupboard and produced a squeegee mop, the type that folded over along the length of the mop head when you pulled the lever on the handle.

Now we're talking I thought as I blocked Pete's greedy little hand as he tried to upgrade his now pathetic broom.

Mr Roberts was explaining that the sponge head on the mop would cushion the force needed to pin the snake down.

I had other ideas and started to unclip the sponge section to leave the wickedly sharp metal plate it was secured to. I gave Pete a superior smile as I ran my finger along the edge of my newly adapted snake decapitator, the French had invented 'Madame Guillotine' and I had come up with the 'Mop Chop'.

"Won't that hurt it" Mr Roberts enquired.

"Not if I'm quick" I retorted.

"Oh I see, you intend to get it quickly" he said, pulling on his white goatee beard as he digested the information.

I was glad that he seemed to be under a misapprehension as to my intentions, if I was unfortunate enough to be the one who found it I was indeed going to be very quick, a quick thrust down with the 'Mop Chop' and that would be the end of the problem, it would also be the end of the snake but I would keep a stiff upper lip and do my grieving in private!

The snake had last been seen by the pond so Pete decided that the first place we should start searching was in the flower bed at the opposite side of the garden. "Why are we looking over here" I hissed.

"Stands to reason, it's got to be in the last place you'd expect it and as far as I'm concerned that's here". With that he shoved the broom into the clump of marguerites and swished it from side to side. The effects were devastating and the majestic upright blooms tottered sideways and fell broken onto the lawn. "I'm sorry Mr Roberts, but I'm really worried that this sort of thing is going to keep happening, it's the flowers you see, they're not cut out for this type of treatment". Pete informed our host with a wink to me.

Mr Roberts tugged on his beard and shook his head in a sagely fashion, "Its ok officer, we have to find the snake otherwise the postman won't call again".

Pete looked over at me, "Well Scottie, you heard what the man said, let's get going or are you intending to leave this to me?"

This was it then, no going back, it was official, I was going on a bloody snake hunt with half a mop and a horticultural psychopath holding a broom. Some days I loved my job, well to be fair most days, but try as I might today just wasn't cutting it. I reached down and tucked my trousers into my socks; there was no way I was going to get bitten where the sun doesn't shine and besides, Pete wasn't the type of team player who would volunteer to suck the poison from my wound. I took up station next to him, slid the mop into the undergrowth and prodded aimlessly in between the shrubs. I had read somewhere that snakes don't like vibration so I had developed a little stomp every time I swished the mop. Stomp, swish, wiggle the hips in preparation for the next swing, stomp, swish wiggle. It was a good easy rhythm and I worked my way effortlessly along to the rose bed.

"What the fuck are you playing at" hissed a bemused Pete, "It's not bleeding 'Come Dancing' you big Jessie".

"Snakes don't like vibration Pete, they are very sensitive creatures and I'm hoping it will have the good sense to piss off elsewhere" I told him, adding "or just attack you instead".

He obviously took on board what I said because when I next looked over at him not only had he tucked his socks into his trousers but he had started to stomp swish and wiggle as well. He had also fallen into rhythm with me and we sashayed together alongside the lawn towards the pond. We only needed a musical backing track and we could have been the Metropolitan Police Snake Samba Team.

We quickly covered the ground across the garden and now faced the task of rooting around in the pond. In our wake were the mangled remains of Mr Roberts pride and joy. Flower heads lay alongside the remnants of the shrubbery, the Somme must have looked like this after a week of shelling and trench building.

Mr Roberts had poured himself a long drink of something cold, and probably alcoholic, to numb the shock. He sat on a kitchen chair he had positioned just outside his kitchen door; close enough to see the action but far enough away to slip inside should the snake go feral and start picking us off. I was under no illusion that we would find the backdoor open to us should we try to follow him into the sanctuary of his house. We were modern gladiators doing battle in the amphitheatre of his back yard and he would signal with either a thumbs up or down to the victor at the end of the contest…be that man or beast.

The reeds and lilies in the pond were quite dense and seemed to take forever to search. Pete had accidentally knocked the fountain so the plume of water no longer tinkled musically into the pond but sprayed randomly over both me and the garden gate. I also noticed that the waterfall was no longer crystal clear but a sludgy muddy mess that oozed rather than flowed.

Pete looked towards me and then over to Mr Roberts, "Drawn a blank here, looks like he is either long gone or is hiding in his burrow".

"Burrow?" I queried, "It's a fucking snake not a rabbit, they live in a nest hence the term 'snake nest' and not snake burrow".

"Alright David fucking Attenborough, either way it's not here is it?"

I couldn't really argue with that, especially as every minute I wasted in dispute with Pete the wetter I was getting from the errant fountain.

"Would you boy's like a drink?" Mr Roberts offered, "Must be thirsty work all that snake charming…" and the old bastard chuckled as he headed to the kitchen to get himself a refill and bring out two cold cans of Pepsi for us.

The drinks were ice cold and we both drank greedily. I had thought about pacing myself and trying to play for a bit of time just in case something tasty came in over my Personal Radio and we could legitimately bugger off and hand this over to the late turn. As is always the case in these types of situations the radio was stubbornly quiet.

"I will let Mrs Jenkins know that you are going to be entering her garden just in case she gets upset". Mr Roberts got off his chair and made to walk towards the pathway that divided the two front doors.

"Well look, we don't want to cause any problems between you and your neighbour, we are quite happy to come back another time if it's going to create any upset" I said hopefully.

"No, no, no officer, I am sure that she will want to get rid of the snake as much as I do and if it's not in my garden then it must be in hers".

Yeah, I thought, along with a couple of lost Amazonian tribes, the dodo and a Second World War Japanese sniper.

Mr Roberts called up to Mrs Jenkins and the upstairs sash window opened with a protesting squeal. A large woman, an extremely large woman filled the opening and shouted back down to him.

"What do you want with all your calling, you old fool" she hollered in a thick Nigerian accent, "I got better things to do than be talking down to you, you know".

"Charming" Pete mumbled, "we would be better off getting rid of her and leaving the old boy with the snake, it would be a damn site friendlier I'm sure".

"Sorry to bother you Mrs Jenkins, but I have two fine police officers here who are searching for a snake I saw in our garden this morning". Mr Robert's manner was gentle and tolerant. "They need to search your part of the garden so they can find it and take it away".

"Have they got a search warrant?" was all she could reply.

"No Mrs Jenkins, I asked them to look because the postman won't deliver until we catch it".

"Why didn't you say that in the first place you old fool".

Pete looked over to me and in a stage whisper said "You know what that means, no postman no giro, lazy cow will have to get off her fat arse and waddle down to the post office to get it".

I knew Pete could be blunt but this was outrageous and typically stereotypical of his views of the obese or unemployed. "Pete, wind your fucking neck in" I mimed.

Mrs Jenkins, having heard all the facts bellowed, "Well get on with it then...and don't go making a mess".

I cast my eye over what had been laughingly described as a garden and could detect a couple of traffic cones, the door from a washing machine and a dozen or so pizza boxes that looked as if the contents had been eaten and the empty box just tossed out from the window above. It would be damn near impossible to make anything any messier.

Sitting in the middle of the wilderness was what once had been a large double sized mattress. Its original blue cover had long since faded leaving only dubious stains and a moulding green slime that possibly had its own eco structure, a veritable micro universe for organisms yet to be discovered by man. I think had Pete and I been perfectly honest with ourselves we would have started our search here. The mattress had everything a homeless reptile could need, bar the neon sign announcing 'snake hotel - room to let" flashing from it.

Being a bit quicker off the mark this time I headed for the corner furthest away from our potential quarry leaving Pete with the unenviable task of tackling the area adjacent to the mattress.

Resuming the search we both fell into our previous rhythm; stomp, swish, wiggle as we carved away across the garden. At this point my radio burst into life; the sergeant wanted a progress report.

"Still searching Sarge, no sign of it anywhere yet" I informed him.

He was in the area so he was going to drop by, it seemed a little suspicious that if he was that close he hadn't already attended being as he was so interested.

"Oh shit!" screamed Pete, "I found it".

You stupid twat, I thought.

"Quick, get over here and give me a hand".

He was standing next to the mattress and I could see that he had his broom pressed down onto something that was writhing in the long grass. I gingerly approached, there was no point rushing, if things turned nasty then at least I would be in a good position to explain to Pete's wife how he died heroically trying to wrestle with the rabid reptile. It would be the least I could do for him.

"For Christ sake get over here and help me". Pete's cries were getting desperate.

"Bollocks" I thought and stepped closer.

Mr Roberts now had a ring side seat; his kitchen chair had been moved from the sanctity of his back door to the corner of the building so that he could get a better view of the proceedings. I did notice however that he was still a lot closer to safety than either Pete or me. I consoled myself that if the snake did turn nasty then all I had to do was outrun Pete. It wasn't a particularly charitable thought, knowingly being prepared to sacrifice your mate, but I was sure that I would get over it.

Pete had indeed found the snake; it was winding itself around the handle of his broom, its blunt head thrashing from side to side and its forked tongue probing the air. It was predominantly grey although it did have little flecks of red on its body but none of the vivid markings I would associate with a python.

"It's ok, it doesn't look poisonous" said Pete who appeared to have become an instant expert in deadly reptiles.

"How do you figure that?" I demanded.

"It's just a plain colour, nature naturally makes things brightly coloured if they are dangerous to warn away other animals" he announced.

"Like the BLACK Mamba?" I enquired, "and I also seem to remember that cobras are dark brown...not much of a colourful warning on them".

"Well there are always exceptions to the rules aren't there?" Pete replied sulkily, "and the cobra has that hood thing that's brightly coloured" he added belligerently.

"Yeah you get to see that just before it bites you...very re-a-bloody-ssuring".

"Stop whinging and get that blade thing of yours on its head".

"Push it away from the mattress, I don't want to be standing with my back towards it" I requested.

"What's the bleeding matter with you? I've got hold of it here".

"Remember snakes live in nests and I bet all his mates and relatives are lying under there just waiting to jump us and free the bugger as soon as we drop our guard".

"Just get a grip and give me a hand". Pete was getting angry at the lack of assistance I was giving him.

"If you remember, Mr Robert's said it was three feet long, that's only about two and a bit feet at a stretch" I cautioned.

"I couldn't give a fuck if he tells everyone he's got a twelve inch knob, we got sent here to catch a snake and I've fucking caught one so the job's a good one, fucking mission accomplished" he snarled "now quit your fucking yap and get that fucking mop over here".

I reluctantly pushed my mop head onto the snakes and pinned it to the ground. Pete, seeing that I now had a firm grip on his captive, immediately pulled his broom away leaving me in sole charge of what was now a very pissed off critter.

"Can't believe you fell for that" he said and winked.

What had been Pete's problem was now mine and I had made a simple rookie error. I had forgotten the golden rule that 'a friend in need' is normally a scheming bastard who is going to try and offload his problem onto you and Pete had shown great aplomb in doing so.

It was at this point I realised that we hadn't really thought the situation through properly; having caught the snake we were at a total loss as to where to put it. It was contained at the moment but was incredibly strong and very agile, it was all I could do to keep it pinned to the ground. My initial idea of 'accidentally' lopping its head off was badly misplaced as it seemed to have a neck the size of a small dog, I would need a bloody big axe to decapitate it and I didn't recall seeing one in Mr Roberts cleaning cupboard.

I keyed the talk button on my PR, "Papa Lima, Papa Lima from Eight One Eight".

The dispatchers voice came straight back, he could obviously detect from the tone of my voice that the call was pretty urgent. "Papa Lima to Eight One Eight, go ahead".

"Yeah thanks, we've got this snake and are going to need some help. Can you get back in touch with the zoo and see if they can send someone to help us box it up and remove it from here?" I asked hopefully.

"Stand by" was his response.

'Stand by, stand by'...it wasn't like I could be doing anything else until someone got their finger out. There was little chance that me and my new pet 'Slippery Sam' were going to be popping down to McDonalds for a burger and thick shake was there?

Mr Roberts was now standing on his chair for a better view "Be careful officer, he doesn't look too friendly" he shouted encouragingly, the beaming smile on his face clearly at odds with his concern. "Mrs Jenkins, come and see what has been living under your old mattress. It's grown big and strong on all those left over bits of pizza you throw down in the boxes".

Mrs Jenkins filled the window frame and bellowed back "Shut up you old fool, them's not my boxes, I'm not allowed to eat them types of things. I have a very serious medical condition you know".

Unsubtly Pete muttered "Yeah your arsehole's only a fraction of the size of your mouth".

"Did you say something officer?" Mrs Jenkins enquired angrily.

"I wasn't talking to you Mrs Jenkins; I'm discussing tactics with my colleague". Pete replied slickly.

"Your tactic should be to remove that snake and your sorry backsides from my garden as quick as you can" she bellowed, adding "you can take them traffic cones with you". She indicated towards the two large orange cones that lay on their sides next to the wall. "I don't know how they even got themselves in here" she declared.

Learning from his earlier close call Pete turned his back away from the window and lowered his voice "She probably had them filled with ice cream and a giant fuck-off sized flake!"

This idle banter between resident and officer was all very well but it wasn't solving my problem...that of what to do with the snake on the end of my mop.

It must have been Mrs Jenkins mention of the traffic cone that spurred Pete into action and he quickly collected one of them and placed it next to me. "Don't know why we didn't think of that before, shove it in the cone and we can keep it there until the zoo arrives".

There were a few flaws that I could see in the plan but it was far better than me standing like a lemon, struggling to pin the damn thing down for the rest of the afternoon. "Great idea Pete but just how do you propose that we get it into the bloody cone. Offer it a pizza slice and then throw it in the cone in the hope that it will follow to retrieve it?" I was a bit sharp but my nerves were getting a little frazzled.

"No Einstein, we lay the cone next to it on its side and you just flick it in".

Actually Pete had a good point so I readily agreed to his plan and in short time we had the cone set up and I manoeuvred my way so I could flick my captive into it. In one slick move the snake was safely launched into the depths of the cone and Pete snatched it up from the ground, holding it like it was the plastic equivalent of the FA cup.

"Eight One Eight, Eight One Eight from Papa Lima"

"Yeah go ahead" I responded.

"Reply from the zoo is that they will not be sending anyone and suggest that you secure the snake in a burlap type sack and bring it to them" the dispatcher informed me.

"Would that be the Metropolitan Police issue snake conveyancing burlap sack they forgot to issue me with at training school?" I enquired sarcastically.

"Yes that would be the one…" The dispatcher had heard it all before and was unfazed by most of the replies he received from the recipients of his messages.

"If they are still on the line you be sure to thank them for me…couldn't have managed without their help". I paused before adding "Just so that you can update the log we've actually contained the snake in a traffic cone and…"

The scream that interrupted me was high pitched and coming from Pete as the snake was no longer fully contained inside the cone and had managed to force itself up inside the tube and now had its head level with his own. Momentarily they were eye to eye and then in the next moment the snake was airborne. Pete in his panic had tossed the cone as far as he could away from himself; unfortunately for me I just happened to be in its direct line of flight. The second scream was mine. I would like to think it was a little manlier than Pete's but I am probably deluding myself. The snake and cone hit me square in the chest and once again I had the beast at my feet only this time it was completely free. It was either good fortune or pure luck but I recovered the quickest and in an instant we were back to square one with the mop pinning it to the ground. In all the excitement I had dropped the transmitter/receiver of my PR and it swung from the battery pack on its cord down by my knee. I could hear the dispatcher calling me and remembered that the last thing they heard would have been both our screams.

"Eight One Eight, Eight One Eight do you receive?"

"Yeah go ahead" I responded.

"I take it that your former statement regarding the snake being secured is no longer relevant?" he enquired.

To avoid further embarrassment I tried to sound as professional as I could "That's an affirmative. We are now back to stage one with it being detained but not secured".

"That's what it sounded like to us here" was all he could say before bursting out laughing.

It seemed like we were keeping everyone entertained today!

Once more the upstairs window went dark as Mrs Jenkins leant out over the sill. "You scream like little children" she sneered.

Pete had recovered his composure and responded with "And you look like you've eaten a couple so why don't you put your head back inside before one of your chins falls out and you end up getting poured out onto the garden like a giant slinky!"

Mrs Jenkins cheeks inflated and she looked like she would explode, and that would have made a terrible mess. "Don't you back talk me" she screamed, "In my country my father is a prince and I will have your job".

Pete took the bait. It was funny that in the past couple of months every Nigerian we had cause to have had dealings with had been the son or daughter of a Prince and the claim was starting to get a little thin. "Have my job?" he enquired, "wouldn't do you any good, they wouldn't have a uniform big enough to fit you".

The air was toxic and even the snake had stopped struggling awaiting the expected fall out (either physically or metaphorically) of Mrs Jenkins response.

It never came; the garden gate opened and in walked Sergeant Matthews who immediately sized up the situation. Mr Roberts, standing on his kitchen chair and mopping the tears from his eyes, Mrs Jenkins, her face puce with rage, leaning dangerously close to the edge of the upstairs window and his two officer's standing knee deep in grass and discarded takeaway pizza boxes both armed with kitchen cleaning implements... something was definitely wrong with this picture.

In a very precise and to be fair accurate manner, Mr Roberts explained the situation to the sergeant. He managed to keep it all together until he got to the part regarding the traffic cone and a fresh batch of tears started to flow down his cheeks. Mrs Jenkins had tried to add her comments but Sergeant Matthews asked her politely to go back inside her flat, telling her that he would deal with her complaints later. Only then did he turn his gaze fully on us. We stood there with our trousers still tucked into our socks, our white uniform shirts soaked from the fountain and the sweat of our exertions. He took a long hard look at what was left of Mr Robert's garden, the broken flowers and battered shrubs. On cue the fountain gave a couple of gurgles and slipped sideways into the murky water and a deathly silence descended in the garden.

"What the fuck have you two jokers been up to" he hissed. "Looks like a fucking tank has driven through the old boy's garden".

"Had to search thoroughly Sarge" Pete offered by way of explanation.

"Oh it looks like you did that alright, a very, very thorough search by the looks of it".

Pete foolishly took it as a compliment and smiled.

"You pair of prats; it must have been bleeding obvious where the fucking thing would have been. Fucking mattress has almost got 'The Snake Hotel' written all over it".

I almost said 'I thought that as well' but decided that discretion was the better part of valour and kept my mouth shut. Sergeant Matthews was a good skipper but he could be scathing when he got upset. It was rumoured that before he decorated his house he would sneer at the old wallpaper and it would just curl up and fall off the walls.

He finally turned his attention to the problem in hand and cast his eyes down towards the snake. It had unfortunately resumed its indignant struggles and was writhing around like a demented demon. He seemed to overlook the fact that I had removed the mop head and that the area I was applying pressure to was now visibly flatter than the rest of the snake's body.

"It's a bleeding slow worm you soft tarts, bloody harmless" he said contemptuously.

I'd seen slow worms before and they had not been anywhere near the size of this thing. "Sorry to disagree Sarge, but that's not a slow worm, that's like comparing Pete's cock to a real penis".

Pete, although not exactly ecstatic with my choice of comparisons agreed that what we had caught wasn't a slow worm.

I added: "Well whatever it is we have still got to take the bloody thing away with us and I have no idea where I can get a sack from let alone one of those burlap ones the zoo mentioned".

"Sod the zoo; they are NFI as far as I'm concerned".

Pete and I nodded in unison with Sergeant Matthew's observations of the zoo being NFI (not fucking interested), it being a common state of affairs when other agencies were supposedly helping the police trying to deal with problems that were nothing to do with catching criminals.

Sergeant Matthews turned to Mr Roberts who had been out of earshot of our group huddle. "Mr Roberts, have you got a bin liner I could trouble you for?"

The old boy nodded and headed back to the kitchen cupboard that had already seen plenty of the day's action. He returned with a black plastic sack. "Is this the type of thing you are after?" he enquired.

"That will do perfectly".

Having given the bin liner to the sergeant he retreated to the safety of his chair and readied himself for the next instalment of frivolity and drama.

Sergeant Mathews opened the sack, "There you go Pete just pick it up and pop it in there".

"Fuck off Sarge...with respect. I'm not touching the bloody thing".

Sergeant Matthews gave him a withering look, we all knew that the 'with respect' comment was almost a get out of jail free card for speaking your mind. It seemed like that simple phrase tacked onto the end of a sentence almost gave you carte blanche to say what you liked within reason.

"Scottie, you'll have to do it then seeing as Pete can't be arsed".

"Stands to reason I can't Sarge as I can't let go of the mop or it will be off on its toes; well its belly" I responded, adding "and before you get the notion of getting Pete to hold onto it so that I can pick it up, I would like to refer you to Pete's earlier answer of fuck off".

We had reached an impasse and all stood looking at each other for some time until Pete suggested, "Why don't you pick it up Sarge, seeing as you think it's only a harmless slow worm and all?"

Sergeant Matthews physically baulked at the idea and pointed to the three chevrons on his epaulette. "Listen sonny, I didn't take the fucking exam so I could be ordered about by a couple of wet behind the ears PC's. Now I'm not the sort of person to pull rank and order someone to do something like pick up that fucking snake, but let's just say that I am the sort that would strongly recommend that one of you did it so that we could get the fuck out of here and get on with the rest of our lives".

The threat hadn't gone unnoticed but neither Pete nor I budged.

"Could always try flicking it into the bag like we did with the cone" I suggested. It was a bit selfish on my part as I knew that I would be the one doing the flicking and would certainly be propelling the snake in the opposite direction to the one in which I was standing.

Pete and the sarge pondered on my suggestion for a few minutes before agreeing that it was the best plan we had and they set about opening the bag and placing it on the ground next to the snake like a giant windsock. On the given signal I thrust the mop forward and the snake skidded across the grass towards the sack. Unfortunately I hadn't got much in the way of elevation with my thrust and the creature went under the bag instead of in it. Despite being a rather portly chap Sergeant Matthews showed a surprising sprightliness in his step as the snake, now free once again, coiled around the nearest object to stop its forward momentum, that being his left leg.

He hopped and kicked out with such force that the creature became dislodged and fell to the ground. Swiftly, and in order to rectify my earlier mistake, I deftly flicked it into the bag Pete still had open…its capture was complete. Pete quickly tied a knot in the end of the sack to stop a repetition of his earlier close encounter with the traffic cone.

Our attention turned to Sergeant Matthews who had gone a deathly white and seemed speechless from his encounter. It would appear that for all his bluster he was as afraid as we were of snakes (or slow worms as he would originally have had us believe). Mr Roberts had been laughing so much it had made him collapse breathless onto his chair and it was odds on as to whether it would be him or the sergeant who was going to flake over first.

Sergeant Matthews regained his composure first and straightened his tie in order to indicate that he was once again back in control of the situation. "Right you two twats; take that thing and dump it at the cemetery".

"The cemetery?" we both said in unison.

"I thought it was going to the zoo?" I added.

"If you jokers think I'm going to let you swan off to the zoo for the rest of the shift you can think again. If they were so keen to have it they could have come and got it but they didn't so fuck 'em".

"But what if it is poisonous?" enquired Pete.

"Then the cemetery's the best place for it, seeing as there are only dead people there".

It was obvious that the sergeant wasn't going to be swayed and that the snake was going to be rehoused a few miles down the road. I did think to suggest that we dumped it on someone else's area. Our neighbours in Peckham were conveniently located and having met some of their residents I formed the strong opinion that it would only be loose for a couple of hours before someone either nicked or ate it. But the sergeant didn't look like he was open to suggestions.

We returned the equipment we had borrowed to Mr Roberts and under Sergeant Matthew's watchful eye apologised for the damage we had caused in his garden. The flowers would take some nurturing, well those that were still intact, and at least the waterfall was no longer muddy silt. The fountain would require a bit of searching for but would hopefully work again. Mr Robert's shook our hands and thanked us for all our efforts declaring that he would remember the day for a very, very long time. He was one of life's gentlemen and I hope he is still able to chuckle when he remembers the whole scenario.

The snake was conveyed to the cemetery as ordered; I had added another knot to the bag and had shut the boot lid of the beat car down on the area between the two knots. The bulk of the bag and its contents hung out over the bumper; my theory being that if it managed to chew its way through the flimsy plastic sack then it would be hitting the road at about thirty miles per hour and we would be long gone before it regained its senses. At the cemetery we cut a slit in the base of the bag and drove around until we felt it was safe to check that our quarry had escaped, it had and the bin liner flapped empty in the breeze.

Sergeant Matthews had written up the message to read that the 'snake' had been a slow worm and relocated. London Zoo never bothered to check and see if we had indeed managed to locate a burlap sack in order to transfer the snake to them. Mrs Jenkins hadn't made a complaint about Pete's attitude, her and Sergeant Matthews had reached an agreement that if she wasn't making a big thing of it then he wouldn't need to inform the environmental people about the state of her garden and the dangerous creatures that inhabited it...all in all it was an incident that looked like it was going to have a happy ending.

The guy who walked into Lewisham Police Station three weeks later quickly destroyed that illusion. He had been walking his dog on the railway tracks close to the cemetery and he had seen a grey snake, about three feet long with red markings on it. Sergeant Matthews had duly noted the description before advising him that as it was on railway property it would have to be reported to the British Transport Police and it wasn't a Metropolitan Police matter. He made the call in front of the gentleman and passed over all the relevant information before adding that before they went to search for it, it would be a good idea for them to get hold of a burlap sack.

***

Patrolling on foot was always seen by some of my colleagues as being a bit of a punishment posting but I have to say that I did enjoy it. It wasn't as adrenaline fuelled as a stint on the area car or being asked to crew up with the divisional dog handler but it had its own perks. Being as I looked like a malnourished teenager (I was in fact in my mid-twenties and fitter than I had ever been) this could lend itself to not being taken seriously but it also meant that women usually wanted to mother me and feed me up. In fact I can't recall ever packing up a lunch box if I knew I was going to be out on foot patrol. One of the beats that I would be asked to cover was the Riverdale Shopping Centre, a modern (for its time) covered mall that boasted most of the High Street giants and plenty of smaller independent establishments. The bigger shops often had canteens that allowed us to get a meal or a cup of tea at staff rates. I always made a point of chatting to the catering staff; I knew from experience that these are the people you need to keep on side. It always amazes me when someone is rude to the very people who cook their food, at the very least you know they are going to get the smallest portion ever and at worse I've seen things added to the dish that have made my stomach turn.

When I was serving on the ships there was a running battle between the salon (where the officers dined) steward and the Chief Engineer; both were raging queens and hated the very sight of each other. The Chief would always be questioning Ada (for that was how the steward was known to us all) about the menu or waiting until he knew that the kitchen had been cleared away and then ordering second helpings. There would be a frantic rummaging around in the slops bin in order to plate him up a meal and he would then insist on examining the kitchen which meant that I had about thirty seconds to plate several more meals in a similar fashion and place them in the hot box, pretending that we always kept a couple back as spares. Ada would always ensure that the Chief had an 'egg' with his breakfast and would hawk up a globule of phlegm and add it to his porridge. It was something that should have been reported to the Chief Steward but I have to admit that I never even contemplated it because as far as I was concerned he deserved everything he got. Those officers who treated the staff with respect would often get an unexpected visit when they were on watch and presented with a favourite sandwich or pudding if we had any going spare at the end of service. It was just mutual respect as we all had a role to play when on board what was a very confined area.

Back in the real world I understood the effort that had gone into preparing the dishes that would be on offer and would always compliment the chef even if they were a miserable sod; let's face it, when you are dealing with staff or the public it can wipe the smile off anyone's face. Over the months that I worked in the Riverdale centre I knew all the canteen staff members by name and a little bit about their lives and for that I would get double portions and more often than not a free cake or pudding.

The smaller shops would always find time to have a quick chat and put the kettle on for a brew. These chats would often result in some useful snippets of information being imparted. I would often know who was seeing to whom, who had changed their car or where they hid it up to avoid getting caught for no tax and insurance, and hear about those who had recently come out of prison and were already immersing themselves back into criminal activities. I would go back to the nick and relay all I had learned to the 'collator', who was by any other description the area intelligence officer. This person would normally be an experienced officer who was nearing retirement and the collator's office was an ideal posting for someone with their vast knowledge and experience. In the age before computers and electronic intel they were the next best thing and just like Wikipedia, the font of all knowledge.

My ability to be able to get invited to have a cup of tea and biscuits didn't only work in the shopping centre and I would usually have plenty of tea stops on whatever beat I was asked to patrol. I would always make a point of calling back to see the people I had originally met under normally quite trying circumstances, victims of burglaries, assaults and domestic violence. Some people were never affected by what had happened to them and didn't need the reassurance of having a policeman call when they were in the area, on the other hand others had been scared witless by the experience and appreciated the visit. Much later on in my career some bright spark (no doubt bedecked with the scrambled egg insignia of high rank or with some fancy Whitehall ministerial Tsar's title) came up with the notion that we should always revisit the victims of crime for a 'reassurance visit'; it was seen as cutting edge forward thinking policing. It's a sad indictment that what was passed down from the old sweats to the new officers as part of teaching the beat craft had been reinvented all those years later at a time when very few officers had the luxury of just wandering around an area in order to show a presence and fly the flag. Unfortunately email, websites and MSN are the new public interface methods for the staff strapped and time poor officers.

During one of my perambulations in a fairly leafy part of Lewisham (well the road had a couple of trees planted alongside it) I was heading to an address where the couple who lived there; Mr and Mrs Pilgrim, had fallen foul to a gang of music lovers who had a hankering for other peoples car stereos. They had been quite pragmatic about the whole affair and even managed to quip that the cassette player was actually on the blink and had taken to randomly chewing up cassettes like a bored puppy. They didn't look like the type that would need any reassurance but you never could tell. Before I could get to their end of the street a young lady ran out onto the pavement and called after me.

"Oh officer, thank god you're here, I've got a real problem. I've locked myself out and can't get back into my flat. I really need to get in as my baby will need feeding any time soon".

I followed her as she ducked back into the small courtyard that serviced a block of maisonettes and pointed out her door, "It's this one" she said expectantly, "do you think you can get in?"

The only house breaking implements I possessed were my size nine boots (which had been used on a few previous occasions to put some scroats door in after they became a little bit hard of hearing when we came calling) and my truncheon which was useful for smashing windows and very little else. "I'm sorry, I don't have the expertise to be able to pick the lock but I can ask the station to call out a locksmith for you" I offered.

"Do the police pay if you call them out?" she asked hopefully.

I smiled ruefully, "No sorry we just act as the middleman in cases like this".

Her face fell, "I can't afford to pay, it's going to be tight this month as it is just to come up with the rent".

I could see tears welling up in her eyes. An emergency call out wasn't going to be cheap and would probably make a dent in most peoples budgets. "Has anybody got a spare key?" I coaxed. "What about your partner?"

"Partner?" she looked blank.

"Baby's father" I prompted.

"Oh him, he fucked off five minutes after she was conceived" she replied, "my mum had one but I had to borrow it last month because I had lost mine" she had the good grace to look embarrassed when she told me. "You must think I'm a right silly cow".

I was surprised that she could read my thoughts so clearly. It suddenly dawned on me that it was just the two of us in the courtyard. "Where's your baby?" I asked, "Is it indoors?"

"Yeah" she replied.

The stakes had clearly been raised and I thought about gently coaxing the door open. This required damaging it but at least I could control where that might be. It wasn't the same as a rapid entry, useful for securing evidence that might be flushed down the toilet or hidden in body cavities. The technique of 'coaxing' the door open relied on locating where the lock was (in this case a single Yale) and then gently applying more and more pressure until the block that captures the locking mechanism is forced from the door jamb. Most are only secured by two short screws and as long as you are methodical and not too violent these will be ripped out of the wood and hopefully won't take half the doorframe with them. If the door has been poorly fitted whereby a large gap has been left so that the lock doesn't fit home snuggly, only then can it be opened using the credit card trick so misused in Hollywood films.

I pushed against the door and could see that there was no chance of slipping the lock, the flat part of the latch was all that I had access to. The maisonettes were a new build and I had noticed that the councils had started screwing reinforcing bars on the door jambs next to the locks to stop people doing what I was attempting. "Have you got a large metal bar attached to the door frame next to the lock?" I asked fearing the answer.

She closed her eyes to visualise the inside of the door and when she opened them she said "Yeah, it's about twelve inches long with four screws going into it. Is that good?"

My heart sank. "Well in normal circumstances I would say yes but it means that I can't force it open without doing a heck of a lot of damage and it will probably be cheaper to get the locksmith". I looked up to the second floor and could see a small transom window open a notch. "Is that one of your windows?" I asked.

"Yeah, it's my bedroom" she replied.

We were game on. Back out on the street I looked down towards Mr and Mrs Pilgrims house and could see what I was hoping for. The last time I visited when they had reported the theft from their car, I had noticed that Mr Pilgrim had the rear of the house scaffolded so that he could replace the soffit and guttering. Resting against the scaffolding was a one piece wooden ladder which would be ideal for what I had in mind. I told the lady to wait in the courtyard and set off to the end of the street to knock on the Pilgrims door, but after knocking several times and receiving no answer I realised they were out. I thought about it for a few minutes before deciding that I was sure they wouldn't mind me borrowing the ladder for a few minutes being as this was a genuine emergency. I shot to the top of it and released the retaining clamps.

Manoeuvring a large fixed ladder without causing any collateral damage is quite a skill and one I had learned the hard way when working as a builder's labourer for my dad. The trick in confined spaces is to keep the ladder upright and balanced against your shoulder. Using this method I was soon able to carry it back down the street to my damsel in distress and as I put the ladder to the wall next to the open window she clapped her hands in glee, obviously seeing an imminent end to her predicament.

The transom wasn't that wide and it soon became apparent that what had seemed like a good idea had potential to leave me in a very embarrassing position, stuck half in and half out of the window, requiring the fire brigade to come and rescue me. There was no love lost between the two emergency services; they referred to us as 'wooden tops' and we returned the compliment by calling them 'water fairies' or 'odd jobs', the latter referring to the fact that most of them had second jobs when they were not at the station. It would be a great loss of face to have to call them out to rescue me and I resolved to chew my arm off first before letting anyone alert them.

The ladder was really far too big for the job and left me at a precarious angle; I was going to have to step off the top and onto the windowsill in order to be able to slide my head and shoulders through the opening. Once I had committed myself to stepping off those rungs there was no turning back as the angles would be all wrong. I removed my helmet, radio and trouser belt before emptying my pockets of all the report booklets and other paraphernalia carried by the modern law enforcement officer. My truncheon and handcuffs followed everything else and I instructed the lady to look after them with her life. A police radio falling into the wrong hands didn't bear contemplating and I knew that if it was nicked I would spend the rest of my career filling in bloody forms explaining why.

I quickly scaled the ladder and using the one piece of kit I had retained; a small plastic six inch ruler, I slipped it into the crack and teased the catch up so that the window could be fully opened. Now came the tricky bit and I tentatively placed my right foot onto the sill. Twisting my body so that I could grip the edge of the window with my left hand caused the ladder to move fractionally and this was my cue to transfer all my weight across and balance precariously on the frame. If I couldn't get my head through the opening I was bollocksed. I carefully eased it into the gap and despite it being a bit tight as my ears passed through, so far so good. I wriggled my shoulders through and hung by my midriff half in and half out the window. There was no graceful way to complete the manoeuvre other than sliding through the opening and down face first onto the bedroom floor. I looked to make sure that I wasn't going to be planting my face into anything nasty when I made that final move as it wasn't uncommon to find in some of the houses I had been in before a pile of stinking used nappies or the odd turd on the carpet albeit human or animal. It had to be said that she wasn't the tidiest of mothers and what looked like a month's worth of washing had been piled up on the floor under the window. This was going to be the first time in my career that a pair of knickers and a padded bra had cushioned my fall.

I landed in a heap, my shins had been scraped raw on the frame as they had followed my falling body through the gap, my knees had clouted the internal windowsill and hurt like buggery. Despite all of this I had managed to get into the premises and allowed myself a moment to congratulate myself on a job well done. During that moment I surveyed the room I had just gained entry to; it was a complete pit. I shouldn't think the carpet had ever been introduced to a hoover or even a dustpan and brush. The bed hadn't been made which isn't something I would normally think twice about but the state of the sheets was something else, they were filthy and stained. Big grease marks had formed on the pillow cases and a large ashtray next to the bed was full to overflowing.

I moved out of the bedroom as quickly as I could and stepped into a small lounge that was in a similar state; the whole place smelt of stale biscuits, dirty bodies and cigarette smoke. I quickly checked the two remaining rooms, the kitchen and the bathroom, and if it hadn't been for the cooker I would have been hard pressed to tell the two apart. Dirty cups and plates littered every available surface in both rooms. Used toilet rolls lay discarded on the floor next to a handful of tampons which fortunately hadn't been used. The bath was full of more dirty washing and a carrier bag bulged under the strain of all the used disposable nappies that had been crammed into it.

The kitchen held a similar bag of nappies and a bulging waste bin. The sink was half full of rancid water and overflowing with dirty mugs and plates. I was starting to get a little panicky as I still hadn't seen the baby; worried, I rushed down the stairs and opened the front door.

"I can't find the baby" I said to her as she stepped over the threshold.

"She's at me mums" she replied.

"I thought you said she was indoors" I replied snappily.

"Yeah she is, she's indoors at me mums across the road, forgot to take her formula over with me".

I felt bloody stupid and had learned a good lesson; never assuming anything. I was sure that the girl hadn't been trying to have me over; she had answered the question truthfully, just not fully.

I relieved her of my helmet and equipment and she snatched up the front door key from the hall shelf and thrust it into her pocket.

"Better not forget that" she said, "don't want you having to come back again do we?" she smiled and I noticed the nicotine stains on her teeth that hadn't yet turned black.

I started to put all my kit back on and refill my pockets.

"I'm really grateful" she said, "do you want to pop back for a bit later and have a cuppa".

I didn't know what the bit was she was offering but there was no way on earth I would drink out of anything in that flat so I made my excuses and stepped out into the fresh air. By the time I had collected the ladder and balanced it on my shoulder she had run down the stairs clutching a baby bottle full of liquid. I smiled as I headed for the road.

"By the way, nice arse" she blurted out.

"Sorry" I asked not sure exactly what she had said.

"You've got a nice arse" she replied and winked.

"Er thanks...I think" was all I could muster. It was hard to move quickly with a bloody great ladder hanging off your shoulder but I made pretty good progress in order to put as big a gap as possible between me and her.

I put the ladder up against the scaffold next to the ladder clamps and was nearly half way up when I was confronted by a very irate Mr Pilgrim who rounded the corner on the scaffold platform to confront me.

"What the fuck do you think you're playing at?" was his opening address. "You stole my fucking ladder and left me stranded on the fucking roof".

It was fair to say that he wasn't that impressed with me.

"I'm so sorry, I did knock before I took the ladder but nobody answered" I stammered.

"Of course nobody fucking answered, I was on the roof you prat" he blustered following me down the ladder so that he could continue his tirade. "What gives you the right to nick someone else's property?" he demanded.

I quickly related the circumstances to him expecting him to understand and calm down.

"That lazy little cow hasn't done a day's work in her life, has a queue of blokes in and out of that flat of hers and now she's got 'em climbing through her bloody window on my fucking ladder" was his response and if anything my explanation only served to make him even more irate.

"I can only apologise" I said in the hope that it would be an end to it.

"Well I'll tell you what you can do young man, you can make a report out for the theft of my ladder" he demanded.

"But nobody's stolen your ladder Mr Pilgrim...it's there".

"I know it's there now I'm not fucking blind, it wasn't there twenty minutes ago though was it? Not there when I wanted to come down off the roof for a piss was it? I've had to take a leak in my new guttering and for the sake of some lazy little strumpet and a bloody sneak thief policeman!" he raged.

"Well you can make a complaint about my actions to the station if you think that would make you feel better" I offered in the hope of placating him.

"I'm making a bloody complaint right now to you and if you don't write it down you'll be in dereliction of your duty" he demanded.

He was actually talking about neglect of duty but it didn't think it would be the right time to contradict him. "Mr Pilgrim, just so that I've got this straight, you want me to record the theft of your ladder as a crime and no doubt expect me to put myself down as the culprit and then what…take myself off to the nick and arrest myself?" It was hard to keep the sarcasm out of my voice.

"That's right young man and I expect to see a copy of the arrest report".

"Mr Pilgrim, I don't want to sound picky and understand that you are extremely upset with me but in criminal law we have to be able to establish certain facts before an offence can take place. In the case of theft the intention in the mind of the person" I indicated to myself, "taking the property" I indicated to the ladder, "has to be to permanently deprive the owner of it" I pointed to him, "and as we can see the property is back where it came from so it cannot be a theft". It was a text book classroom explanation outlining the rudiments of the theft act.

"What a load of bollocks" was his response, "what other sort of law is there?"

"Well there is civil law" I answered helpfully.

"Hardly fucking civil having to piss into your own guttering is it?"

"Like I said I'm really sorry about that". We were going around in circles and I just wanted to get back on my beat. All thoughts of Mr and Mrs Pilgrim possibly needing a reassurance visit had long gone, if anything it was going to be me who needed counselling if I stayed much longer.

"So can I report this as an offence against civil law?" he asked.

Tired of the whole thing I replied "I don't know Mr Pilgrim, I don't have any training in civil law matters, you will need to speak to a solicitor for that".

"So it's going to cost me money to see a bloody solicitor to see if I can report my ladder as stolen is it? What's this fucking country coming to?" Fortunately he didn't go on to give me the benefit of his analysis. "When you get back to the station, be a good lad and find out for me will you". With that he turned and started to climb back up the ladder.

I remembered the reason for me wanting to see him in the first place, "Mr Pilgrim, just before you climb back up, I had originally come to tell you that we weren't any further forward with identifying who stole the cassette player from your car".

He paused mid tread and turned to me "OK son, didn't think you'd get very far with that, not really got much to go on have you. Don't expect to see that back again and besides the new one is a much better model and doesn't eat the tapes, that old one was costing me a fortune. Thanks for taking the time though" and with that he continued up onto the scaffolding.

I'd never met anyone at that time with a split personality but that was probably the closest I had come. I scuttled back to the nick and reported to my sergeant the whole sorry saga.

"So let me get this right. You took his ladder and stranded him up on his scaffold before playing Sir fucking Galahad and storming some maidens castle to rescue a baby that wasn't there thereby forcing the owner of the aforesaid ladder to have to take a leak in his nice new shiny guttering?" he asked.

In summary he had succinctly covered all the salient points albeit in an acerbic manner. I nodded my acquiescence.

"Quite a morning, young Redington; quite a morning", was all that he could say before sending me back out onto the streets.

Before my shift was over I phoned Mr Pilgrims number. Fortunately he was still putting the finishing touches to the guttering, no doubt also disinfecting his new ad hoc urinal. Mrs Pilgrim answered the phone and after I had introduced myself I explained that as far as I could find out there wasn't anything in civil law that covered her husband's query. The phone went dead for a few seconds and then she burst out laughing.

"Young man I'm sorry he's put you to all that trouble. I think you did a very kind thing and I nearly wet me drawers when he told me what had happened. It's bloody hilarious that he was stuck up there on the scaffolding, he's been fannying about with that guttering for days now trying to get it right; I should have taken the ladder away myself. Don't you pay no mind to him lad you've got a hard enough job as it is".

I hung up feeling a whole lot better about the day, especially the fact that I apparently had a nice arse!

The Shit machine

At one stage in my career I thought that I would like to be a dog handler, they had the pick of the calls for the area and always saw plenty of action. Having a snarling, snapping companion to back you up also seemed like an interesting prospect. My first introduction to the dog section was the time I was cornered on a fire escape by one, that could have all ended badly for me but the dog chose to ignore me and ran past. As my career developed my interest became common knowledge and it didn't take long to get a posting onto the dog van if the driver was singled crewed. It made sense for them to have a radio operator who knew the area; often they would be double crewed with another handler and their dog but sometimes staff shortages meant they ran solo. It was a prestigious posting and only sanctioned by the handler if he trusted that the officer assigned to him was up to the job.

In those days there was an 'RT course' (radio transmitter) that was held at Hendon where selected officers would learn the art of pursuit commentaries and the use of accuracy, brevity and speed when on the radio. This ensured that the airways remained as free as possible for the longest periods; it was very evident when listening to transmissions to tell if the radio operator was indeed trained. With the course under my belt it made me eligible for quite a few plumb jobs.

***

Parade started for the night duty and officers crammed themselves into the long thin parade room. It had been a hot and balmy day and threatened to be the same overnight. Already sweat stains could be seen developing on the officers; their white shirts damp both under armpits and between shoulder blades despite the windows in the hot sticky room being open, but there was no available breeze to circulate the tepid air. The occurrence book was read out by the shift inspector and a couple of memos from the chief superintendent added to the overload of information. Apparently the practice of hanging one's clip-on-tie on the PR straps in the shirts was now frowned upon and definite threats were being made by the boss towards those who chose to ignore the warning. We were getting several murders a month and house burglaries were going through the roof but our illustrious leader was more concerned about our neckwear it would seem.

Once the duties were read out officers were posted to various foot beats or nominated a particular vehicle. Those officers on the area car would parade an hour later, their shifts designed to overlap so that there would be at least one car out on the area during changeover. The crew of the area car (or RT car to give it its historic name as it had been the only vehicle to be fitted with a radio transmitter) were given a month's posting so that they knew in advance that they were to come to work an hour later. It was one of the best postings, as the area car always got the best calls directed to it first. The drivers were trained to an extremely high level; the licence classification system denoting an officer's ability to handle the car, a class 1 driver was top of the tree and became one of an elite few. Because I had undertaken the RT course I was often posted as operator and enjoyed the close working relationship one developed with a full time partner albeit only for a month.

I had just had a posting on the car so I was back in the melting pot of potluck with regards to available duties. For a bit of sport it was not unusual to find that the duty sergeant had placed a piece of card in your tray with a big black spot on it. If you got it you knew that you were going to be getting a foot patrol and quite likely very wet during the course of the night because every other officer on parade was going to be hunting you down in order to give you a good soaking from either a water pistol, or adapted washing-up liquid bottle.

The rules to this game were very simple; you would be given jobs over the air so you were required to give the controller your position. This meant that the other officers knew exactly where you were and where you were heading, they would then converge and soak you if you were foolish enough to get seen. The only proviso was that the public were not to be alerted to the fact that this game was taking place. Calls of a serious or sensitive nature would also place the owner of the black spot out of bounds; it wouldn't look very professional turning up at some poor unfortunate's door to inform them a loved one had died whilst dripping water from your freshly soaked uniform onto their lounge carpet.

It was a very subtle ploy on behalf of the shift skipper as it meant that the officers would be constantly on the lookout for their intended victim therefore fighting the urge to find a quiet back alley and grab a quick forty winks. The recipient of the spot would also learn how to get from point A to point B without using main thoroughfares; using back alleys, railway embankments and footpaths being more preferable than being out in the open. In short you learnt to patrol your patch in the same manner that a villain would be looking to avoid detection. It was a fairly common occurrence to find that a local burglar was slipping through the same hole in the fence you were intending to use and several very good arrests were made as a result of this unconventional practice.

I was relieved to find that when I had opened my drawer it just had the same bits and pieces I had left in it the previous day. It soon became apparent who had the spot; it was a young probationer who had been nicknamed Joe after the children's TV character 'Joe 90' due to his oversized specs and the rather wooden manner in which he walked.

Poor Joe was struggling with his new vocation; he was a gentle soul who should have been working for the Social Services and not at one of the roughest nicks in London. I am sure that when the divisional postings were handed out at Hendon some perverse bastard thought that it would either make or break him. He was certainly heading for the latter and I had found him on a couple of occasions curled up in the corner of the locker room crying. It wasn't as if the shift were getting on his back, I had hated it when that had happened to me and now that I held a bit of sway with my peers I would make sure that that my displeasure was felt should anyone go over the top with the new guys. With only a few exceptions, virtually everyone had tried to teach him some street craft, if only to keep him safe and out of trouble. Unfortunately it seemed the harder he tried the further he fell. It was getting to the point of him becoming a liability and once that happened he would most surely get binned and 'asked to resign' (a term used just prior to your being sacked).

His last episode had seen him heading in the opposite direction to an urgent assistant call when one of the girls on shift had taken a bad beating from one of our nastier scroats. He had claimed that he hadn't known the location and was looking for it; the jury was out with regards to him being believed. He was probably the only person on shift who could use this excuse as he had been found wandering on numerous occasions' miles off our patch. Whenever I was on a neighbouring beat to Joe I would team up with him and try to get him to learn the area. A trick taught to me was to say the name of the street you were in as you turned into it and then repeat it along with the name of the intersecting street every time you approached a junction. The theory being that if you needed help you called out your location first because if that was the only transmission you made then the rest of the details could be sorted out when the cavalry arrived. Joe was on his last chance; purposely not backing up at an 'urgent assistance' call was professional suicide as you would never be trusted by colleagues no matter where you were posted.

Knowing Joe had the spot made me nervous; foot patrols were always posted with a partner on nights and I knew that the skipper thought that I was the most patient member of the team with him. I wasn't looking forward to having to drag his sorry arse around the ground trying to avoid the rest of the shift and a bloody drenching for the rest of the night.

"Scott," the sergeant's voice cut through my thoughts, "the shit machine is short tonight and have asked for you to operate for them".

In short, 'the shit machine' was local parlance for the dog van and I had been given the job of crewing it for the night. Not only that but it seemed that the driver had specifically asked for me which was evidence that I was getting to be a face that was known to the dog section. Any applications for the team would involve the 'dog sergeant' (as he was affectionately known) canvasing his staff as to the pedigree of any would be candidates for the post. If your face didn't fit then you would have more chance of winning the pools than ever getting a hound.

"Who's on the van Skip?" I asked.

He smiled "PC Granger and Demon".

The room hushed and I went white, Demon was one of the ugliest dogs I had ever seen, a long haired German Shepherd that looked like a cross between a pit pony and a crocodile possibly the result of a mad breeding experiment undertaken in secret at the Met's puppy farm just outside New Addington. I had witnessed Demon take down a group of Leeds supporters after a particularly violent football match against Millwall. There had been bad blood between the rival supporters for years, and a cup tie pitted them against each other and gave them a chance to renew their animosity. I had been posted as a supporters guide and got the crap job of being one of the team who had to get onto the Leeds supporters coaches and direct them via a safe route into Coldblow Lane, the infamous home of Millwall FC. The 'FC' in this instance not being an abbreviation for Football Club but providing an apt description of its supporters.

When I got onto the coach I was greeted with jeers of derision and a few of their many football chants and songs that were foul mouthed and violent. As we reached the hot zone I warned the driver not to stop regardless of what happened. I then informed the Leeds 'crew' that we were approaching ambush territory and that they should cover their faces with their jackets in case the windows got bricked. The singing abruptly stopped and an air of unrest descended. One of the supporters asked me if there had been any trouble so far and I explained that there had been several nasty fights, some serious injuries and a dozen or so arrests. The same guy then asked if any Leeds fans had been injured; I informed him and the rest of the coach that the fighting had so far been just between the Millwall fans as they warmed themselves up for the main event.

The occupants of the coach looked mortified, if the Millwall mob were prepared to put each other in hospital just what the hell would they be capable of when confronted with rival fans. I noticed the scarves that had been adorning the windows were quickly removed and jackets and coats were being placed over the owner's heads as they ducked down in their seats. I chuckled to myself; it was a trick that worked every time, there hadn't been any problems so far and I didn't want any now; especially as I was the only copper on the bus. When we arrived at the ground, officers who had also been tasked with escorting supporters on the coaches gave me a knowing look as my occupants quietly and quickly evacuated the bus and headed for the sanctuary of the penned terraces.

The match (if it could be called that) was a spiteful and violent affair and the fans baited and taunted each other for its entirety. Although the supporters were all separated by metal fences there was still a real fear that if the Millwall fans could get at the opposition there would be a blood bath and the thin blue line trapped in the middle would get a right good kicking. A friend of mine Gaz, from my early days on shift, was posted in 'the cage', a small narrow strip of no-mans-land that separated the opposing sets of fans. Iron grilles helped to keep the area sterile and Gaz would patrol between the fences, wrapping knuckles with his truncheon of those foolhardy enough to put their hands or fingers through the narrow openings. It wasn't unusual for him to end his shift covered in spit and other dubious fluids, gifts from the animals penned either side of him. I asked him why he never complained about being put in there after one particular match and he answered me by simply emptying his pockets which were full of coins.

The fans, unable to reach each other would throw coins, probably in the hope of injuring their arch enemies, and the majority of these would hit the grilles and fall short; at the end of the game Gaz would scoop them up and claim them as spoils of war. He would make at least five pounds a match and was looking forward to beating his all-time record of twenty five pounds with the forthcoming fixture.

At the end of the match the Millwall fans were all shepherded out of the ground and walked away from the area, the Leeds fans were kept penned in the stands. Gaz spent twenty minutes collecting up his rewards and I saw him shovelling money into his pockets until they bulged, the smile and thumbs up he gave me being a good indication that he had achieved a new record.

Deprived of a punch up with the Millwall fans the Leeds supporters took out their frustrations on the stand they were trapped in. The toilet block was constructed from corrugated asbestos and the fans completely demolished the tatty building and turned it into missiles which they threw over the large metal doors that corralled them and onto the heads of the officers standing outside.

When the gates were finally opened they burst forth with snarls and chants about killing police officers. The reception committee that awaited them soon subdued their gusto as there were up to thirty police dogs waiting for them. They were formed into an impromptu line of fur and teeth, a corridor that would funnel the fans from the stands through to the gates and out onto the street. The long narrow passageway lined with baying hounds and snapping teeth was an extremely sobering sight. Anyone not prepared to just walk quietly through the middle of it would see the nearest dog handler release a couple of feet of lead and allow his charge to lurch forward towards the errant fool who wanted to make a name for themselves. Soon a pile of ragged jackets, trousers, shirts and skin began to build up either side of the path.

Waiting at the reception end of this line I saw what looked like the aftermath of a charge on the Somme, the walking wounded sporting injuries that in some cases looked quite severe. The concrete concourse was stained with blood as the fans limped or were carried away by their friends in order to get clear of the snapping jaws. Whatever fight had been in them when they burst out of the pens had been well and truly knocked out of them by the time they got to the gates.

Slowly the groups were herded back onto their coaches and most seemed to be relieved at arriving alive if not totally in one piece. Wounds were bound from either the meagre first aid kits on the coaches or from scraps of clothing that had not already been torn from their bodies. There wasn't time to let the St John ambulance crews administer first aid and their uniformed officers walked to the doors of the coaches and literally threw bandages and antiseptic creams in through the open doors so that the injured could self-medicate and dress their own wounds on their way home.

Not all of the Leeds fans went quietly, a small group hyped up on bravado and alcohol decided to make a show. Breaking away at the coach park they charged down one of the streets hoping to get to the nearest underground station where they assumed the Millwall fans would be waiting for a scrap. I was amongst a group of officers who were quickly rounded up and sent after the escaping fans. They didn't know it but they were running into trouble as the street was quickly being cut off at the other end by a few dog handlers who were being hastily deployed from the ground. Twenty fans were suddenly confronted by six dog handlers, they either had to go through them or confront the squad of officers who were approaching from the rear. Twenty against six were good odds in their favour and in preparation the more savvy members of the team removed their jackets and wrapped them around their arms. If the dogs should bite them it would lessen the impact.

This was the first time I had ever come across PC Rob Granger and his dog; I had heard the fables and stories but had never had the privilege of seeing him in action. A fact that was about to change and add a fresh chapter to Demons' legendry antics.

The twenty fans roared and charged as one and as the gap between them and the dogs started to diminish it looked as though the officers would be quickly overwhelmed. When the mob was less than twenty metres away the dogs were released. First out of the traps was Demon who, with huge bounds covered the ground between himself and his prey quickly; those unlucky enough to find themselves at the head of the group started to proffer their protected arms against the oncoming animals. However, they were to quickly learn that not all dogs want to just bite as Demon lowered his bull like head and crashed through the front ranks, scything them down like skittles. From where I was standing I could see grown men airborne and tumbling through the air as a result of the impact. Having lost his speed advantage due to the collision he leapt into the air and let his bodyweight crash chest height into the remainder of the group, his giant jaws snapping as he did so. By now the remainder of the dogs had entered the fray and began chewing arms, legs and any another body parts they could get a grip on.

Demon crashed to earth on top of a fat and unhealthy looking man who aimed a punch at the shaggy head that loomed over him. He watched in horror as the dog completely ensnared his fist before biting down onto the unprotected wrist, the screams of the recipient evidence that he no longer wanted to play. The charging line had faltered and lay scattered across the tarmac and all six dogs worried at their hapless victims. Occasionally someone would wrestle their injured limb from the jaws of their attacker only for the dog to find another place to bite and the screaming would start afresh.

The half dozen fans that had been the vanguard of this motley crew quickly assessed the situation and thought it more prudent to turn themselves into the officers behind them. The worst that was going to happen was that they might get a slap or a kick, a far better alternative to what they had seen happening to their friends. With their hands held high to denote their surrender they knelt calmly on the road and waited for salvation to arrive.

Those unlucky enough not to be in this small group continued to struggle and try to fight their way out of trouble. Demon was in his element and even the other dogs seemed happy to just sit back and admire his work as the other handlers caught up with their charges and called them off. PC Granger was howling at his dog to return and was being blatantly ignored by the animal that seemed to be relishing his task.

The cry of "Come here you hairy cunt" echoed down the street, Demon pricking his ears to the call but slyly ignoring it. Eventually he conceded that his fun time was over and responded to his master's voice. Somewhere in his dense skull he failed to register that he still had a good grip on a Leeds United scarf, which no longer bore any resemblance to the one its proud owner had adorned his neck with earlier that day as he had set out for London. This item was torn, bloodied and still attached to the wrist of the wearer who was being dragged unceremoniously along the road behind the hairy beast from hell who had attacked him and all but severed his wrist.

Once safely back with PC Granger, Demon decided that he would show his prize to the handler and sat wagging his tail with both scarf and supporter dangling from his mouth. PC Granger could quite clearly be heard trying to encourage his dog to release the scarf but a three way tug of war was starting to develop. Trying to control his dog and the prisoner was all starting to get on top of the officer and his shouts of "Let go you fucker" to his dog and "just lay still you silly twat" to the supporter could be clearly heard to the end of the street. By this stage those supporters who had surrendered had been placed in handcuffs and we all stood and watched PC Granger struggle, there was no way either I or any of my colleagues were going to put ourselves on offer and interfere between man, beast and prey.

Eventually PC Granger managed to boot Demon in the bollocks and he relinquished his grip to the relief of both the officer and his injured victim. The dog glared at his handler with his malevolent piggy eyes and licked the area that had just been struck. One of the fans who hadn't yet been bitten, a podgy fat lump of acned lard shouted, "Look he's giving himself a blow job"; Demon postponed licking his bruised balls and turned to face the owner of the voice.

A low growl started way down low in his vast chest and he began to slink forward, snatching covert glances across at his handler who hadn't noticed the subtle movement. He slowly inched his way towards his next victim who was now trying to push his way behind the officer who had arrested him.

"Where do you think you're going sonny? *You* fucking wound him up so *you* can take what's coming, I don't want the arse ripping out of *my* trousers" the officer advised him as he shoved the half-witted lad back towards the angry animal.

Before the dog could spring, the sharp voice of the handler rung out "You sneaky fucker, I know what you're up to. Come back here".

Demon flicked a look back at PC Granger and then gave one long menacing growl at the fat fan before returning to his master's side and resumed the examination of his undercarriage.

Of the twenty arrests in that road PC Granger and his dog went down on the arrest sheet for eight of them and straight into the annals of folklore.

***

My next meeting with Rob Granger was some months later when I was once again posted on the dog van. I recognised him immediately and felt a little overwhelmed; I was going to be working with a living legend. He seemed a down to earth chap and we hit it off straight away. Over a cup of tea he explained that things might be a bit different to what I had experienced with other handlers and their hounds.

"When you get in the van Scott, don't make eye contact with him, he hates that. He sees the van as being his territory and he can be a bit funny".

I recalled him being a 'bit funny' at Millwall and didn't want any of that to fall at my door.

"Also he doesn't like it when anyone eats when he hasn't got something, but for fuck sake don't offer him anything".

I was trying to take all this in and must have looked a bit perplexed.

"Someone gave him some chips once and it must have given him indigestion because since then he views anyone other than me who feeds him as trying to poison him".

To say I was nervous was an understatement, the shifts I had been on with other handlers had only included the warning 'don't get between the dog and the bad guy'. This was a whole new scenario and one that could end badly if I got it wrong.

I must have looked nervous because Rob laughed, "Don't worry, after an hour or so he will treat you like one of the family".

"Have you got family Rob"? I asked.

"What with a fucking psycho dog in the house?" he grunted, "You must be mad, I have a job just getting laid. If I'm planning to take someone back to my place I have to bribe one of the other handlers to look after his nibs as he does tend to lower the tone and ruin the mood".

So much for being treated like one of the family then I thought.

I spent the next hour avoiding eye contact and not even daring to think about opening my lunchbox lest I upset the beast behind me. Our first job of the evening came and went; some insecure premises that didn't interest the dog in the slightest and he just snuffled around a bit before wandering back to the van and pissing up the back wheel. A suspect fleeing a stolen car generated a lot more enthusiasm and as soon as the blue light started revolving on the roof of the van I could hear Demon giving off a high pitched whine.

"He does that because he senses he is going to get some action...probably got a hard on as well" Rob informed me.

I certainly didn't want to check, if Demon got upset with a little eye contact he was going to be well pissed off with me having a gawp at his erect todger.

Upon our arrival there were a couple of officers I knew standing by the open door of a car that had been driven into a tree. Rob quickly established that the car had been TDA'd (taken and driven away) and that nobody had gone running after the scroat once he had bailed out. This meant that Demon would have a scent that hadn't been contaminated by anyone else.

Rob put the dog on a tracking line and we set off at breakneck speed. I had taken the heavyweight rechargeable Dragonlight torch from the van and attempted to keep up with the team and light up the way as we went. Demon worked hard at sniffing out his quarry; firstly he seemed to be relying on transferred scent where the runner had brushed against something but very quickly he started to track an airborne scent and our pace quickened. I saw a set of car keys laying next to the track we were on and scooped down to pick them up, a pound to a pinch of shit they were for the motor I had just seen wrapped around a tree.

After ten gruelling minutes even I could have tracked the fleeing driver, he was crashing through the undergrowth like a rutting rhino and I fancied I could smell the stale sweat from his unwashed body on the air. The dog was frustrated that we couldn't go any faster and he took several seconds every now and then to spare me an evil glare that promised retribution if this villain got away and spoilt his fun. I on the other hand was breathing through my arse.

The weight of the Dragonlight prevented me from being able to pump my arms when I ran and by the time we got to the point where Rob had shouted out his challenge of "Police, stand still or I will release the dog" I was about ready to dump the bloody thing in the hedge.

The initial call was ignored and Rob commanded Demon to speak. The night air was shattered by the guttural rasps of the animal as it sensed it was getting close to 'playtime'.

"Last chance" Rob yelled and reached down to release the tracking line and harness.

At the eleventh hour a pathetic shout came from the darkness, "I give up, I give up, don't let the dog go".

A thirty something dishevelled beanpole of a man emerged from the thicket, his hands arms and face scratched in hundreds of places from the twigs, brambles and branches he had collided with on his headless flight. He nearly passed out when he saw the size of the animal that had chased him and you could see him running the scenario of the dog being released through his mind over and over again as Demon went wild with hysteria and annoyance. Rob had thrown him his ball which is supposed to represent a reward for the game they had just played. That may work with a lot of dogs but this one wanted flesh and blood to play with, toys were for lesser animals. Totally ignoring the ball as it lay on the ground Demon cocked his leg and pissed up a tree next to where Rob was standing, splashing his handlers leg.

"You did that on purpose you dirty bastard" screamed Rob as he bent down to retrieve the dog's ball from out of the way of the steaming piss that was heading its way.

I grabbed the prisoner and cuffed him, making sure that I always kept him between me and the mouthful of teeth that were never too far away. Rob also made sure that he had a good grip on the animal as he knew that the bugger would nail the driver given half a chance. I looked over to Demon as we walked back to the officers at the scene of the crash.

"Well done..." I suddenly realised that I had never heard Rob call him by name, only by the first profanity that came into his head. I didn't even know if his proper name was Demon. I couldn't believe that the Met would give their breed programme puppies Demonic name's, it just wouldn't be politically correct. The dog was still looking at me expectantly to finish my sentence, "Well done you big ugly bastard" I said. He seemed pleased with the compliment, gave his tail a wag and wandered off to see if he could find a rabbit or a squirrel to chase.

It took several tours of duty before Demon actually accepted that I had a right to patrol with him in his vehicle. On the few occasions he softened his demeanour I got a couple of unsolicited licks and he'd nudge my hand with his big head until I scratched his ears. After months of trying to find out from Rob what the hounds real name was I eventually approached the dog sergeant who informed me that his official name was Loki as in the Norse god of mischief.

***

On this particular night shift however Demon was particularly bad tempered and was letting loose some foul smelling farts that even he looked disgusted with. I climbed into the dog van and made sure that I didn't make eye contact with the beast in the back.

"Thanks for this Rob, thought I was going to be stuck out on foot patrol with Joe all night. The skipper has given him the black spot so he is going to get creamed as will the poor sod who gets teamed up with him" I uttered as I made myself familiar with the previous crews logbook entries.

"No problems mate, although you might not be thanking me in a couple of hours. Numb nuts in the back has gone and got himself a bout of stomach upset which is making me gag" Rob replied as he eased the car out from the nick onto the road. We turned right and pulled up at the junction of the High Street, "What do you reckon, left or right?"

Left led towards the centre of London and right towards the outer boroughs.

"Left" I said, "Catford is due some action" and based upon a choice as simple as that, you are either in the right place or not when a job comes in. I had a reputation for being lucky, always being in the thick of things and getting the arrests that mattered. At the back of my mind I resented the fact that my arrest rate was attributed to luck, I worked bloody hard at playing the odds, being observant, tuning in to peoples body language and to top it all off I didn't mind getting stuck in when the poo hit the fan. Usually calls between the main three stations of Lewisham, Catford and Deptford were pretty evenly balanced. The last few nights had seen Catford get a bit of a reprieve and in my mind that couldn't possibly last.

At first it seemed as if I had given Rob a bum steer, a couple of 'dog jobs' came up on the air but the van from the neighbouring districts were nearer than we were, they were also bored so took the calls.

"Don't worry, they'll just be PADFA jobs" I reassured him. PADFA was an abbreviation used to write off the job sheets that were created when the station got a call or a visit from the public. Each job was laboriously written out and then resulted by the end of the shift; the inspector would then have the dubious pleasure of reading through them to ensure they had all been suitably resulted. PADFA actually stood for Police Arrived-Did Fuck All. There were a myriad of other abbreviations ranging from the obvious; LOB (Load Of Bollocks) to TMAC (The Mans A Cunt) and my favourite FATWOB (Fuck All To Do With Old Bill). These acronyms were used on a daily basis thirty years ago and will have disappeared into the annals of time but I am sure with the modern day technology and policing available most officers would recognise the type of jobs these were attributed to as they will still be attending them.

Rob was the first to notice the lad step out of the dark alley, clock us and dart back into the shadows again. He was out of the car like a shot and into the alley just in time to see him starting to climb the side wall that separated the alley from a rear garden. Rob caught a trailing leg and the lad was unceremoniously dragged back to earth, knocking them both to the ground. I rounded the corner at this stage with the Dragonlight clutched in one hand and the van keys in the other, I wasn't too bothered about the van being nicked I was just worried that someone might be stupid enough to get in it with dog still in there.

Rob was lying between me and the lad he had just confronted; the young man had regained his feet quickly and pulled a knife out of his trouser waistband. I had to make a quick decision; do I run towards them both and possibly get Rob stabbed or do I get the dog and hope that he will do the work for me. Rob had regained his feet and was putting some distance between himself and the threat. I could hear him coaxing the youth to put the knife away and the lad was slowly trying to back up the hundred or so metres of alley while keeping the copper at bay.

I opened the rear door of the van and slipped the lead onto Demon, he wasn't happy but I hadn't enough time to fuck around or be frightened of him. "Get out you ugly fucker" I commanded as I yanked him out the back of the vehicle and pulled him over to the entrance of the alley. What seemed like two tons of reluctant, belligerent animal suddenly perked up and all but dragged me down the narrow passage. He had seen Rob and realised that there was trouble, and now he wanted in on the action.

"Stand still or I'll release the dog" I yelled, imitating the numerous times I had heard Rob give the challenge. Demon was straining so hard it was all I could do to hold him back and there was a very good chance that he would attack with me being towed behind him. The image of him dragging the Leeds supporter across the road by his scarf sprang to mind and I had no illusions regarding his physical prowess.

"If you let it go Mister I'll gut it", the lad flashed the blade from side to side to emphasise the point.

"It's not my dog mate" I called back "it's his, and this fucker loves to play with little boys and their knives".

"He's a bollock biter" Rob added helpfully, "if I was you I would make sure you kill him with the first stab because that's the only thing that's going to stop him from ripping off your crown jewels".

The small three inch bladed knife in the lads hand looked useless when matched up against the hound from hell that was slowly dragging the policeman attached to him closer and closer. The boy considered his options and let the knife fall to the ground.

"Ok Babylon, you win this time but next time I'm having a machete and taking his head off". The lad offered out his hands for Rob to cuff, never taking his eyes off Demon.

"You might want to add a bollock protector to your war chest just in case you don't manage to cut it off with the first blow" Rob added with a wink as he grabbed the lead from my hands.

I felt as if my arms had been pulled from my sockets and when Rob had a firm grip of his pet monster I could feel my muscles quivering with relief.

Demon, totally confused with the past ten minutes of his life, edged towards the lad and stuck his nose up against his crotch giving a low growl. The lad nearly pissed himself and begged Rob to keep the dog away from him.

"Told you he likes nuts didn't I?" Rob replied as the lad was placed in the prisoner van I had called.

Once the van had left for the nick I climbed into the van with Rob. "I hope I wasn't out of order getting him out of the van like that?"

Rob looked over "Fucking diamond mate, fucking diamond. I thought the lad might have a go and I can tell you my arse was going. You did well getting him out the van without losing your face let alone holding onto him when he saw the twat with the knife".

"I think it was touch and go on both counts" I admitted, "What's he been nicked for apart from pulling the knife?" I enquired as I still didn't know what he had done prior to him threatening Rob.

"No idea" said Rob. "He was walking instead of talking and that was good enough for me. I'm sure we'll find out soon enough once we get him back to the nick".

Demon just let rip with a god almighty fart, grunted and laid down on the floor of the van.

The lad was well known to the local lads and he had been out burgling houses when Rob spotted him. I still don't know to this day why neither of us called for urgent assistance, a call that would have seen half the Met descending upon our location knowing one of their own was in trouble. I know that I could never have held the dog had he heard the approaching sirens and things could have turned very ugly. Rob quite rightly went down as the arresting officer and Demon got his name on the sheet for an assist, I got a phone call from the dog sergeant telling me that I had done well and that the incident wouldn't be forgotten. For a short time I revelled in the reputation of being the bloke who dared to get the Demon out of his box.

***

I returned to Lewisham nick at the end of my shift. News of the incident had already spread and I got some back patting when I entered the front office to put away my paperwork. Despite this there was a subdued air hanging over the place and I could hear the inspector having a rant at the skipper some place out of sight of the shift.

Gaz it seemed had gone a little over the top with the water soaking of poor old Joe. He had noticed that someone had left a bag of clothes in one of the recessed shop fronts on the High Street and had got control to call up Joe and ask him to investigate. Gaz in the meantime had returned to the nick and filled up a couple of large plastic bags with water before getting up onto the roof of the shop from the shopping centre service ramp. He waited until Joe had stepped into the recessed frontage and had heaved the bags over the edge with the intention that they would both explode on the pavement and soak poor Joe who would be standing in the doorway. But Joe had stepped out of the shelter of the shop and stood directly in the flight path of the giant water bombs, one of which had hit him squarely on the shoulder and given him a suspected broken collar bone. He was currently sitting in Lewisham hospital with Gaz of all people, waiting to see a doctor. When the inspector had been called to the scene he had gone ballistic as there was no denying that the culprit had been a fellow officer; both the shattered bags clearly bore the MP Metropolitan Police logo.

The good news was that Joe hadn't been hurt badly and after a couple of days he returned to work where Gaz took him under his wing and helped him sort himself out. The bad news was that the black spot practice was knocked on the head and I never saw it played again.

Many years later and after I had transferred out of the Met I was visiting the Hounslow shield training facility in my capacity as a Police Support Unit instructor (riot police trainer). To my delight I bumped into Joe (who now wore contact lenses) who was undergoing some refresher training. He seemed settled and was enjoying the job, even laughing at his initial months out of Hendon when he had felt like chucking it all in. It was Gaz's help that had tipped the scales so at least the 'black spot' soaking had led to a positive outcome.

Urban myths

Police officers are natural story tellers; there is a lot of downtime in the job, waiting at court to give evidence, sitting on standby at a demonstration or just parked up on observation. These boring hours need to be filled and a good story teller is a great asset; weaving tales of incidents they have dealt with around a thin fabric of truth. It came as no surprise to hear someone else relate tales of jobs that I had actually attended only to find that my recollections were vastly different from theirs. For a profession that is based upon the faithful and honest recollection of incidents I suppose the yarns are a therapeutic alternative, as there is little likelihood that the teller will be cross examined or called a liar. They are taken for what they are.

When I worked on the IRU (Instant Response Unit) we spent hours and hours on 'standby'; a term that would send shivers of dread down my spine as it meant hours of wasted times just sitting in the back of a police station yard or tucked up in some backstreet in the rear of a transit van. The object of the exercise was to have a unit of officers on hand and close to a situation; quick enough to deploy rapidly if the need arose but not close enough to cause confrontation. We were a bad smell that nobody wanted lingering in their vicinity. Funnily enough though, when the shit hit the fan we were like a breath of fresh air as we waded in to sort it out. It wasn't so bad if we were on our own district as we were known to our colleagues and generally regarded as being professional in our approach. The problems came when we were 'off our ground' and working elsewhere as there was always a danger that we wouldn't understand the local politics or status quo with regards to certain areas that may be deemed as sensitive. A heavy handed approach in such an area could easily cause full scale public disorder that would rage on for weeks, while the officers would just return to their van and bugger off home leaving the locals to pick up the pieces.

To ensure that these visiting patrols could be easily identified, A5 size melamine plaques were issued to each crew and these had to be mounted on the top right hand corner of the vans windscreen. It was a good idea but not that well thought through. Our sergeant who just went by the nickname of 'H' was a resourceful man; he ran his own haulage business from either the police station or from local payphone kiosks (there were no mobile phones in those days). He also relied on the fact that during his time on the IRU he would have certain freedoms that he wouldn't normally be afforded if he was station bound.

For a start we had the remit to patrol anywhere on the division, which was handy for him as his haulage yard was only just off the area and meant that he could 'just pop down' to brief drivers and sort out problems should the need arise. The IRU could also 'disappear' out of the area to assist somewhere else and allow H to nip to the other side of London to sort out his extra-curricular tasks. The fact that we now had to have identification plaques plastered over the windscreen was going to seriously curtail his roving's. Unperturbed by the new rulings H turned up for work as usual, however his business briefcase was slightly bulkier than normal and it didn't take him long to reveal why. He had spoken to a 'friend' who had made him up a collection of these name plates for the areas we most often frequented. As we crossed divisional borders we just changed the windscreen identification and nobody was any the wiser.

These plaques later became proof of identity in order to obtain packed meals when deployed on long operations that would prevent the teams from being able to have a scheduled meal break. This gave the ground commander more flexibility with his deployments and the crews were expected to eat on the hoof or when a suitable period of time became available. The downside to all this was that you invariably didn't get any time to kick back and enjoy a refreshment break, it would be a case of stuffing a pork pie or a sandwich into your mouth as you hurtled around on blues and twos getting nowhere fast. The other problem was that there was only the minimum amount of food to keep you satisfied. Boredom breeds hunger as one of its by-products. Sitting on your arse for a couple of hours will kick start your stomach into looking for something to chew on and a packed lunch that's only fit to satisfy a five year old doesn't last long in this type of situation.

The solution was to hope you got posted close to a fish and chip or kebab shop or try to get another box of provisions. At one point this was quite easy, you walked up to the distribution point, assessed what divisional IRU wasn't present and then pretended to be them. The food was duly handed over and your mate would then go up and collect your own. This was a task generally carried out in shirt sleeve order as you could slip your divisional epaulettes off and remain incognito. It was a simple, cunning ploy that kept us well fed on many occasions. However this hadn't gone un-noticed by the catering manager who would be faced with hostility when he tried to assure the hungry crew of an IRU that they had already collected their lunch and wouldn't be getting anything further. It therefore made sense to have the officers present their vehicle identification plaque as a prerequisite for their box of goodies. The system worked very well and the shortages became a thing of the past, however H's bagful of false flag identification plaques allowed us to continue our ruse undetected for many more years.

One of the teams we liked to impersonate were the lads from Q district as there was a certain amount of rivalry between us. It all stemmed from the fact that we would share crowd control duties at Crystal Palace Football Club and they would always engineer it so that they would be able to get away early from the match. They were given assignments that put them close to their van so they could quickly jump on board and shoot round to the ground commander who would then deploy them to follow the away supporter's coaches. A short escort trip to one of the arterial roads which would lead them on to the M25 would then leave the officers free to go home. We on the other hand would have to hang around the ground until the away team players had finished titillating themselves in the shower and quaffing their permed hair (it was the eighties' and the era of hideous suits and hairstyles). It would take hours before we could be released to head for home much to the amusement of our colleagues. No matter how fast we tried to get back to our van after the final whistle they would always be on their bus and ready to pull away once they had finished giving us a barrage of insults.

During his travels while making deliveries for his transport company, H acquired some fairly noxious stink bombs with a smell akin to the release of CS gas. I once set one off at a 'Stop the City' demonstration where the protestors were sitting, arms locked and refusing to move. I dropped one of the vials on the road behind them and smashed it with my boot. The odour went from unpleasant to downright nasty in only a few seconds. Those who could; walked promptly away, those who were making a point of their resistance sat stone faced trying desperately to ignore the stench that was assaulting their nostrils. The great thing about these particular bombs was that they were builders; the fetid smells just keep multiplying and eventually the resistance of the demonstrators caved in and they got to their feet and moved. Having seen the success with my group, the rest of the team began deploying our secret weapon along the length of the street and the whole place smelt like an open cesspit. Of course there were shouts of foul play but all is fair in love, war and demonstrations.

Having seen the effectiveness of the nasty little vials I had a cunning plan that involved us unleashing them on our Q district buddies. At the next Crystal Palace game two of us sneaked back to where the police vans were parked while the game was in full swing. Although securely locked these vans were very easy to break into; all the glass (apart from the windscreen) had been replaced with Perspex as it didn't smash when struck with rocks or bars. Its non shattering capability had a downside though; it was a lot more flexible than glass. This didn't matter if it was secured within a frame, but in the case of the rear sliding window a constant and firm tapping with the flat of one's hand would cause the metal locking clip to vibrate loose and the window could then be slid open. I was small enough to be able to wriggle one arm and shoulder through the opening and release the rear doors allowing us to gain entry.

Every seat was booby trapped by placing a glass vial between the cushion and supporting spring; as soon as somebody sat on the chair their weight would push the fabric down and squash the glass tube against the metal springs and snap it open. Having done our work I secured the rear doors and window before carefully climbing out of the driver's door and locking it on the handle release.

The trap was set.

At the end of the game we got a flyer and raced down the concourse only this time is wasn't an attempt to beat the Q district guys it was to watch their imminent distress. As predicted, their team were well ahead of us and seeing us emerge through the stadium gates they bolted into their van and the engine fired into life. As they drove towards us I could already see some of them gesturing through the windows and laughing. The van travelled another hundred yards or so before it pulled violently to the kerbside and ground to a sudden halt. The doors were flung open and heads appeared through the side windows, those who could quickly exited the vehicle only to stand dazed on the pavement coughing and spluttering. Those trapped inside the vehicle were retching and strings of saliva hung from their mouths and noses. The smell from where we were standing was startling and pungent; inside the confines of the van it must have been hell. By the time we had reached our own vehicle and covered the distance to where our stricken rivals stood several officers had vomited onto the pavement. H asked our driver to pull over and as we slowly drove past he called out through the open window "Now that's what I call a fart"; he then signalled the driver to take us to the ground commander for our next assignment. He looked confused when we turned up first but shrugged his shoulders and directed us to follow the supporters coach.

We didn't see the stricken crew from Q for a couple of weeks; by now word of the practical joke had spread. Most of the lads who had been gassed were fairly pragmatic about the whole episode; a couple wanted our bollocks on a plate but you will always get some who can't see the funny side and as the age old saying goes…if you can't take a joke, then you shouldn't have joined.

As word spread, H was doing a roaring trade selling his smelly stock; it would seem that it wasn't just us who wanted to dish out some payback.

***

H was a great skipper; by the time he got to work he was so tired from his haulage commitments that he would invariably fall asleep, giving instructions that he should be awoken only if hell should freeze over or if a senior officer make an appearance, and as there was more chance of the former happening he was pretty assured of catching up on his kip during work time. The problem was that he would insist on retaining the one and only Personal Radio (PR) and would often be cosily settled in the land of nod whilst the radio merrily tried to summons our help. What H had failed to realise was that most of us were on the IRU because we liked the busy aspect the duty provided. It was a three month posting for the opportunity to escape the mundane, with the chance of being deployed to a large scale public order incident and a potential bonus of using the shields.

We trained for this type of deployment every week and were experts; the training even included throwing petrol bombs at us so that we would get past our inbuilt fear of being set on fire. We could debus and deploy shields and be formed into two teams of five in less than ten seconds. We were then able to switch to the police version of the old Roman Legions turtle formation, where one team forms a roof over the heads of their colleagues enabling the unit to assault a building in one swift and fluid movement; a manoeuvre that would enable the team to withstand heavy objects dropped from rooftops as we forced open a door to gain entry into a building. But all this training was of little use if the person in charge of the radio didn't monitor it. The call would eventually be out over the main set but vital minutes and some professional ethos would be lost if you had to be hunted down to take a job.

The sad fact was that H needed to be taught a lesson.

The plan was simple, we would wait until he was asleep and then head into the Pepys estate on Deptford's ground. The high rise jungle was a villains playground that was interlaced with narrow alleyways, underground car park's and concrete skywalks that gave the shit bags who plagued the estate a bird's eye view and advance warning of everyone's comings and goings be they potential victim or the Old Bill. Officers who had the misfortune to have to come on to the estate would make sure that they kept away from the sides of the buildings seeking the relative safety of the paths underneath. To fail to do so could mean you faced some pretty serious consequences. Human faeces being the preferred missile of choice would be dropped from the roof tops or out of the high rise windows and it said something about the type of person who was able to lay their hands on a couple of turds at a moments' notice. Bricks and bottles could be stockpiled on the balcony or by the kitchen window but just how do you have a ready supply of shit to hand?

Mind you, if you were ever unlucky enough to get lumbered with executing a search warrant in some of the flats the answer would have been obvious. I ended up being involved in a couple of such warrants and in each case I ended up calling out a social worker as I feared for the safety of the children within the household. In one case the toilet had been blocked, blocked for some time judging by the thick crusty scum that had built up on the surface of the water that filled the overflowing pan. A bucket had then been used as a temporary measure until that had also become full, the bath was the next fitting to be drafted into use and this was three quarters full of human excrement, a large shit covered stick had been thrust into the mass close to where the plug hole would have been, no doubt used as an auger to help drain away the liquids. Used sanitary products bobbed alongside turds in this devils concoction and I would have gladly pushed a couple of H's stink bombs up my nose to freshen the air I had to breathe.

The flats were council owned but the tenants hadn't bothered to let them know about the plumbing problem, just what would have happened once the bath was full God only knows. They would have probably reverted to just shitting out of the lounge window onto the footpath below. The worse thing about the whole affair was that they had two lovely children living with them, two bonny little things who had radiant smiles but emaciated bodies. I went home late that night and looked in on my daughter who was sound asleep in her bedroom. The enormity of what I had seen hit me hard and I sat in the darkness in the armchair and wept for the two little mites I had seen in the flat that day. Up until then I had been quite good at separating my work life from home life, the thirty minute ride home on my motorbike clearing away the dross of the day, but seeing something like that doesn't just vanish and it stayed with me for a very, very long time.

***

As we headed into the Pepys estate H was sound asleep. I had briefed all the crew on what to do, the driver sat poised for my signal and when I nodded the van shot forward at break neck speed before screeching to a halt. The doors were flung open and we all bailed out and ran into the garage complex. In the commotion H had woken to see his team running like madmen into the estate and out of sight. By force of habit rather than by choice he keyed the PR and called up that we were chasing suspects and as he said it the uneasy feeling of not actually knowing where we were and for what reason pushed its way to the fore of his mind. The PR was linked to the main set and now all of the South East of London listened in to see what we had and if we needed assistance. It was good fortune that H had worked the Deptford area and quickly recognised his surroundings.

"Papa Three One, Papa Three One from MP, location, direction of travel and reason for the pursuit please" the bored voice of the Scotland Yard dispatcher requested.

"MP from Three One, we are on the Pepys estate Deptford..." and that was as much as he knew. Because we had all split up when we left the van he couldn't really give a direction of travel as there were so many.

"Three One, from MP I say again, direction of travel and reason for the pursuit please" the dispatcher continued with his demands.

From where I was hiding I could see that H looked like a floundered fish; his mouth gaped as he wandered from exit to exit inside the complex looking for either a member of his crew or divine intervention. I could hear the wail of a siren and guessed that the local units would start making their way towards us and that was something I didn't want to happen, the joke had gone on long enough, hopefully a lesson had been learned and it was time to call off the support, the last thing I wanted was for anyone to get injured when responding to a bogus call. I walked out of the shadows and H ran over to me, it was the fastest I had ever seen him move. The dispatcher was still demanding information as he thrust the handset towards me.

"MP, MP from Papa Three One, cancel, cancel. We had a couple of locals square up to us but they are long gone. Thanks for your assistance". I handed the set back to H and waved to the others to join us.

"What the fuck was all that about?" demanded H.

"If you hadn't been asleep H you'd have known" said our driver.

"If someone else had the radio you wouldn't have looked so bloody daft on the main set" added another member of the team. "If that had been for real, we would have been up shit street relying on you for back up. You were fucking lucky you knew where we were".

H looked like he had swallowed a wasp, "What the fuck do you mean, 'if it had been for real', don't tell me you fuckers set this up?" he looked at us with menace in his eyes.

We started to get back into the van and left him fuming on the pavement. As we found our seats he sauntered into the van and plonked himself down where he had only a few minutes previously been enjoying a quiet nap. "You bunch of twats" was all that he said before unclipping the PR, handing it to me and then closing his eyes to resume his nap.

Nothing more was ever said on the subject but I know of at least three officers who have told that story to me who were never there…story tellers one and all.

***

On most weekends life on the IRU was hectic and busy, if you were nominated as Commissioners Reserve it meant that you could be sent anywhere in London (or as happened to us, outside of the Metropolitan area to assist our county neighbours). Trained to the top level in public order control the units would cruise from pub fight to pub fight backing up their divisional colleagues. Used as extra staff for football matches it was a case of us being the people the officers called when they needed help. I loved working on the unit, similar minded people willing to put graft in for their wages. We trained hard as it was a taxing job if you got deployed to a riot situation that required the use of shields as there would be very little let up until the situation was under control.

It wasn't all pub fights and public order; often we would be used for mundane jobs that nobody else wanted. Being used as glorified doormen or security guards wasn't unusual. A deployment anywhere near Covent Garden on a Friday or Saturday evening was also fraught with a different type of danger as this was 'the place' to have your hen party. Patrolling an area that's packed with drunken women who all seem hell bent on having a good time brings the words sexual harassment to mind. When men grope women and make sexual innuendos towards them it is quite rightly deemed as being out of order and often unlawful. When women do it to men there seems to be a degree of leniency and an element of 'they are only having some harmless fun'. I have seen the most cocksure officers look pale after the onslaught of a hen party's wandering hands, I can tell you that it's often not the officer's hat that they want to try for size!

American tourists could also be accused of being very forward and would want photographs of themselves posing with a real 'British Bobby'. On one such occasion we had been posted outside an Israeli airline office in the centre of London, it was a Sunday and as boring as could be. We took it in turns to stand outside the glass fronted building that was closed for the day in our pointy hats and gabardine macs. It was a cold, dry late autumnal day and there was nothing to relieve the boredom. When they were not standing outside the door of the building the remaining officers took off in pairs and just wandered aimlessly around the nearby streets. If someone had intended to blow up the building, a dozen or so unarmed, unmotivated and brain dead cops were not going to be presenting them with much of a challenge.

The tourists though took full advantage of the immobile officers and grabbed any photo opportunity they could. Some wanted to wear the 'Bobby hat' and others wanted to hold my 'billy club' which I believe is their word for truncheon…if not I guess I missed out on what could have been a much more exciting afternoon! I decided that to make things more interesting I would slip my arm out of my coat and then tuck the empty sleeve in between the buttons down its front. The one armed policeman was an instant hit; I stepped inside the confines of the front door of the premises to isolate myself and just stood and stared blankly into space waiting for the public's reaction.

People are really funny about disabilities, everyone immediately noticed the missing arm from the coat sleeve but nobody said anything directly to me. It didn't stop them talking about it though as if I wasn't there.

"Jeez honey, that poor guys only got one arm; you wouldn't be able to be on the force at home with only one arm".

"Maybe that's why they have him on door detail because he can't do anything else".

"Get his picture honey".

"I can't just go and take his picture, it'll look too obvious. Guy's probably a bit sensitive".

"Then get a shot of me with him in the background".

Similar conversations went on with other tourists using the same lines for the rest of the day. We took it in turns to play the one armed bobby and I suspect that dozens of people returned to the US with tales and photographic evidence deriding the state of the UK police officers.

I should really apologise for the deception, but a one armed officer patrolling the streets of the capital...come on guys get real!

***

Bravado is often alcohol fuelled and can push someone well beyond that point where their mind is screaming 'Don't do it'.

This Saturday night had been quiet; quiet for a weekday let alone a weekend. There had been very little radio traffic and jobs for the local units and absolutely nothing for us. On this day I was travelling in the rear of the van on what we referred to as the jump seat, a single seat adjacent to the large side door. It was the place to be if you wanted to be the first person out of the van and into the action. The winged door was spring loaded thanks to the fact that the riot shields we stored transversely behind the driver and front passenger bench seats were too long. These shields were flexible Perspex and about an inch and a half wider than the interior of the van. By releasing the door catch the door would spring open which could be used to clear a crowd so that you didn't have to step out of the van into a hostile situation. If the door was assisted by the foot of the officer in the jump seat it could swing open at a rate of knots and woe betide anyone who tried to stop it.

I loved sitting there as it was the busiest place to be. However when we were on a public order deployment I would sit up front with either the sergeant or inspector and take on the role as scribe which entailed recording all the calls that were made to us from the operations commander and listing any deployments, arrests or things of note. It also meant that I was the radio operator and this gave me the chance to shoehorn us into any situation that sounded a bit tasty.

On this particular Saturday night however, we were patrolling the streets of Penge and not being overtaxed with our workload. The unit was on standby status and jobless, left to our own devices and free to roam where we wanted within our own division or to provide support to a neighbour. We had patrolled the High Street and a couple of residential areas where spontaneous parties had a habit of springing into life in the early hours of the morning. Hundreds of youths would attend the gatherings, abandoning their vehicles in the street and causing gridlock until their owners deemed to move them. The parties could last the whole weekend and the residents not involved in the festivities were often driven from their homes just in order to get away from the repetitive base and beat of the nonstop loud music. However on this particular day no large sound systems had been seen on the move so it looked like the neighbourhood was going to get a break.

On our third trawl of the High Street we noticed a group of young men standing by the zebra crossing. As cars drove along one of them would slowly walk out onto the crossing, causing the vehicle to stop and then just before they got to the centre of the road another member of the group would then walk out and thus keep the poor motorist stationary for a long period of time. It was a silly prank and when they saw us coming they quickly disappeared into some alleyways. We gave them twenty minutes before circling again and sure enough there they were standing by the side of the crossing. We were the only vehicle on the road so there was going to be little chance they would play their silly game with us; well not unless they wanted to get nicked for obstructing the highway. As we crawled along, one of the group walked out to the middle of the road; standing in the middle of the crossing with his back towards us he waited until we slowed and then dropped his trousers and pants to half-mast and mooned the police van.

I have seen some daft things but never this blatant, he might just have well painted "nick me" on his arse cheeks.

His mates were falling around laughing as he slowly turned around with a big grin on his face. His smile fell the minute he recognised the big white van with Police written on it. I opened the side door and beckoned him over; he sheepishly walked over to the open door.

"Inside young man and sit on the floor" I instructed as we didn't have any spare seating capacity.

He climbed in and sat on the floor between the seats and I closed the van door as we drove off leaving the remainder of the group apoplectic with laughter.

"What the fuck was that all about?" I enquired.

"Sorry" he mumbled "I didn't know it was a police van, they just said a car was coming and dared me to do it". He sat in silence for a few seconds. "Bastards must have known you were the Old Bill...I mean the police" he said indignantly.

"Oh yes, they were pissing themselves long before we stopped and you dropped your keks. Stitched you right up they have" piped up H.

"It's my stag night and the last thing the missus said to me was don't get into any bother" our mooning mate added.

H looked over to me and winked, he indicated with his thumb that we should chuck the lad out and give him a break. I didn't want to be tucked up for the rest of the shift with this guy, he'd been a twat but his mates had been worse. I nodded to H and he spoke quietly to the driver who turned off the road and did a circuit back to where the guy's friends were. They were still laughing amongst themselves when we came into view but the smiles dropped as it became clear that we were going to be stopping. As the van pulled up against the kerb I opened the door and told the lad to get out. He couldn't believe his luck and quickly headed for the door.

"Early wedding present from the Met Police" I said as he left the van thanking us all profusely. I asked him to send his Best Man over and he returned to his mates to a chorus of cheers and back slapping. Eventually a gangly young man who looked worse for the drink he had consumed lurched over to the van.

"You the Best Man?" I asked.

He nodded.

"Best you get your mate home before he gets into any serious trouble and you have to phone his family and future wife to explain he's been nicked" I cautioned.

"Sorry about this" he mumbled, the prospect of having to make such a phone call finally dawning on his addled senses.

As he walked away I shouted "Going to make a great Best Man speech I should think".

He stopped and turned back to the van, a big grin breaking out across his face. He raised both thumbs and re-joined his friends.

Night Duty

Bizarrely I loved night duty, being on the streets of London when everyone else was asleep had a certain buzz to it. This was the time when we had the villains on a level playing field, not getting waylaid with calls or accidents (they weren't collisions in those days) to deal with; it was strictly us against them, no rules, and the winner takes either the spoils or the prisoner.

Some of my less enthusiastic colleagues would like to grab forty winks when the opportunity arose and if we found them parked up in a back street, headlights off and seats reclined there was often some sport to be had. A couple of house bricks in front of the wheels and a wet newspaper stuck across the windscreen would often suffice to cause a mad scramble if they were rudely awoken. A tin can tied by string to the rear towing eye, reminiscent of a bridal car was also used as a means of letting your mates know they had been caught.

I hated sleeping, not for any other reason than when I did sleep I practically died. I didn't hear or feel anything and would find it extremely hard to wake up without feeling exhausted and sick. I used to work with one guy on the area car who could take a twenty minute cat nap that would keep him going for another eight hours. He and his wife had an autistic son who wouldn't sleep and they would take it in turns to stay up with him; eventually their bodies learnt to cope on an erratic sleep pattern. His mother-in-law used to stay over on alternate nights when he was working.

There have been a couple of occasions though where it seemed damn rude not to get my head down...

Once, a few days after my son had been born, I had pulled an overtime shift on a large siege at the Libyan embassy. Police Constable Yvonne Fletcher had been shot down in cold blood whilst policing a demonstration outside the building. It was the first few days of a siege that was to last nearly a week, right in the heart of London. Incidents like this make you realise just how vulnerable you are and losing one of your own is terribly sad. Over the previous days I had been getting up in the night to feed the baby as it was one of the conditions of my wife being allowed out of hospital. I enjoyed it and understood the bond that she had developed with my daughter when she would wake up and instantly know the baby had woken. I now found myself being able to predict the wakening moments of my son before he cried. However, the previous few days had been particularly tiring, I was knackered and glad to be going into work and earning some extra money.

Our role at the siege wasn't going to be either exciting or taxing as we were told on briefing that we were just going to be sat up in a side street unless the shit hit the fan. I can remember climbing into the van and putting my feet up onto the stack of shields in front of me; the rest of my twelve hour shift is a blur. I was awoken and surprised to see that we were still at the nick and was even more surprised to find that I had slept solidly throughout the whole tour, even missing a couple of meal breaks where the crew had left me in the van happily snoring away. Even after all these years it was the easiest overtime I ever earned.

Despite my lazy shift I was once again given the opportunity to earn some extra wonga on the siege. This time it was on a late shift so I would have to remain awake as we were to conduct foot patrols around the embassy cordon. The roads off the square had been screened with green netting and every so often we would snatch a glimpse of the four police hats laying abandoned on the road next to where Yvonne had fallen. It was a sad and forlorn site and one which was beamed around the world on numerous news briefings.

During the course of the evening an officer from Lewisham walked to the inner cordon, brushed the screen aside and bravely walked out into the square that had been so empty for so long. He went to where Yvonne Fletchers hat lay and collected it so it could be placed on her coffin at her funeral. He walked from the square and back to the sanctuary of the cordon straight into a shit storm where he was quickly returned back to Lewisham police station and told to present himself before the Divisional Commander in the morning. Having been told that his actions could have sparked more shooting, there having been a breakdown in dialogue between those inside the embassy and the negotiators, he must have known the shit he was in was deep.

I don't know the full ins and outs of what happened other than what he told us but apparently after his bollocking for irresponsible behaviour from the boss he was told that 'some people' were pleased with his act of defiance towards those in the embassy. He kept his job without any form of punishment and shortly afterwards was made a Freeman of the City of London and able to herd his flock of sheep over London bridge.

Clive, I thought you were a hero then and I still do.

***

There was another occasion when I was told that I was going to have to babysit a surveillance camera that was in an observation point (OP) opposite a jewellers shop. They were suspected of fencing stolen gear taken as a result of street robberies and dipping (pickpocketing). The shop was shut during the night but the observation gear was deemed far too valuable to leave in situ unaccompanied and on this particular night I was nominated as its security. Having sneaked into the OP, within an hour I was bored witless, my packed lunch had been eaten and the flask was empty. I wasn't allowed to put any lights on or use a torch in case it gave the OP's presence away.

The premises we were using as the OP belonged to a picture framing company although at the time I wasn't aware of this fact. The room I was confined to (apart from the smelly toilet) was bare apart from the camera on its tripod, a high backed wooden chair and a dirty lino floor. What looked like a work bench stood against one of the walls, a six foot long oblong that was raised up on a couple of trestle's with a felt cover that had been thrown over the surface. I sat in the uncomfortable chair and looked enviously at the workbench until temptation got the better of me and I stretched out on top of it. I snuggled down under my overcoat, propped my head on my rucksack and felt a hundred percent better. I could feel the drowsiness creeping up on me and knew that I would soon be powerless to resist. Not wanting to have to explain why I slept through the theft of the surveillance camera I jammed the wooden chair under the door handle to prevent any unwelcome visitors, be they uniformed colleagues or villains. The following six hours passed very abruptly, my sleep only being disturbed by the occasional sound of something cracking. At first this invoked a complete search around the room to ensure that everything was secure but as the night wore on I would just casually glance at the camera to make sure that its dark shadow was still there before drifting back off to sleep again.

The morning found me quite refreshed but none the less happy to see the detective who was taking over from me for a day of filming. I told him that everything had been quiet before slipping away into the back alleyway and heading to the nick. No sooner had I returned and the shift was stood down. It wasn't until I removed my overcoat that I noticed the thousands of small glass shards that were stuck to the back of it. I shook off the worst and resolved to give it a good brush down before the commencement of the following days shift.

The following night it was the turn of Julian, another probationer to have to babysit the camera and I was able to get on with some real police work out on the streets. Halfway through the shift Julian called up in a panic from the OP and requested that the sergeant attend his location. Believing that he had been under attack or that the premises had been compromised the rest of the shift headed that way just in case.

Using the alleyway, the sergeant sneaked into the OP and crept back out again ten minutes later. My crew mate Chris and I picked him up in our unmarked cavalier; as he climbed into the rear of the car he was already in mid-stream, questioning the parenthood, capabilities and IQ of the officer he had just spoken to.

"Fucking moron" he bemoaned. "Not only did he decide to have a fucking kip when he was supposed to be watching the camera, the twat takes his nap on a fucking stack of glass panes they use for the picture framing. Whole fucking lot collapsed underneath him, there's fucking glass everywhere. I'm going to be typing this shit up for the rest of the bloody shift".

He was still muttering when we dropped him off at the nick. I hadn't said a word during this time and once we got back out on the road I realised that I also hadn't been breathing. Finally I let out a long breath and Chris laughed, "Sounds like you had a lucky break...if you'll excuse the pun".

Poor Julian had done exactly the same as I had done and had been caught out by pure bad luck. He didn't last very long at Lewisham and was promptly moved on to a quiet backwater, the nickname he earned that evening following him. I don't know how long 'Crystal' lasted in the job and sympathised with his plight…however it could have worse; it could have been me!

***

In order to join the Met I had uprooted my family and moved to London. I had said that it was only going to be a temporary thing but I was having fun and making a name for myself. For the first time in my life I was good at something and people wanted to be me. However there was no point in denying it, after five years my wife wanted to move back to the country and had more than fulfilled her side of the bargain. At that time Suffolk Constabulary had a change of mind with regards to recruiting officers from other forces (or maybe they were just anti Met), Norfolk were just not recruiting, and as a matter of principle I wouldn't go to Cambridgeshire as they had had their chance once before and blew it.

It was obviously a destiny thing, the stars or fate aligning themselves and all that old tosh because within a couple of weeks of me making my initial enquiries I was phoned by my mother who had seen on their local news that Norfolk had just been given the go ahead to recruit twenty new officers. I contacted their recruiting department and got an application form by return post; the dice were cast and I had a feeling that I was going to be one of the lucky applicants.

Meanwhile at Lewisham, my inspector was fighting off transfer orders for me to be moved within the Metropolitan Police area. Some bright spark had come up with the idea that you should move officers every five years so that they get the benefits of working both inner and outer London stations. It was a pathetic waste of everyone's skills, knowledge and street craft especially as these moves often involved shunting an officer from P district to M district just for the sake of it. I saw officers who knew everyone on their beat transferred across the road from Lewisham to Peckham. There was no way they were benefiting from working outer London as they had just been moved from one boiling cauldron to another and both within spitting distance of the other. The only difference being that the officer from Lewisham who, after five years at the station would know all the local villains, informants and every inch of his patch would now know absolutely fuck all.

I had already had a stay of execution; my inspector had argued that I was an experienced officer who was a point of reference to the junior officers and supervisors alike. I only had five years' worth of experience in total so it just goes to show what dire straits the job was in at the time. Whether I liked it or not things were going to change so I might as well have them change to benefit my family.

I was given an interview in the Norfolk Police Head Quarters in Norwich. The building looked massive and I was impressed at the size of the operation I was now hoping to be a part of so it came as a bit of a shock when I realised that the police only rented a small corner of the building from the County Council.

The interview went well, my operational experiences far outweighing those of the reviewing panel. At the end of the interview I was told I had the job and that I was being posted to East Dereham as this would be equidistant from where my wife's and my family were living. I thanked them and left the room wondering where the hell East Dereham was as it was now going to be my place of work. The inspector in charge of the interviews was of great help and he pointed out the town on the large county map.

"You lucky bugger" he said. "It's a quiet market town in the middle of nowhere. Plum posting that, it's really quiet and nothing ever happens".

I was gutted, I wanted action, I wanted busy, I certainly didn't want a graveyard for knackered old officers. The inspector also gave me a good bit of advice and that was to buy a house in the East Dereham area as it was central to most police stations in the county, so if I ever got posted or specialised in a particular department I wouldn't have to move house. He couldn't have possibly known that the property prices in the area would rise steadily over the following years.

I went back to the Met and told my inspector who seemed genuinely pleased for me and helped to sort out my leaving date which was going to be just over two months in the future. This gave us a chance to sell our bungalow and find somewhere to live in Norfolk, a prospect I wasn't looking forward to as I hate moving house.

The weeks ticked by quickly, we had a buyer for our bungalow the day it went on the market and had found a cottage we loved in one of the villages outside East Dereham. Everything was going well although I still couldn't get my head around the fact that I would be leaving the only nick I had ever worked at, despite my colleague's envious remarks about leaving a sinking ship.

During this time I attended a call for back up from a beat officer who worked one of the less salubrious areas in Lewisham. He had been called to a domestic between one of our local idiots and some children who had been playing football in the street outside his house. The guy was trouble and always kicked off whenever he got arrested or stopped. I jumped into a car with a good mate of mine called Danny and we shot off to Campshill road where the problem was still ongoing.

Danny and I went back years and were now stalwarts on the shift having the younger officers come to us for advice. This advice was not just restricted to policing matters either, problems with their love life or finances were included. It seemed strange to me that I was barely twenty nine years old and acting as an agony uncle to kids only a few years younger than myself.

A few years previously Danny had been involved in a foot chase down Lewisham High Street. An armed robbery had taken place and the bad guy was away on his toes with Danny in hot pursuit. As Danny got close the guy turned, pointed his handgun at him and pulled the trigger. Danny saw the hammer drop but the gun miss-fired. The shock of it all caused him to collapse onto the pavement, stunned to still be alive. Unbeknown to the rest of us, our last contact with Danny had been that the guy had a gun and was threatening him…then nothing. I was riding shotgun in a passing police van, it slowed to pick me up as the driver was from off our area and was responding to the urgent assist shout Danny had put up. As we went towards the large shopping centre a crowd of people had gathered around the inert form lying on the pavement. Danny, prostrate on the pavement, looked like he had been seriously injured and calls were already going into the control room requesting an ambulance for him. The guy with the gun was both armed and dangerous.

The public kept pointing the way for us, gesturing to the service road that led to the rear of the Riverdale Centre that would give access to the numerous shops trading there. I jumped from the van and started to make my way up the ramp hoping to catch a glimpse of our man going to ground somewhere. He had run a long way and must have been breathing out of his arse so it would make good sense for him to hide up in someone's stockroom for the rest of the afternoon until the coast was clear. My colleague in the van took the exit ramp so at least we had some form of containment on the area. However I knew that there were a myriad of stairwells and exits that could give him access to the shop floor and the chance to blend in with all the shoppers going about their business. Years of working in the centre came in handy as I was able to call over one of the security guards who was having a crafty fag and get him to warn his control room. They had CCTV cameras, and armed with this guy's description could start scanning the concourse for him.

The steady thud, thud, thud of the helicopter rotors above me let me know that we had an eye in the sky as well as on the ground. Based upon what had been seen and what we knew, the Service Deck of the centre was going to be the first place a search would commence. A warning; stern and to the point, was transmitted across both airways stating that armed officers were being deployed to the scene and that all non-uniform officers should vacate the area. All civilians should be moved away from the place of the search until it was assumed that it was clear. I warned the security staff and they started ushering members of the public and staff away from the search area. My adrenaline was pumping, my colleague was lying, shot (as I believed at the time) on the pavement and the bastard responsible was hiding somewhere nearby.

The search was starting on the far side of the Service Deck and would work its way back to where I was. At this point a door opened that led into one of the stairwells; I was on alert but could clearly see that the guy didn't fit the description of the gunman.

"Sir, please go back inside, we have an armed operation here and it's not safe" I called out. The guy hesitated and I ran over to where he was standing, "Sir please leave the area".

"What's happened?" he enquired.

Rather than just reiterating my command to leave I thought it might be more prudent to tell him and scare him off the Service Deck. "There is an armed robber hiding up here somewhere, he's already shot a policeman so he's got nothing to lose".

"Is he wearing jeans and a red top?" he asked.

"Yeah, but he may have dumped the top to change his appearance" I muttered as I tried to get my rubbernecking bystander back into the stairwell and safety.

He pointed to a flat rooftop close to a service bay. "There's a guy wearing jeans and a red top on that roof" he said , "just saw him duck down when he spotted you".

I thanked the guy and turned back to where the witness had seen my quarry. What I should have done is call it in and get the armed team and the helicopter to break off their search and come to where I was. I didn't do that; memories of the piss taking I had got from my tutor years before looming large in my mind. I hadn't seen the guy myself and only had some random bloke's word that *he* had; if I got this wrong and the gunman got away I would lose my credibility with my shift and virtually everyone else. I decided that I would go and make sure that there was someone on the rooftop before calling it in.

Using a tall, cage-sided storeroom trolley I pushed it to the side wall of the single storey building the witness had indicated. Using the caged side as an improvised ladder I climbed to the top and took a sneaky peak. A pair of jeans and a boot loomed into view. They were under a ventilation shaft but I couldn't see the wearer or the rest of their clothing. My heart was pumping and so was my arse, I needed one good look to satisfy myself before calling in the cavalry. I placed my hands on the top edging of the concrete coping and dared myself to put my head up high enough to see more. This was no longer me playing cops and robbers, the reality of getting seriously injured was screaming out its protests and I was doing my best to ignore it. One quick look and then get the fuck out of there and call it in.

I steeled myself and started to pull myself up.

"Look out mate he's got a gun".

The shout rang out and I froze. I tried to look back to where the shout had come from and saw my star witness ducking back into the stairwell. I was trying to get down off my impromptu ladder and keep an eye on the roofline in case the gunman was going to come after me. It was a matter of seconds, normally just a quick blur, but time stretched as I misplaced my footing and fell the remaining few feet back down to the ground. The stacking trolley I had used as an impromptu ladder clattered against the brickwork of the building and I smashed both my knees into the concrete. I lay dazed on my back staring up at the roofline I had tried so hard to look over expecting to see the gunman appear at any moment. Both my legs were numb from the knees down and I half scampered and half stumbled into the loading bay where I collapsed in to the shadowy interior. I radioed up for help and then just laid back letting the pain wash over me.

It wasn't the first time I had been hurt, I'd been put in hospital on a couple of occasions. It was however the first time I had been scared shitless and hurt and I sat back and listened to the action unfolding around me. The guy had made a break for it (no doubt after my not too subtle exit) and had climbed through an open window into a wages office. It didn't take long before he was located and arrested, bundled into one of the numerous vans in attendance and taken to Catford nick.

One of the security guards gave me a hand to his office where I found out that Danny hadn't been shot but had just collapsed. I called up the nick to try and get a lift back to the station but nobody was free, the calls had been stacking during the search for the gunman and were getting urgent. I limped out onto the main road and started to walk towards the hospital. Within a few minutes I realised that I had seriously damaged both knees as sharp pains radiated from them every time I put some weight down or tried to bend my legs.

A black cab pulled up and the driver called out "You alright mate"?

I shook my head, "I think I've knackered my knees, I just had a bit of a fall".

"Hop in pal, I'll run you to the nick, it's only just down the road".

My knight in shiny black armour dropped me off outside Ladywell nick and helped me up the front steps into the public office. I was quickly ushered into the canteen and then driven to the hospital. That evening with both legs heavily strapped in bandages I was driven home where I started a ten month long cycle of physio, operations and more physio. Despite the pain from my legs which eventually healed I had struggled with something else during that period, something which lurked in the dark of night and woke me in a sweat and fright. Nightmares of lying on the hard concrete floor watching the barrel of a gun appear before pointing down at me. It very rarely fired, I would wake up before that happened. The times I never woke in time left me feeling depressed and annoyed with myself.

I thought that I was going soft; couldn't hack it when the going got tough. It wasn't something I was proud of and hid it from my wife, family and doctor; on a good day I was even able to hide it from myself.

It wasn't until I returned to work and was posted on the van with Danny that the subject was broached. It seemed that we both had our demons from that job and talking to someone I respected as being a 'hard man' and a good copper I found it easier to accept.

Years later, during training to become a firearms officer, we had a talk regarding Post Traumatic Stress Disorder and I wasn't that surprised to find that I had experienced most of the symptoms described. Mine was such a silly incident and I take my hat off to those who are able to recover from greater PTSD's than I had.

I did an awful lot of research into stress as a result of the way I had felt and I think I was then able to spot and help other officers return to work a lot easier than I had been able to. Having big stressful moments and coping allows one to deal with even more stress the next time. It's not something I would advocate but it does take the positives from a shitty situation.

***

Back at Campshill Road Danny and I were hurtling out of the nick to support the beat officer dealing with Mr Campbell, our resident gobshite. We had told the officer to wait until we got there before he laid hands on him as Campbell could kick off spectacularly, especially as he was almost outside his own home. These pearls of wisdom fell on deaf ears and in the two minutes it took us to get there Campbell was in full swing and his family were starting to bundle out of their house to help and support him. We were out of the car and straight into the shit as I watched the beat officer disappear over a low wall into someone's front garden after a good a shove from someone in the melee. Danny was swinging his fists and lashing out. I knocked someone to the ground who was shouting obscenities at the top of his voice. It was a street brawl and we were now the enemy.

Something struck me across the back of the head, it was a hard blow. A large group of Jamaican males had emerged from somewhere and before I could fight my way free an arm the size and thickness of my leg was wrapped around my neck and I was yanked off my feet and dragged backwards. Danny had gone down in a hail of punches and I could hear the sirens in the background as I was dragged into a house. After a barrage of insults being shouted at me I was released and rammed into a wall. It was that Tweety Pie moment when you get sparks and little birds floating around inside your head. Instead of happy little birds though I got lights, lots of them, I also got a punch in the guts to accompany the kicks my legs were receiving. I could see Danny was also inside the house and getting the same treatment, his hand was reaching for his stick and I remember thinking don't do it, they'll fucking kill us if you get that out.

Women emerged from the kitchen area brandishing knives and a rolling pin; the room darkened as the curtains were shut and we were shut off from the outside world. Campbell was going mad, screaming and shouting into our faces, the spittle flecking from his mouth as he shouted "die Babylon, die".

The older and bigger males were laughing but telling him to quieten down; the sirens outside were still arriving and I could hear the officers shouting for us to respond. My PR (personal radio) was reduced to a piece of junk, the cable had been so violently pulled that the handset was only attached by a few stray wires. Someone had dropped the battery from the bottom of Danny's unit and that too was now unserviceable. I covered over my face and took the punches to my midriff. I had done quite a bit of freestyle full contact karate before I joined the job and knew that I had a good core strength that could soak up some of the punishment. I would be alright until someone cracked a rib but I hoped that help would arrive before then.

I could hear voices outside the house trying desperately to locate us; we were effectively hostages and in a very dangerous situation.

Tired of hitting me, one of my assailants pushed me across the room and in to the locked front door. As my back hit the Yale lock I raised my elbow and used it to smash the small window light in the centre of the door before slumping to the floor.

That stroke of luck gave our location away to our colleagues outside and the occupants of the house were given the choice of opening the door or having it put in; an inspector from a visiting IRU (who had responded to the urgent assistance shout) had taken charge of the situation and was negotiating for the door to be opened. Two of the shift who were on the area car pushed past him and started to kick the thing off its hinges, I was lying next to it and each thud made my head swim. The occupants conceded and daylight flooded in through my escape route back to civilisation and freedom.

Young Campbell, the instigator of the whole incident, had barricaded himself in his upstairs bedroom and was throwing large pieces of his stereo out of the window at the officers below. The inspector, seemingly happy with this situation stated "It's only his own stuff he's destroying; we'll just leave him to it". The fact that this little shit had just assaulted two policemen (he didn't get round to having a go at me) and was actually throwing heavy speakers at other officers and vehicles didn't appear to register with him.

I pointed out to him two of the people I recognised as being in the group who assaulted me and he just nodded.

"They need nicking; they've just kicked the shit out of us in there". I informed him in no uncertain terms.

He turned towards me and I could see that he was totally out of his depth, a fresh faced kid, no doubt with a good degree from university and career prospects spanning the stratosphere but totally fucking clueless.

Already I could see the guys responsible for the assaults going back inside the house and changing their clothing to fuck up any evidence continuity we might have had. I looked over at Danny mouthing obscenities at the inspector who chose not to notice.

"Come on Danny, let's go back to the nick" I said and took him by the arm, "this is fast turning into a cluster fuck and the boy blunder here is going to fuck it up even more the longer he stays".

We climbed back into our vehicle and drove to the nick, our inspector was in the back yard to meet us. Danny gave him the full low down on what had happened, pulling no punches when it came to describing what the IRU inspector had done. The boss went ballistic and snatched the keys from Danny's hand and the old cavalier beat car screamed out of the nick with the hooter blaring. I wasn't present when the two inspectors had their 'meeting' at the side of the road as the police doctor had arrived at the nick to treat Danny and me for our injuries. The conversation between the inspectors was apparently very one sided, as was the finger pointing and cursing until the 'young pretender' jumped into his van and sped off. With our shift inspector now in charge at Campshill road the suspects were quickly arrested and soon the nick was bulging with prisoners.

I wrote up my notes then junked the PR after completing another lengthy report describing what had happened to it. Our shift inspector hauled us both into his office and apologised for what had happened. The IRU inspector had blotted his copy book before but still seemed to be well thought of by the hierarchy; well thought of and seemingly well protected too. It was the way of things to come, rapidly promoted officers who were great on paper but a liability out on the streets.

I only had a few weeks left before I transferred out of the mad house and for the first time I started to look forward to it.

Rush Hour

The first few days in Norfolk were quite an adjustment, my last duty as a Metropolitan police officer had been at the Notting Hill carnival and despite the general good spirits of most of those in attendance there was always a small minority who went looking for trouble. Several officers had been slashed with knives and there had been many other injuries of a less serious nature so it had been a couple of evenings of adrenaline fuelled deployments. We were mostly designated foot patrols and that made us susceptible to being ambushed. The crowds were densely packed and you couldn't see trouble coming until it was upon you and by then it was too late to group together and fend them off. It was a fitting end to my days as a Met officer…all wham bang and very little thank you mam.

In stark contrast, my first duty in Norfolk was on a Sunday morning in October, it was a warm bright day and I had been double crewed on the area car. The shift started when everyone eventually crowded into the small space that doubled as a briefing room, control room and general meeting place. It abutted a larger area that housed the front counter and public access.

Briefing was a leisurely affair, tea and coffee were handed out and I was introduced to the officers I was going to be working with. I was the youngest member; most having a good ten years' in both service and age than I had. It's always hard when you start at another nick especially if you are new to the area or the force. Officers want to know what your pedigree is, can you be trusted not to bottle it in a punch up, do you go to the supervisors and report colleagues if you think they haven't handled something correctly, do you deal with problems or cuff them off onto someone else? These were all things I had never had a problem with in the Met, I was known as being a thief taker and a sound copper amongst my peers. These guys knew nothing about me and wouldn't be able to make a phone call to a mate to check out my background.

In this small market town police station I was just a young whippersnapper with shiny shoes, pristine uniform and ratty moustache on his top lip. Norfolk Constabulary had previously taken a few Metropolitan Police transferees and apparently had a mixed bag, some officers worked hard to establish their credibility whilst others caused resentment with their constant bragging about 'when they were in the Met', a phrase that still made me cringe right through to the day I retired.

I had chosen to come to someone else's force and felt it only right and proper to do things the way they did; if I thought there was a better way of doing something then I would suggest it and not take offence if it wasn't adopted.

Briefing on this particular day was short and sweet; there wasn't anything to be handed over from the night turn and no intelligence to share. Daily crime for the area was in single figures and mainly theft related. I got a quick run-down on how calls coming into the police station were logged and dispatched and how they were filed once they had been dealt with. It wasn't too unlike the system we had used in London when I had first joined, before everything had become computerised and complicated. What did surprise me though was the low numbers of calls received throughout the day, there were on average about thirty logged incidents which would have taken less than an hour to achieve in Lewisham. Despite this disparity the shift strength was of a similar size, three beat officers, a town officer, two officers on the area car and an officer staffing the radio and front counter. In charge was a shift sergeant who was overseen by a shift inspector. I found out that the night shift were greatly reduced in staffing numbers as virtually nothing ever happened; a fact borne out by the crime logs and I found myself wondering just how I was going to cope with the lack of activity. The area the nick covered was massive. There was a fairly busy market town with a small air force base nearby which was being slowly mothballed and situated within the rural beat were dozens of small villages and hamlets; this all sat squarely in the middle of the county. There were two other smaller market towns that the sergeant and inspector had supervisory responsibilities for, these outlying towns had fewer officers than Dereham and we were expected to drive the ten miles or so to back them up should they get sent to anything tasty.

On my first day we had no sooner finished our morning tea when the phone rang; it was control room wanting to book the vehicles and their crews as they had a job that needed allocating. Our controller 'Greybeard' started to take down the details. "Sounds like a job for the area car and our new whiz kid" he joked, winking at me at the same time to show that there was no intended malice in his comments. He scribbled down the instructions and handed them across to me.

My first ever call in Norfolk was going to be dealing with a Shetland pony and a donkey that were wandering along one of the main roads and a potential hazard to traffic. I had driven to work on the same road and hadn't seen another motorist; just how they could be an imminent danger to anyone was beyond me. I jumped into the area car which was a clapped out old Vauxhall Chevette, my crew partner 'Sammy' explained that the usual vehicle was in for a service and that we would have to make do with the spare car. The radio set inside rattled in its fixings and the speaker was a cheap affair that squawked with dubious clarity. This combination along with the broad Norfolk accent of the controller found me struggling to understand what was being said. It reminded me of my first days in the Met trying to tune in to the airwave traffic, desperately trying to avoid being left behind.

I needn't have worried about missing anything important on this particular morning as most of the radio chatter the headquarters dispatchers were engaged in was just them passing the time of day with their patrol colleagues. I missed the quick disciplined professionalism of the Met dispatchers whose mantra was accuracy, brevity and speed as this promoted a response in a similar manner from the officers on the street. This was however a much more friendly and personal way to get tasked with something.

We drove through the streets of the deserted town and out onto the main road, hitting the outskirts of the urbanisation before heading into the sticks. It didn't take us long to locate the two errant equines as they meandered along the side of the road, stopping occasionally to tear at some grass on the verge. Sammy quickly assessed the situation, "There they are" he said needlessly, "we'd better get a couple of head collars before we try and grab them". He pulled into a seemingly deserted farmhouse and disappeared round the rear of the premises. It's one of those country things that virtually nobody uses their front door and callers will always be expected to knock at the back door. These were the small things I needed to learn in order to get the locals to accept me or I would need to get used to standing like a lemon outside a door that had probably never been opened since the house was built.

Being a new boy, youngish and from London wasn't going to go in my favour here especially as I wasn't a local lad. I hadn't entirely lost my Suffolk accent which was probably only marginally better than me having a cockney twang and I made a mental note to try and round off my vowels and pick up a few colloquialisms. I had already learnt that instead of having a chat, people here had a 'mardle' with each other. Another localism was to include landmarks that were long since gone in any directions they gave. Doing the job was going to be easy, fitting in with the locals was going to be a lot tougher.

Sammy returned to the car with only one head collar, "There wasn't anyone about and I could only find one". He threw it over to me, "Just have to see what we can do with that" he said.

I felt like this was some sort of initiation test, something to test out the new lad and see how the city copper faired against a couple of ponies. Fortunately I had been hanging around farms and horses for most of my adolescence and didn't feel fazed at having to deal with them; my problem would be what to do with them once they were caught. Sammy drove around the pony and stopped the car indicating that I should get out. I exited and took the head collar with me, it had a lead rope attached which was good as I had a feeling that these escapees were not likely to come quietly.

As I closed the door Sammy called out "I'll go and find somewhere to stick them until the owner contacts us" and with that he drove off. I was now in the middle of nowhere with no idea what to do, not the first time in my career but it was certainly not something I had experienced for a very long time. I congratulated myself on having had the foresight to help myself to a few carrots that had formed part of a huge pile at the farm. I called out to the animals and watched them as they eyed me suspiciously and holding the head collar out of sight I extended my hand with a plump carrot in it. The donkey looked nervously from the pony to the carrot and back again; at least I had established who the lead animal was. I gently called out to the pony and slowly it edged nearer, the lure of a quick snack overpowering its sense of self preservation.

When it was about a metre away it stopped, I turned my back on it and walked off a few steps making sure that the rope and tack were out of sight. The pony followed, stopping short again but a little closer than it had been before. We played this out for several minutes until it was close enough behind for me to step beside it. It nuzzled the food I had and I spoke softly as it crunched its way through the treat. I turned slowly and fed it the rest, slipping the head collar around its nose and up over its ears. The cheek strap was still loose so I looped the lead rope around its neck and we had a small tug of war until I could tighten up the strap and secure it. Its eyes rolled white with anger at being betrayed and it struggled against the rope. I let it trot around in circles, making them shorter and shorter; the lure of another carrot wasn't cutting any ice this time but I hoped that it would review the situation once I had some semblance of control over it. I also wanted to ensure that I had something to keep its teeth occupied as it was getting a bit snappy.

Once I had the pony under control it was now a case of seeing if his long eared mate would follow where I led them. We set off to where I had last seen Sammy and the area car disappear in the hope that I could find either, and I was relieved to see the donkey happily following behind. I was desperate to offload my charges as I was fast running out of carrots and the pony was still not predisposed to being friendly towards me.

After a good half mile walk along the main road I glimpsed the chequered stripe of a police car across a large field. The car was parked outside another farm but there was no sign of Sammy. The most direct route was across the field so my entourage and I stepped off the tarmac and onto the fallow ground.

When we arrived at the farm Sammy was still nowhere to be seen. I called out his name several times and hailed him on the radio but all to no avail, however at least I was able to tie the pony to a metal post and leave it standing there albeit glaring at me for my sheer audacity. I knocked at the backdoor and it was opened by a ruddy faced gentleman. "How do, young man, you'll be Sammy's new partner" he said beckoning me inside.

I entered the large kitchen and found Sammy sitting at the huge wooden table which dominated the room. A steaming mug of tea sat half drained in front of him along with a plate on which sat two large wedges of bread with bacon and a fried egg squashed between them. A couple of large mouthfuls had been taken from one of the huge breakfast sandwiches and Sammy's jaws masticated the most recent.

I must have looked livid, as he hastily swallowed before guiltily announcing "I was just about to come and give you a hand but Frank", he indicated to the farmer, "said you had it all under control". He pointed to the large pot of tea on the cooking range, "Frank, pour the boy a mug of tea, I think he's earned it".

Frank and his wife Betty were great; they knew who owned the pair of escapees and promised to phone them later in the morning before returning the head collar to the other farm. Everyone seemed to know everyone else and be on the lookout for each other, it made a welcome change from neighbours not even knowing who lived next door, let alone caring what happened to them. Betty delivered a second plate to the table overflowing with two similar sized sandwiches to Sammy's, she pulled out a chair and beckoned me to take a seat...if this was what Sunday morning early turns were like, I thought that the transition from Met to Norfolk might not be quite as difficult as I had imagined a few hours earlier.

The shift sergeant had heard from Sammy (as no doubt had all the rest of the shift) that I had handled the situation well and the fact that I hadn't gone bleating about being left to fend for myself after Sammy had pissed off for breakfast had also not gone unnoticed. The sergeant informed me that I would be spending the following days out with him so he could introduce me to key members of the community; I suspected that there would be a few more mugs of tea and sandwiches to be consumed.

The pony call was the only job we had at all that first day, the remainder of the populous surfaced around midmorning and the town slowly came alive. By midday the local fish and chip shop was doing a roaring trade as was the ice cream van that had parked up in the market place. Stopping close by, Sammy took charge of the two proffered 99's from the owner. As we sat and worked our way through them Sammy took the opportunity between mouthfuls of chocolate, cone and ice cream to point out the local villains, explaining their particular traits and MO's.

Despite the unexpected heat of the day one bedraggled family bedecked in thick coats and woollen hats shuffled out from the car park entrance and as one all stopped when they saw the police car. Their furtive eyes darted about as they all but sniffed the air for danger. I knew that they were a dysfunctional family before being told so by Sammy. Villains were villains wherever you were in the country and this feral looking bunch were ringing warning bells in my subconscious fit to deafen Quasimodo!

"Meet the Woodcocks" said Sammy nodding his head in the family's direction, "the ratty looking one at the front is dad, Peter Woodcock and the fat lump behind him is his eldest retard, John. Those two drive motors that have been nicked by the dids".

I looked blankly at him.

Sensing the gap in my education he elaborated, "Diddicotts…gypsies".

I had heard the term before; it was just that I hadn't heard it being used so blatantly. Utter anything like that in the Met at that particular time and it would have been construed as being a slur on an ethnic group of people and you would have been outed as a racist and thrown to the wolves at professional standards. Officers had stopped ordering black coffee for fear of upsetting some eager beaver looking for a name and promotion. Maybe political correctness hadn't arrived in the shires yet but I was sure that it wasn't going to take very long.

I watched as Peter Woodcock acknowledged Sammy's presence with a sly nod, the smallest Woodcock surreptitiously slipping us the finger.

"Who's the little one flicking us the bird?" I asked.

"That's Peter junior, he's not even got enough sense to be a halfwit" he answered, "mind you he is the most likeliest to take a swing at you if he thinks he can get away with it".

"I can almost smell them from here" I mused.

There is an unmistakable stench that only a body that hasn't felt the caress from a bar of soap can emit, especially if it has been encased in clothes that have never seen the inside of a washing machine on a regular basis. Someone had termed the phrase 'beany' to describe the smell and 'Eau de beany' was a very potent fragrance. If perfume manufacturers could identify the cloying agent that made the stench linger for such a long time they could make a fortune just so long as they could eradicate the smell.

"You've not smelt anything until you've gone to go to their house" replied Sammy. "We've had officers be physically sick when they have eventually emerged".

I had a horrible feeling that it wouldn't be too long before I was going to be testing out Sammy's claims. As the final member slithered out of the car park and headed towards the chip shop, I asked "Is that all of them?"

"Christ no, Mrs Woodcock is like a battery farm, knocks out a new one every year. We reckon she gives the old man a couple of months off before she wants servicing for a new brat".

I looked at Peter Woodcock senior and he didn't look like he had a good fuck left in him. He was a husk of a man, systematically drained by his demanding wife while the rest of the country paid for their dole and child benefit. "How many of them are there?" I asked.

"Well there are three more boys who live at home and two other younger ones in care. Strangely enough they were able to keep Peter junior...probably found that Battersea dogs home wouldn't take any more of them".

Sammy soon lost interest in the Woodcocks and disappeared around the back of the chip shop only to emerge ten minutes later with a couple of bags of chips. "Lunch" he said as he dumped half a kilo of fried potatoes in my lap, "my niece works there so I get discount" he explained. It transpired that his 'discount' amounted to free chips... and lots of them.

I had barely been in Norfolk for four hours and I could feel the pounds starting to pile on around my waist. Before the shift had finished I had added several more cups of tea and a couple of large chunks of farm cooked cakes to my calorie intake. It was lucky the area was quiet and crime free as I couldn't have chased after anyone even if my life had depended on it.

***

The following day the sergeant was as good as his word and we headed out of town together after briefing. Our first port of call was the RAF camp and we entered the base and drove straight over to the canteen.

"They do a good breakfast here young Scott", he informed me.

My stomach was already protesting as the prospect of another calorie packed shift looked ever more likely. I was duly introduced to all the staff and given a whistle-stop tour of the base, the sensitive areas being pointed out as we drove around the vast area. The thought of having to respond to an incident on the base was a daunting prospect as the MOD police would take several hours to even get to the county let alone find their way to the airfield. We were the first responders and our job would be to hold the fort until they arrived…if they ever did turn up as there had been several occasions when they just hadn't responded at all.

We eventually returned to the police station for a meal break, a large bag of chips supplied gratis from the chippy, just how they made a profit was beyond me as they seemed to be supplying half the constabulary with a free lunch. Members of the shift congregated in the tiny control room, each taking advantage of my offer to take a handful of chips from my huge pile. The office stunk of fried food and this couldn't have gone unnoticed by the members of the public who attended the front hatch. The sergeant didn't help matters when he lit up his pipe and filled the confined space with thick dense smoke. Eating in the front office was frowned upon at Lewisham and smoking was positively banned, the inspector would have had a shit fit had he witnessed this particular scene. I had wondered about how I would cope with the discipline in a county force, the Met had a reputation as being a bit lax but Norfolk was so laid back it was horizontal.

In between emitting great clouds of noxious smog the sergeant turned to me, "Young un, you've got to stop calling me Sarge all the time, my names Tom".

Sergeants had always been 'Skipper', 'Skip' or 'Sarge' to me, even when they were mates I socialised with outside of the job, when we were at work it was a mark of respect for the rank if not the person. This was all very alien to me and it took me the best part of the next six months to manage to occasionally call Tom by his first name, some things are just too far ingrained.

After lunch, 'Tom' drove out of the station with me riding shotgun and we joined several other vehicles at the only set of traffic lights in the whole of the area. We were in a queue of six and Tom started moaning about being caught up in the lunchtime rush hour! At first I thought that he was taking the piss, in Lewisham's morning rush hour it took so long to get through the lights that as a probationer I used to stand in the middle of the queue and spot the drivers who didn't have tax. I would then be able to walk alongside them and report them for the offence, check out their other documents, do a computer name check on them and their vehicle all before they actually reached the bloody lights.

"I expect I'll get used to it Sarge" I said keeping my face as straight as I could.

***

I had only got a few days under my belt when Tom threw me the area car keys on briefing for my first night shift. "I don't suppose you are going to want to get your head down tonight" he said "too bloody keen you young 'uns" he muttered as he took his sleeping bag up to the police stations bar and function room.

It was surreal, the station didn't have a canteen but it did boast a fully kitted out bar, complete with wall mounted optics, pumps and packets of peanuts and crisps. Each evening the grilles would be lowered and the barman (a serving policeman who ran the social club) would then clear away the empties and lock up. It then seemed that the night duty crew would occupy the room and bed down for the night. A full sized snooker table was also available for those who couldn't sleep. It appeared as though I hadn't entered another force I had somehow slipped into another dimension of space and time!

As usual there was nothing to hand over at briefing, the late turn had adequately handled the six jobs that had been allocated to them before slipping up to the bar for a quick half to beat closing time. There were no intelligence reports or information to pass on other than the fact the area car driver on the late turn had forgotten to fill up the car with petrol; his beery breath an indication that he hadn't forgotten to keep himself topped up.

I filled the area car up with fuel from the station pump as there were no 24/7 service stations within a hundred miles, the middle of Norfolk had gone to bed and it was my job to make sure that all the lights had been turned off.

***

I now had the chance to patrol the area on my own while the rest of the world and my shift slept. It seemed like a good idea; I would be able to start to build up a picture of my 'patch', it was a good opportunity for me to see if my policing skills would stand the transition from city to the middle of nowhere.

Tom counselled me before I left the nick. "Now just be aware young 'un that this isn't like the big city you're used to. Don't go rushing in expecting the cavalry to follow you. Even if you happen to know where you are the chances of anyone else knowing where that is will be slim. Use your eyes and your mouth before you use your fists".

I had never had a reputation for using my fists; well not unless someone I was nicking decided that they were going to have a pop at me. I didn't know how to take what Tom had just told me. Would nobody have a clue where I was and come to help? Sammy came over to me after Tom had gone to stake out his claim on one of the comfy armchairs.

"What Tom was trying to say is don't go rushing in, people don't go very far in this county so if you can get a good look at them then there is every chance you'll cross their path again at some point. Talk to people the way you'd expect to be spoken to, most people still respect the uniform here so you don't have to go in hard to get a result".

With their words of advice still ringing in my ears I set off on my first solo rural patrol. I have to admit being lost more times than I knew where I was, but I kept to the main arterial roads that I knew, darting down smaller roads to find quicker means of getting from A to B without visiting the rest of the alphabet beforehand.

The RAF camp was a good visual reference point as I could follow the perimeter fence back to the gatehouse and then find my way back to the nick from there. The red flashing light on top of the high mast could be seen for miles so I didn't stray too far from that. The radio was dead, even the ever present static and Dutch trawler men that cut across the airways every so often had seemingly turned in for the night.

I had just driven past the main gate on the airfield, mildly annoyed that the canteen I had been frequenting for most of the week was shut at night; in fact the whole base was locked down as it was being mothballed and didn't possess any equipment of tactical value. I could do with a cuppa but couldn't be arsed to drive the ten miles back to the station to make one. I followed the fence down a small lane to see where it led to; it was a narrow track with grass growing up through the tarmac. Annoyed that it looked like it was leading back to the 18th century I tried to find a place in which to turn around and had to continue another mile or so before I found a hard standing that was covered in a huge pile of slurry. The tyres squelched over the slimy surface and the smell of rotted vegetation and cow shit wafted up through the floor. "Fucking marvellous" I thought to myself "that's gonna stink like fuck all night".

Heading for the concrete with slightly less bio waste than the rest, I noticed another set of car tracks which led to a beaten up old motor parked at the back of a slurry heap close to the perimeter fence of the camp. There was no way a car like that could be legal; it couldn't have held a valid MOT for years. The neglect needed to get it into its present state didn't happen overnight, somebody had taken a long time of not bothering to get it into such a mess. I ran the number through the PNC operator on the radio, they initially seemed a little indignant that I had disturbed them and the airwaves. After a few minutes I was told rather sullenly that the vehicle didn't exist on their data base. That confirmed to me that there was something definitely wrong.

I grabbed the torch from the foot well, a plastic Pifco affair that threw an insipid yellow light a couple of feet in front of me. I had always coveted the aluminium Mag lights the American cops had, a couple of the lads I had worked with in London had bought their own and I was impressed with the quality of the illumination and the sturdy nature of the unit. The torch could also be used as a makeshift truncheon if push came to shove and you were being attacked.

I had seen one thrown at a car windscreen once when the driver decided that he would run over the officer who was flagging him down. The torch hit the windscreen in front of the driver and caused him to swerve away from the officer he was aiming the car at. The vehicle continued and those of us on the roadblock watched as the Maglight cartwheeled high into the sky, its light beam spinning like a Catherine wheel. It travelled thirty feet or so before coming to rest in the middle of a patch of grass, the end sticking into the soft turf and the beam of light reaching skywards. The only damage it sustained during this incident was a small chip on its sleek black handle. Unfortunately I couldn't justify the expense of buying my own; they were hellishly priced and cost far too much for my disposable income to cover.

I walked over to the car, a turd brown Morris Ital that hadn't been particularly chic or desirable when new, and certainly not one of British Leyland's best efforts. It had seen better days, plenty of them, and had it been a dog someone would have shot it a long time ago, although personally I didn't consider it even worthy of the cost of the bullet. The bonnet was warm indicating it had been used recently; the smell of unwashed bodies and stale B.O helping to confirm my theory.

The ignition barrel had been broken and a screwdriver protruded from the sheared column. I removed it and placed it in my pocket, it was hardly going prevent anyone from driving it away but it might slow them down a bit. I also cast the dull beam from my useless lamp on the ground and sought out a thickish tree branch from which I snapped off a chunk with a well-placed stamp of my foot. The piece of wood I had broken free was then jammed underneath the back of the clutch pedal. If the bastards managed to start the car they were not going to get very far if they couldn't depress the clutch and get the car into gear.

The fence close to where it had been parked had a gaping hole in it and there was a small pile of coiled copper wire next to the gap, laying just inside the base perimeter. I trotted back to my vehicle and called it in to the control room on my main set radio, the controller seeming slightly less annoyed than when I had asked for the PNC check.

They said that they would phone the nick and let them know of the situation. My PR wasn't getting a response from the station but this was something I had been warned about; the huge radio mast on the RAF base seemed to knock the signal out and make the small radios useless. That and the fact the bastards were probably snoring their fucking heads off in the bar.

Taking care not to put myself on offer I slipped through the fence and struck off in the opposite direction to where the wire was laying. After a short walk I turned off the torch and retraced my steps back to the gap in the fence. The pitch black shadows absorbed my form while I closed my eyes in order to hasten my night vision. I found a good spot to hole up in and waited, the bad guys would have had to have been deaf daft and dumb not to have known that I was on to them. I guessed that they would have seen me long before I would get the chance of seeing them. By walking away I was inviting them to make a quick exit and get away while the silly plod tramped down the perimeter fence. It only took a couple of seconds before I saw shadows moving, two people were sitting in a small bush waiting for the coast to clear. Seizing their opportunity they both sprinted for the Ital, one of them swept up the coils of wire and threw them unceremoniously onto the back seat before getting into the passenger side. I could see the shadowy figure of the driver rooting around in the glove box no doubt looking for his spare screwdriver so that he could start the car.

A torch beam briefly illuminated the interior of the vehicle to help the driver locate what he was looking for and those few seconds gave me a glimpse of two of the rat-faced Woodcocks I had seen the previous Sunday. The light was quickly extinguished and the engine turned over twice before it burst into life and I ran over towards the car, my torch beam raking into its interior. Both occupants slunk down into their seats and put their arms over their faces trying to protect their identity. The gears crunched and I could see the driver franticly trying to depress the clutch; the cogs chewing frantically on each other but the car remaining stationary. I still had a bit of ground to cover and Tom's advice sprang to the forefront of my mind…"Use your eyes and your mouth before you use your fists". The odds were not in my favour, two against one and their desire to get away was probably greater than mine to wrestle with them both on the shitty concrete. The doors suddenly burst open, was it going to be fight or flight?

"Woodcock, you and your son are getting nicked for this" I shouted. It stopped them dead in their tracks; the odds had changed now they had been recognised. Their options were now limited, they could take me out…but it would have to be permanent as I could recognise them. That's a big, big step to take for a bit of copper wire. Just to make sure that they wouldn't even contemplate this course of action I shouted into my defunct radio "Its old man Woodcock and his son, positive identification". I hoped they could hear me and believed that I had now informed the rest of the world.

It did the trick and both of them legged it in opposite directions.

I didn't bother to give chase, I knew who they were, had the evidence and even got their old banger. I knew roughly which village they lived in and even with my sketchy knowledge of the local geography knew it was miles away and a bloody long and miserable walk for them while contemplating when the axe would fall and they would get nicked. These were the days before mobile phones, and with very few phone boxes (that may or may not have been vandalised), doing a quick ET and phoning home for a lift was not going to be much of an option.

The Woodcocks were nicked a couple of days later by the CID; they claimed it was a case of mistaken identity but their fingerprints all over the crime scene, wire and car proved otherwise. At court they pleaded guilty along with a collection of other offences they had committed; the community service order they were handed down by the bench seemed a laughable punishment for two career criminals who had been caught red handed.

For me it was a great way of showing my new shift that I was reliable and on a personal note it convinced me that I could transfer my skills, adapt them (I would never have backed off in London, I would have gone steaming in for the arrest and no doubt a bout of fisticuffs) and still get a good result.

***

My days on the beat at Dereham were educational; I kept telling the officers just how lucky they were to still have the support of the public. Lewisham had been a war zone; them versus us and no quarter given to either side. The pace in Norfolk was much slower, well to be truthful it was sedentary but that meant I wasn't getting bogged down with rubbish calls like sorting out a noisy dog or a stroppy neighbour. We did get our fair share of peculiar requests though and I remember one old lady who rang the station one night to tell us that her tap was leaking and she was afraid it was going to flood her flat.

It was 1am when Mrs Smith phoned. PC Greybeard hadn't got his head down yet so the phone was answered promptly. "Dereham Police, how can I help you?"

The frail voice at the other end of the line forced PC Greybeard to push the receiver closer to his ear. "There's water running and I can't stop it".

"Where is it running from my love?" he asked kindly.

"It's coming out of the taps, where do you think it's coming from" the not so frail voice barked back.

Although slightly shocked at the sudden transition in this meek caller he continued in his calm voice, "I take it you have tried to turn the tap off then and it won't stop?" he coached.

"Of course I have! I'm old not bloody stupid" she replied caustically.

The conversation progressed very slowly, the tap was running and wouldn't turn off. She lived in a maisonette and the only stopcock she knew the location for was in the footpath outside her building and that also turned off the water to the other five residences in her block. She didn't know a plumber and no the situation couldn't wait until the morning. This was an emergency and she expected some action.

I was given the job to go and sort it out; it was after all past most of my colleague's bed times.

I pulled up at the address and located the bell for the top flat and Mrs Smith's emergency. I rang it and waited, then rang it and waited some more before the hall light illuminated and she came to the door. She was obviously pleased to see me. "You're a bit bleeding impatient aren't you; you'll be old one day and see how long it takes you to get to the door".

We were off to a cracking start.

"Wipe your feet before you come in, last time the doctor called he trampled dog shit right up the stair carpet".

I wiped my feet and checked for turds of any denomination before following her up the stairs into her tidy flat. It smelt of Estee Lauder, lilac soap and boiled vegetables, a cloying mix that's not that uncommon in nursing homes if you include some Dettol.

The kitchen tap was dripping with a solemn and regular beat into the stainless steel sink. It was a slow leak caused by a knackered tap washer and nothing that couldn't be sorted out by a competent (or even incompetent) plumber in ten minutes. Leaving it wasn't going to make things any worse as the escaping drips dribbled merrily down the plug hole of their own accord.

"See" she said and pointed at the offending tap, "I can't have it running like that all night".

It was hardly going to drain the local reservoir and cause a national drought but it was obviously worrying her. I opened the under sink cupboard and quickly located a stopcock that serviced only her flat. I gave it a couple of twists and the tap stopped dripping. "There you go Mrs Smith; that should hold it until you get a plumber round in the morning".

She disappeared into the bathroom and turned on the bath and basin taps both of which were devoid of water. "There's no water in them, that's no good".

"I've isolated the supply Mrs Smith so the tap won't keep dripping" I replied patiently.

"You've turned all the bloody water off, that's what you've done" she puffed. "Turn it back on and fix it properly".

Despite my best efforts she seemed to be mistaking me for some sort of uniformed plumbing service and nothing I could do or say was going to sway her. She couldn't have the water off because she always bathed first thing in the morning and it would be too hot without the cold tap working. She also needed to have a cup of tea to start the day and then have another with her breakfast. When she realised that the toilet wouldn't flush you might have been excused for thinking that I had suggested that she stuck her backside out of the window and shat on the pavement below.

Back at the nick I had a tool box in the boot of my car and I was pretty sure that I had a small box of tap washers in it. I had re-plumbed my central heating system when we had lived in London and knew my way around a tap replacement or two. Convincing her that I would return with my tool box was almost as difficult as convincing her to just turn the water off and get a plumber out in the morning.

My luck was in, the box of washers was in the toolbox and I was able to return and fix the problem which incidentally took me less time than it had to try and convince her to just shut off the stopcock.

I had the water flowing on full bore before twisting the tap and shutting it down, "There you go Mrs Smith, good as new" I said.

The old cow untrustingly completed the same operation a couple of times just in case I was engaged in some elaborate con. "Seems to be working fine now" she said begrudgingly before sneaking off to the bathroom to check the taps and the flush in there.

I gathered up my tools and put her under sink cupboard back in order as I didn't fancy a reprimand for shoddy aftersales service. "Well that should save you a few bob Mrs Smith. No need for a plumber now". I chose not to mention the fact that I had been there for forty five minutes and she hadn't even offered me a cup of tea.

"I wouldn't pay for a plumber" she informed me, "these are council owned, they have to pay for all that sort of thing. I can barely find the rent each month".

I was gobsmacked, I had just done the work of the local bloody council because the dozy old girl couldn't be arsed to wait until the morning. I snatched up my tool box, "Well if that's everything I'll leave you to it" I told her.

"Well my toilet still isn't flushing properly from the last time they came out" she informed me as I beat a hasty retreat down the stairs and back into the sanity that the rest of us call Planet Earth.

***

As the years passed the town and surrounding villages grew bigger and bigger, the workload also became more and more demanding. Small developments on the outskirts of town became huge estates that merged seamlessly into one massive housing area. Nobody slept on nights anymore; as demands for officers, increased cut backs and staff re-alignments robbed staff from the 'sticks' and beefed up the city patrols. Nearly a thousand square miles consisting of three market towns and nearly a hundred villages were patrolled by two double crewed cars. Backup was light years away and if your crew mates couldn't get to you because they were off the area with a prisoner then you were in deep shit if it all turned nasty. In one incident an officer was single crewed and ended up being chased around his patrol car by a machete wielding lunatic. It was only good fortune that the night duty traffic car happened to be passing through the area at the time and the incident didn't end badly.

By this stage I had shown a bit of aptitude when it came to getting results and being able to interview people. On one such job I had been asked to work a couple of hour's overtime to assist the CID with an investigation into some damage that kept occurring at a caravan dealership. New caravans that were due to be collected or delivered to customers were mysteriously developing dents which had to be repaired at great cost and leave the expectant new owner having to wait much longer for their new purchase. The owner had sat up for a few nights to watch and see if anyone was getting into the yard and causing the damage. He had seen someone he had fallen out with park his car next to the fence and then heard a whack on the side of a van awaiting delivery the following day. Upon inspection he found damage similar to the dents he had previously been experiencing but as it was his word against the other guy it wasn't going to be going very far in the courts. An independent police witness would make all the difference and that was going to be me.

I sat up with the owner for several nights and nothing untoward happened, he apologised and felt bad about wasting my time. The CID had hoped to see a return on their overtime investment and very quickly cancelled the operation. A week later I bumped into the owner of the dealership, who looked tired and knackered and he informed me that he was still sitting up watching over his stock each evening. He had been informed of why the observations had been stopped by the police and understood the reasons for it; he was after all a businessman and knew the need to see a return for monetary investment. I thought that I would give him a bit of moral support; I was on early turns so didn't mind doing my shift and then coming back in the evening for a couple of hours to give him a hand. If he witnessed anything when he was there on his own we would be back in the same boat he had started out in, his word against the other guy.

After work I went home, had dinner with my family and then returned to work in civvies. I let them know at the station that I was going to be doing some observations and grabbed a radio. At the dealership I had barely finished my first cup of coffee when car headlights illuminated the chain link fence that ran around the perimeter of the site. The lights were quickly extinguished and the area plunged into darkness; it was the car that had been seen on the previous occasion and it seemed as if our man was back. I slipped out of the workshop we had been using as an OP and ducked into the shadows. Slipping from under one van to the next I made my way to where I could see the outline of a man's shadow. He was walking alongside the fencing but I managed to get under the caravan next to where he stopped and could see he was carrying a long walking stick. I had left my PR in the building, I didn't want one of the night shift squawking out an order for fish and chips and giving my position away. I watched as the man lent over the fence with the stick and gave the caravan a mighty belt with the end of it. The thud must have been reassuring because he scuttled back to his car and left the area.

The following day I went to his shop to arrest him, giving him the option to attend the police station voluntarily to save embarrassment in front of his customers. As we walked the short distance towards the station he started to pump me for information. The owner of the dealership and himself were old adversaries and it didn't take him long to get to the point that it would be one man's word against another. We were still talking when I took him through to custody and formally arrested him; he was arrogant and full of swagger, telling me that I had been manipulated and lied to as part of a vendetta against him. The custody officer asked for details of the offence and I filled him in regarding the suspect having being seen by an independent witness striking the caravan and causing damage. His cockiness started to wane now that he thought a third person was involved. In typical arrogant manner he demanded to know who that witness was and when I told him he collapsed onto the bench realising that his morning was taking a really bad turn for the worse.

He didn't say a thing in interview, not until I showed him the result of the search I had made at his house. The walking stick I had seen him carrying the night before now had its ferrule wrapped in a forensically sealed plastic bag. We both knew that the end was going to match the damage; I also hoped that it would fit in with some of the other marks that had been left on previous occasions. Some weeks later I found out that they did, a positive forensic fit…game set and match!

He wasn't however a man to take his problem pragmatically. I noticed that my home telephone was giving off some high pitched feedback whenever I placed the receiver next to the body. A man ran from my garden after I had been out for the evening with friends; we had returned early and a dark figure sprinted out from behind the hedge and disappeared into the cul-de-sac opposite, ten minutes later a car sped off without its headlights on. From then onwards I would make a point of picking up the phone and saying good morning or goodnight, wave out of the window before I closed the curtains and slip out of the house under cover of darkness with my old Met truncheon and check the shrubbery and bushes in my garden. My 'stick' hadn't seen any action for years but I was sure that it would remember what to do if we found a snooper on the premises.

BT came to the house a few weeks later as I had reported the fault. Under my front window and behind a large laurel bush he found where the wires had been stripped back and the imprint of crocodile clips had scarred the surface. He was pretty sure that someone had clipped a recording device to my landline. I couldn't prove anything but now it had become personal.

The court case was a humdinger of an event, a Stipendiary Magistrate had been called in and I was facing a QC who had been called in to act on behalf of the defendant. I have given evidence in the Old Bailey and most of the High courts in London; I have also been cross examined in Crown Courts across the land. They had all been civilised affairs. This small County Magistrates Court in the middle of nowhere suddenly became alive with supporters of both the defendant and the victim. To the chorus of "liar" and hisses and boo's I rattled out my evidence, it was pure drama. The Magistrates were threatening people with expulsion and contempt whilst I paused theatrically for effect when the crowd intervened. I left the witness box to a chorus of hisses (hopefully from the defendants side but you never know with a fickle public).

The evidence given by the forensic scientist however quietened the gallery to a whisper as he told the court that beyond any doubt the defendants stick had caused the damage to that caravan and several others, the ferrule being the perfect match. The crowd's hero had stitched himself up like a kipper and they quickly realised that they had hitched their support to the wrong man. The guilty verdict came as no surprise and despite the sentence being lack lustre; justice had been done for a change.

A few weeks later I was told that the CID aid programme, which was a chance for officers to have a short period on the department to show off their potential, had been reconfigured and I was now on the next attachment. It came as a bit of a surprise because I hadn't put in for it and the posting was extended until a full time position became available for me. The following three years of service saw me become an office bound detective and I quickly became swamped in all the paperwork that goes with the job. The excitement of zooming around London was but a distant memory.

I got bogged down in an endless pile of bounced cheques, credit card fraud and the aftermath of pub punch ups. There was little reward for all the effort I was putting in and I started to resent it. The lack of continuity as to where I was working was also an issue; as I lived in Dereham I would get posted there if there was a sudden crime spike or shortage in the office. This was fine in one respect as it would knock an hour and a half off my travel time every day and save me a fortune in fuel costs. However, as soon as the problem at Dereham was sorted I would then be moved back to Thetford and was expected to pick up where I had left off. Crime files and investigations would have to be handed over to a reluctant recipient which made me as popular as a turd in a lucky dip. Also as a consequence of this toing and froing, the informants that I had cultivated would be handed on to another detective and I would have to start over again only for the same thing to happen three months further on. Being able to tune in to local affairs and pick up on the under currents is essential to being an effective detective. It gives you the edge when you interview and helps build a trust between you and the person sitting across the table.

I was working at Dereham when I attended my CID course in Wakefield; it was very intense, front loading acts and sections and points to prove. Situated next to the classroom I was in was the Armed Response Unit and I would watch with envy as they went charging out of their office, jump into their cars and speed off to sort out a problem involving firearms or weapons. It encompassed all the excitement I was yearning for.

I passed the CID exam and came back to Norfolk with a glowing course report; my reward was being told that I was now going to be working back at Thetford as they were short. As far as I could see I had jumped through all their hoops over the previous couple of years and was getting treated poorly. I was getting great results at Dereham due to the fact that I knew most of the people I was dealing with and they knew that I would treat them fairly. A couple of weeks later I noticed that Norfolk was setting up its own ARV and I wanted to be included.

I had a long chat with both the Detective Inspector and Divisional Chief Superintendent and informed them that I wanted out of CID. I explained that financially I couldn't afford to keep travelling half way across the county and requested being transferred back into uniform. Eventually they agreed to let me go and I was posted back to Dereham. It felt strange, at the time it was something officers just didn't do, go from the mighty CID back into uniform, unless there was a promotion involved. However, despite the suspicions that I had somehow cocked up and been sent back, I enjoyed getting stuck in again and doing what I did best; proactively nicking people and not spending countless hours going through lists of bounced cheques.

A few years earlier I had undertaken a firearms course, before I had officially been given a place on CID, and after only a couple of months I had been told that I could no longer keep my firearms authorisation as the Department wasn't going to release me for classification and training days. There was a ruling that if you went any longer than two years without classifying then you had to retake the basic course. The day I decided to revert back to uniform I phoned through to the firearms training wing and discussed the issues with the chief instructor. I had been fortunate enough to have been given the 'Top Student' award when I had originally passed the course so this gave me a few

Brownie points, and despite the fact that I had exceeded the two years by a narrow margin I was told to get my backside down to the firing range the following day and get some scores on the doors. I had to sneak off at the end of my shift and drive to the range so that the bosses didn't get wind of my scheme.

Now I was back in uniform I was once again an Authorised Firearms Officer (AFO) an essential qualification if I was to work on the ARV's.

The ARV's didn't get enough firearms jobs to keep them gainfully employed so they were amalgamated with the Roads Policing Department (or Traffic as it was always known before fancy title names became the order of the day). Foremost you were expected to be a traffic officer before being a firearms officer and that meant dealing with day to day collisions, traffic process and overweight vehicles. It wasn't something I relished doing I have to say but if I had to do so I would. I had never had a problem dealing with accidents; sorting out the confusion, injuries and mayhem was quite satisfying. In fact I had been given a couple of bollockings while on CID for dealing with collisions I had stumbled across when going to see witnesses. Rather than leave the scene or call for a uniform car to deal with it I had reported the incident myself much to the consternation of the DI and DS. I tried to explain that to have left the scene and pretended not to have seen it (as they had suggested) would be a dereliction of duty and that the time spent waiting for a uniformed officer to attend and take over was no longer than sorting it out myself. By dealing with it this way the department would also gain the respect of the patrol officers and it showed that we were not elitist.

But apparently we *were* elitist and I was expressly forbidden to deal with any future collisions. Mind you, neither the DI nor the DS were willing to give me written instructions to that effect or sign my note book to say they had given the order.

My first application for the ARV earned me an interview, this didn't go very well though as the superintendent of roads policing couldn't understand why I had wanted to leave CID and work on a traffic car. I tried to explain the virtues of having a trained detective working alongside trained traffic officers and cross pollinating skills but it fell on deaf ears and I didn't get the job.

Six months later the ARV's were recruiting again, staff were leaving for promotions and because they were disillusioned with the training and workload.

Once again I submitted an application and this time I didn't even get a response; someone was blocking me and as he was the boss of the Roads Policing Department I was not in a good position. My superintendent at that time was brilliant, blessed with common sense, enthusiasm and empathy for his staff he really stood out in the crowd. Known locally within the force as 'JCB Jonnie' due to his use of a digger to open the shutter doors at an illegal rave; he was a man who wasn't scared to make big decisions and the troops loved him for it.

I was just leaving for home after a night shift and a little despondent as the ARV course was starting the following week and I wasn't on it. The superintendent always tried to make a point of getting to work in time to speak to the night duty and be there when the early turn got in, he wasn't averse to sorting out the brews either which was another reason he was so well liked. He asked if I had heard anything and when I told him I hadn't and that it looked like I had missed the boat again he asked me to hang around for a few minutes while he made a phone call. He rang his counterpart and my new nemesis at roads policing enquiring as to what was happening. My fears were confirmed; I had been black balled and had no chance of getting on the ARV while he had any say in the matter. Jonnie sat on the edge of his desk and bestowed my virtues down the phone, explaining that I would be a loss to his division but a gain for the ARV. After five minutes he hung up and told me I was on the course, like I said JCB Jonnie was a real copper's copper.

The course was hard work; the MP5 was an absolute dream to shoot but a nightmare for me with regards to the stoppage drills. I was all fingers and thumbs when it came to sorting out the gun if it had a jam, it could be a matter of life or death if that happened on a job and I couldn't fix it. The harder I practiced the more difficult it became and I would just get a mental block. It seemed that the biggest hurdle to getting onto the ARV was me.

We moved away from the shooting and handling aspects of the MP5 and concentrated on the tactics; deployment from the vehicles and working with the cars to execute hard stops. I loved it and enjoyed every minute of the training, from the setting up of road blocks to the forcing of vehicles to stop at gun point. Talking the occupants out of their cars and controlling their movements until they were safely in custody was all that I had hoped it would be.

When we eventually went back to the range the instructors loaded up my magazines; they put empty shell cases in with the live rounds so that I would get stoppages in a real live fire exercise. It was just what I needed and by the end of the shoot I had the magazine off, breach cleared and mag back in in one fluid motion. Not only that, I achieved a perfect fifty out of fifty on the targets and had really tight groupings; I had buried my demons and went on to love the MP5 and appreciate it for being the fine piece of engineering it truly was. I have to say that I can barely remember a time when I actually missed the target; even the 100 metre shoots we undertook on the rifle range just using the ring and post iron sights were accurate enough for me to be confident to have taken a shot if the situation had required it. There is something satisfying in seeing the small man sized target in the distance slowly developing a dark patch in the middle of the chest area; this 'patch' being the groupings of the rounds as they punched a tight hole through it.

When the course finished I was a fully trained ARV officer and the fun was just about to start.

***

I was no stranger to putting in loads of training time on the firing ranges we used. At that time there was one situated on a battle area just outside of Watton, sitting on the corner of the Thetford Chase forest, a vast area that the army used for large scale manoeuvres on its wide and open plains. There was even a river running through it for the soldiers to play bridge building on and it also housed the FIBUA (Fighting In Built-up Urban Areas), a purpose built mock-up of an Eastern bloc town. In those days the Cold War was still a real threat so it provided the troops with a layout of the type of urban area they could be deployed to. This really was a big boys (and girls of course) playground that allowed the ARV's to be driven into a scenario as they would be in real life.

As Norfolk didn't own its own range we hired a variety of places to shoot on; converted chicken sheds that were owned by a small bore gun club and an outdoor shooting club that had both a 30 metre shoot and a 400 metre rifle range. Granted the chicken sheds were great in inclement weather but they were absolute hell in the height of summer; the residual smell of chicken shit had never quite been eradicated despite the amount of cordite that permeated the walls. It was dark and cramped and extremely noisy. The onset of my tinnitus can be traced back to these huts and every night I get a constant reminder of the place.

But by far the worse was the battle area where a field would be designated for our use by the range master and an impromptu range set up for the days training. It was awful, a bleak and desolate place with no cover from the elements. The grass had never been cut and grew a couple of feet high in places, hiding the uneven ground that would cause you to trip over or twist an ankle. Grazing sheep (removed before the firing started) and rabbits (who generally fucked off right sharpish when they saw us arrive) had left little piles of excrement for the unwary or those unlucky enough to lay or kneel in when taking their turn to shoot. When firing from the prone position you could often see your rounds cutting through the grass en route to the target. The targets would sway in the wind whenever there was the slightest breeze and with very little in the way of natural features to diffuse it, that same breeze would cut through you like a knife. Sunny weather provided no cover at all and officers would finish the day with blinding headaches, dehydration and sun burnt faces. Getting a good score on this range was a credit to the officer's skill and resilience. Of course the training staff would tell us that it was character building, that we were practicing in the types of weather we could most likely expect to be deployed in. It was scant consolation when you are wringing wet, shivering in the cold, covered in animal shit and have failed to shoot straight all day.

The chicken sheds may have been smelly and uncomfortably hot in the summer but they at least had toilets and a canteen area where you could make hot drinks and wash your hands. Incidentally, it was in those chicken sheds that I first strapped on a gun and felt the weight on my hip and the feeling of the responsibility that goes with it. We had been taken there on our selection day and given the opportunity to fire six rounds at a target just to see how we reacted. It was a surprise when a couple of people dropped out after having got that far; it was a brave and extremely honest thing to do. There is a difference between the wish to do something but then facing the reality of what that entails. The first time that gun kicks in your hand and rips a hole in the target in front of you it is a statement of your intent and commitment; that you are, in the right circumstances prepared to do that to another human being should the situation require it. It is a big moment and those that don't see it as such should perhaps rethink their reasons for being there. Ultimately you are signing up to say you are prepared to put yourself in harm's way and react accordingly, even if it could have fatal consequences. There is no extra pay for having this type of skill set on your record, no improvement in your promotions prospects and every opportunity to drop yourself into some very deep shit should the wheel ever come off.

The chicken sheds were also the first time I ever 'shot anyone' during a training session. The guns were without bullets, either blanks or chalk rounds, the scenarios were set up to make you fail, it was the first day of the course and we knew the square route of fuck all about tactics. Working in pairs we had the simple task of apprehending a man with a pistol; he offered no resistance and complied with the instructions we gave him. His brief was to comply exactly with those instructions and he did so with great aplomb and when my partner told him to place the gun on the floor he did so... and pointed the business end straight at him. I had a split second to react; did the gunman mean to point the weapon in such a menacing manner, was he intent on pulling the trigger as his finger was pressing on it? These questions flew through my head quicker than I could register them. The answer came back quickly and I shot the man in the chest from less than five metres away.

In real life the .38 bullet would have ripped a hole in the centre of his chest and it would have almost certainly been a fatal shot. In reality all that happened was that my pistol dry clicked on an empty chamber, leaving me to call out that I had fired. To say that I felt sick was an understatement, was this something I wanted to do for real, put myself on offer for the shit storm that would collapse on me if this had been a real incident?

Having made my decision to 'shoot' I was asked to explain why I had done it, the reasons I gave were as they expected; poor instructions. The exercise served to reinforce the message that once you had a person under control then you talked them through every step of what you wanted them to do. If you didn't, you placed them and others in peril. It was a lesson that stayed with me for the rest of my career.

We had all been told what to expect should we ever be involved in a 'contact'. A guy from another Force had spoken to us about his experiences after a fatal shooting and it left us without a shred of doubt that the hierarchy would turn their backs on us, ensuring that in the public eye and the press they themselves were beyond reproach. This guy had reacted to a genuine life or death situation; a gunman had refused to comply and then deliberately tried to use his weapon, it had resulted in him being shot dead and in my view quite rightly as there were no other options than to risk him killing an innocent bystander. As soon as his Force realised that someone could lose their pension over the incident they quickly ensured that it wasn't going to be one of them.

The officer had been removed from the presence of his colleagues, his weapon seized and he had been driven to a police station where he was kept segregated and isolated, effectively under arrest. His clothing had been taken and he was given the one piece paper suit generally issued to prisoners, and a pair of slippers. The slippers were odd sizes and didn't match and the whole process smacked of a total disregard and lack of respect for the officer involved. He wasn't allowed to contact his family and let them know what had happened, in many ways he was given less courtesy than the guy he had shot would have been given if he had let him shoot his intended victim. The officer was later cleared of any misdoings and commended on his actions by the coroner, scant compensation for the PTSD (post-traumatic stress disorder) he was experiencing due to the bullish behaviour of his superiors.

The message to us new recruits to the firearms department was clear; even if you do your job professionally you will most likely end up in the same situation.

***

Eventually Norfolk splashed out on its first purpose built range that we could finally call home. It was a much better environment to train in, the fact that it would flood on the odd occasion was neither here nor there. Later, when the Force relocated its headquarters to outside Norwich, it brought with it the opportunity to have a second new range attached to the training wing and the construction of a purpose built state of the art area that could accommodate vehicles and live fire tactics all at the same time.

Prior to all the high tech facilities being available, there was always the question of who had the best personal issue kit, it being something of a one-upmanship affair. In the early days of the conception of the ARV's there was great scope for the vain to invest in their own Gucci equipment. This extended to the purchase of various makes of combat style boots, the SFG (Special Firearms Group) were all issued with the latest in lightweight, supple Gortex footwear which were based upon military spec. The ARV's were their poorer cousins despite the fact that we were doing the job 24/7 and the SFG were on a call out only basis, most having other policing roles to undertake when not on a firearms job.

Most of us wore the boots we had been issued with for PSU (Police Support Unit) duties and they were designed specifically for that type of use; steel toecaps, rigid ankle support and corrosive proof reinforced inch thick soles...subtle they were not! Driving a high performance vehicle while trying to keep the gear changes, braking and acceleration smooth in this type of footwear is akin to making Sebastian Vettel race in diver's boots. Being the consummate professional he would probably still give a great performance but I bet he couldn't deliver the same smooth telemetry readings he would normally achieve. Not being a naturally fast and smooth driver I always felt the pressure to ensure that my crewmate was given a good drive when it was my turn to push and having a couple of boulders on each foot made it almost impossible.

Buying a pair of boots similar to the spec of those issued to the SFG was cost prohibitive but Hitec came up with a good alternative when they introduced their hybrid trainer boot called the Magnum. It had the same structure as a training shoe which made it lightweight, leather and nylon uppers which gave it flexibility and a padded ankle rib for comfort. They were also much cheaper than the Gortex versions and officers who had purchased them swore that they were the dog's bollocks. At the same time another company quickly released a similar product that looked every inch to be the same boot but were marketed at an even lower price; this tempted me to buy them instead of the Magnums. My crew partner Gray bought the upmarket version and we both raved about the improvement they were over the other boots we had previously been wearing. During the summer months they were a godsend, the nylon gusset allowed air to circulate around your feet so that you weren't a bio hazard when you removed your footwear at the end of the shift. The leather was also of a good quality and it was easy to keep a good shine on them even after a day of dusty training on the range.

It annoyed Gray that he had paid more for his boots than I had and hadn't really seen a return for his additional investment as they seemingly performed exactly the same as mine did. Both pairs were put to the ultimate test one very wet Sunday afternoon when we were called to some serious flooding on one of our main arterial routes. A section of carriageway was under three inches of water due to a river bursting its banks and our job was to keep the road open until the highways team could deploy and sandbag the area. Within seconds of stepping out of the car and wading into the water I realised that the manufacturer's waterproof guarantee might have been a bit over ambitious, either that or I was a bit ambitious in my expectations as to what constituted waterproof. My feet were both sodden and would have squelched audibly with every step had they not been almost permanently underwater. Gray looked over to me "How are your boots holding up?" he asked.

"Great" I lied, "feet are as dry as a bone. How about yours?"

"Same" he said "feet are really toasty".

I was feeling cheated and the thing was that I had cheated myself, for the sake of a few quid more I would have had nice dry cosy feet too. However I wasn't going to let on that small fact to Gray, the last thing I needed now was wet feet and him gloating about how dry and snug his were. The Highways department didn't try and set any records to get to us quickly; in fact we had dug a relief channel with our lightweight self-assembly plastic shovel and had reduced the torrent to a trickle before they arrived. We would have done better but the wind caught the shovel and it floated away down the river never to be seen again.

Weight was always a factor with the armed cars, the heavy bullet proof doors and gun safes we carried put a huge strain on the vehicles payload and measures were always being looked in to ways of cutting down on the type of kit we carried and what it was made from. We had collapsible plastic cones that folded up and fitted neatly into a box instead of the conical dunces hat type carried by other police vehicles. In keeping with this we, as the crew would make a concerted effort to do our bit; Hector, another ARV crew member being the only person not to understand the need not to bring the kitchen sink with him when he went out on patrol. After a couple of serious crashes it was found that despite everyone's best efforts the cars were grossly overweight on their rear axles and liable to break away when pushed to the limit causing the back of the vehicle to try and swap ends with the front. Why our workshops had never realised that the bump stop rubbers they were replacing on the cars on a regular basis were not indicating a weight problem and a potential tragic accident waiting to happen I don't know.

Just why the fleet manager hadn't bothered to have the vehicle weighed in its ARV trim would have been comical had lives not been put at risk.

***

After several hours of wading through the floodwater we were eventually relieved by the Highways guys who promptly threw out a couple of sandbags and cured the problem of the river spreading across the highway. They looked over at us as if to say why couldn't you have just done that in the first place and saved us the trouble of having our Sunday lunch disturbed. We climbed back into the vehicle and I set the temperature gauge to maximum, the blower to full speed and directed it down towards my feet. For the first time in hours I could feel some warmth starting to radiate around my toes. As we drove away Gray executed a couple of lumpy gear changes which was highly unusual as he would always be silky smooth. I looked across at him quizzically.

"OK, I'll admit it; my boots leaked so much my feet are numb. Bastard things were supposed to be fucking waterproof" he let rip, "I paid more for them than you did for yours, but your feet are bleeding dry".

He wasn't happy, but I was. "Can't believe yours let in water" I remarked. "When did they start doing that?"

"Soon as I stepped out of the bloody car" he said miserably.

"You lying toad" I exclaimed. "You told me your feet were dry".

"Yeah well I didn't want you standing there with a smug grin on your face did I?" he replied.

I squelched my toes up and down a bit so that he could hear just how dry they actually were. He looked over towards me, "You lying fucker, your feet are as wet as mine...can't believe I've stood there all that time cursing the fact I didn't buy your boots instead".

We quickly established that the boots were waterproof for a light shower of rain and anything beyond that was liable to end up with us getting trench foot, although the nylon gussets were good in some respects as they allowed some of the residual water to run out if you raised your foot high enough. We headed back to the nick and fired up the gas oven. Stuffing our sodden footwear with newspaper we balanced them on the open door, two pairs of wet socks hung down from the grill housing and we both luxuriated in the ambient heat in our bare feet.

***

On a firearms operation little things always went wrong, they were after all live incidents that permitted very little in the way of preparation time. Often the planning stage was being thrashed out between the crews of the two ARV's as they sped across Norfolk to their RVP (Rendezvous Point). The training we received was based on the fact that two crews, four officers, would be attending and initially dealing with the job. Often the two cars would be fifty or so miles apart from each other and this required some pretty fast driving with some frantic planning and coordinating over the mobile phone network.

Our primary role was to attend quickly and either contain the situation or neutralise it without any further risk to the public. It was a dream job...drive fast cars, meet bad people and then thrust a gun in their face. Of course the reality was that we would be scrambled and break our necks getting to some god forsaken corner of Norfolk where we would then be on 'stand by' for hours on end, only to be sent back to our areas without seeing an angry person (my crew partner not included), let alone some gun wielding villain. It wasn't unknown for us to order the odd pizza to be delivered to our lay-up point, the delivery guys often more intent on what sort of kit we were carrying than sorting out the right change.

As the law of sod will dictate sometimes everything that can go wrong will...

"Tango Charlie Two Four, Tango Charlie Two Four...Zebra Zero Two" the radio was playing our favourite tune. 'Zebra Zero Two' was the call from the control room inspector giving us authority to arm. The location given was a well-known estate in the Norwich area and the call related to a potential hostage situation. Our role was to contain the block of flats so that the SFG could be called out, briefed and then deployed. Our training included 'dynamic entries' but only as part of an emergency action; that being a house entry to prevent the immediate loss of life to a friendly. The SFG's trained specifically for this type of thing and were with no doubt the experts.

As we had a fair way to drive; about thirty miles combined and the fact that it was a static job, I agreed with my crew partner 'Hector' that we would arm up once we got there. It was a lot more comfortable in the car if we didn't have to don our ballistic body armour and buckle on gun belts festooned with kit. Having a couple of MP5 carbines wedged between the seats and centre console wasn't desirable either, although in some circumstances where people were on the move on foot or mobile in vehicles, it would be foolhardy not to have all your kit to hand and be ready to strike at the first opportunity. Our speciality over the SFG was that we were the experts in what was termed 'hard stops' where we would literally force a vehicle to stop and then by the art of gentle persuasion (point firearms at them) control their actions and arrest the occupants. The whole basis of our training was to ensure that through our tactics and firepower we didn't have to use the weapons other than as a deterrent to stop our quarry from doing anything rash or stupid.

The MP5's, spare magazines and smoke grenades were housed in a metal gun cabinet that was attached to the back of the rear seat and two Glock pistols sat in another gun safe in the centre console between the driver and passenger seats. This enabled us to be able to get to our side arms extremely quickly should we come across a situation that needed us to be armed.

Hector wasn't my normal crew partner, he worked on another team within the unit, but it wasn't unusual to mix and match partners to cover leave and court appearances. Luckily we mostly all got on well with each other; those that didn't managed to tolerate each other for the period of their eight hour tour.

On this occasion Hector and I took advantage of a comfortable drive and called up our sister crew call sign TC25 who were the Norwich based team and therefore only minutes from the job.

The phone rang and the dulcet tones of Big Pete came booming over the loud speaker "Is that 'Tango Charlie Too Late'?" he enquired with a chuckle. A good proportion of the jobs were based in the city or at Great Yarmouth which often meant their crew would arrive before us and hence their amendment to our call sign.

"Greetings 'Tango Charlie Two Teas', I take it that you are already on plot?" I asked. As they were inclined to arrive at the RVP first for briefings they would be tasked with sorting out two mugs of tea for us when we arrived.

"No time for tea today Scottie we are on plot and about to get eyes on the building. We've just spoken to a couple of the local guys who think it's genuine".

The story was that a drug deal had gone sour and the tenant of the premises owed some nasty people a fair amount of money which they had apparently just come to the flat to collect. Not bothering with the niceties of calling beforehand or even ringing the bell they had simply put in his front door; armed with knives and a crossbow negotiations regarding the repayment of the loan were going to be very one sided. Our intended victim managed to climb out through a window neglecting to take either his wife or their young daughter with him. He had managed to find the time though to snatch up his mobile phone before leaving his family to fend for themselves. The bad guys had phoned him and said that if he didn't return then his family would be getting what was supposed to be coming to him, the screams of his wife in the background testament to their intent. Having spent a lifetime avoiding the law our drug addled 'victim's' first port of call was the nearest police station demanding sanctuary and help for his family. As the oath we all take when we join the job mentions 'without fear or favour' the whole hostage rescue team was launched.

It was the back end of the rush hour and we had a relatively straight forward run to the RVP. Big Pete had periodically given us updates during our blue light dash and informed us that he had assigned us to 'white face' and they were setting up on 'black face'.

Premises are given differing colours to denote areas of responsibility, white is what will be deemed for all intents and purposes as the front of the house, black the rear with red and green denoting the sides. On this op we would have the front door and as Big Pete had already pointed out, there wasn't a rear one so they had taken the area the lounge windows overlooked. The job sounded like it had good potential. If we had to go in quickly before the SFG arrived, Hector and I were going to be first through the door, and whilst

Hector relished this prospect, I wasn't looking forward to it. A crossbow is a strange weapon with so many variants you can never be sure if it's something from the stage set of William Tell or a Special Forces one bought from Russia. The William Tell type is good for shooting apples off heads; the Russian Spetznat one is good for shooting heads off shoulders.

We pulled up into a cordoned area and started kitting up, first with our personal weapons, followed by other bits of kit that we all toted about with us. I had a Leatherman multi-purpose utility tool kit that my son had bought me for Christmas; I also had a gravity knife that extended a four inch blade at the press of a button. These types of non-issue kit were heavily frowned upon but I knew that the hostage release knife we all had strapped to our belts or body armour would be pretty useless if faced with an aggressive dog as they were not designed for stabbing.

***

Years before and on my very first firearms deployment I had found myself in a ditch in the hedgerow of a small field staking out a caravan in the middle of nowhere. I had been partnered by an experienced officer who was there to make sure that I didn't make any silly mistakes. During the night and under cover of darkness, our role was to put floodlights up that would bathe the caravan in light, giving us a clear view of any goings on and to shield what we were doing behind the bright glare. The generator was rented and hastily acquired when it became apparent that it was going to be a long and lengthy siege. What hadn't been factored into the equation when the kit was collected was just how long the electric cable would need to be in order to power the lights from a safe distance. The cable was woefully short and in order to make the best of a bad job the generator had to be located in the middle of the field behind some straw bales.

A second major flaw in this great plan was the short amount of time the generator would run before its fuel tank emptied itself and plunged us all into darkness. Every three hours my partner and I had to crawl from the cover of our ditch the two hundred feet to where the generator would be coughing and gasping as the last remnants of its fuel was being consumed. The guy in the caravan, aware of what we were doing would open the caravan door and encourage his dogs to 'find them'; the hounds would then start baying fit to bust.

The first time we had to top up the generator it had completely conked out, it had wheezed twice and the lights had dimmed before silence descended along with the darkness. As we leopard crawled arm over arm across the damp and muddy field the dogs could clearly be heard barking and snarling; they were outside the van and looking for trouble. I had no intention of getting some mangy mutt attached to any part of my anatomy having witnessed first-hand the mess a dog will make of someone given half a chance and a bit of encouragement. I drew the .38 Smith and Wesson model 10 pistol I had been issued with earlier in the day and prepared myself to use it if the hounds attacked.

"What the fuck are you doing?" asked my chaperone "you'll never get a clear shot off in time".

"I'm going to wrap my left arm in my jacket and let it bite down on that, then I'm going to blow its fucking head off" I informed him while rapidly removing my woefully thin coat.

"Are you fucking mad? You're going to let it bite you?" he asked in horror.

"It's not as though I'm likely to get any say in the matter is it? It'll grab the nearest bit of human and latch on to it. I'd rather it was my arm and not my nuts" I replied tersely. The barking was getting closer as the dogs were getting braver.

"If you're going to go all Tarzan on its arse then you'll have to stab it instead" he suggested while removing his own, somewhat thicker coat "if you fire a shot and miss or it goes straight through, God only knows where it might end up". He waited until I holstered the pistol. "You have got a knife haven't you?" he added.

I pulled the small pen knife from my pocket and extended the inch and a half blade.

"Fuck me if that's all you've got then you are well in the shit" was all he could say. I heard the sound of what sounded like a sabre being drawn from its scabbard, the slick rasp of metal on metal seemed to last an eternity until he held his own blade in front of him. I looked over towards his silhouette and could see the dull sheen of what must have been eighteen inches of bayonet. He grinned, "I've put an edge on both sides, I'll skewer it like a kebab" he said with a wicked grin.

If one of the dogs came for me I'd have more chance of sticking my arm down its throat and choking it to death than trying to stab it with my puny penknife. Whoever said that big is not always best has never lain in a field with the Hounds of the Baskervilles baying for their blood or their bollocks.

The dogs were called off before they got close enough to cause us any more consternation but for the rest of that operation I definitely suffered from knife envy.

***

Hector was well known for his love of extra kit, his grab bag was twice the size of everybody else's and he would struggle to haul the dead weight from the locker room to the rear seat of the car. Nobody knew for sure what he kept in it and I'm pretty sure that Hector didn't know either. One morning another crew working from our base got into work early and loaded an old Olympia typewriter into his bag and stifled their laughter as they watched him struggle down the corridor with it. He didn't notice until the end of the day when he went to get something out of it and found he had his own semi-permanent office with him.

Practical jokes were a way of life for the teams and we would plot and plan against our non ARV colleagues as well as each other. We were divided into teams of three, the reasoning being that two officers would staff the ARV and give the other member a day where he could just perform normal duties. We were attached to the traffic department and if not gainfully employed on a job we were expected to attend accidents and generally carry out the work expected of an officer on that department. We were a mixed bunch, some officers had been recruited from the traffic department itself and others like me from CID or beat patrols. Although not natural bedfellows the mix of skills made the ARV guys extremely efficient with an all-round knowledge bar none. The ability to quickly assess situations, take control and deal with it made them a welcome sight whenever there was trouble. All this seriousness had a joker mentality flip side and practical jokes and wind-ups were a way of life. Only a fool was silly enough to leave their packed lunch unattended in the crew room fridge, because as soon as their backs were turned it would be placed in the freezer for several hours and then replaced seconds before the owner returned to the office for their meal break. Take some annual leave and forget to hide your mug or boots away and you would return to find that some joker had grown a crop of cress in them for you. On one occasion I came back from leave to find that Hector had banjoed (forced the door) my locker open and placed my jacket in a plastic bag which he sealed and then put in an even larger plastic sack which he then filled with fifty litres of water before shoving the whole lot into the freezer in the kitchen. After two weeks holiday I was faced with the biggest ice cube I had ever seen and there in the middle of it was some of my uniform. Fortunately for me the kitchen was on the first floor and I dropped the whole thing out of the window causing it to explode like a mortar shell. It took two days before the ice residue it left behind finally melted. Hector had hoped that I was going to have to melt the whole thing under one of the toilet hand dryers for a couple of hours in order to free my stuff before being able to go out on patrol. He also admitted that it had been his second attempt as his first try had seen him split the bag as he tried to fit it onto the shelving; he flooded the kitchen floor with water which took him an hour to mop up before he repeated the whole process again but on this occasion he used a little more finesse.

By way of retaliation my crew partner KP (so named because he was fucking nuts) brought in an advert from one of the Sunday newspapers. We filled in the application form which consisted of an invitation for Hector to attend a health spa and be pampered like a lady; it did however require him to be dressed as a lady as it was a cross dressers jolly that we thought he might enjoy. A brochure and booking form arrived at the police station addressed to him. It was a laugh watching his indignation as he ranted, wondering how they had got his details and why would anyone think that he would be interested in such an activity.

The joke unfortunately had serious consequences as during the following weeks he started to receive all manner of pamphlets and paraphernalia relating to gay pornography; our prank was quickly turning into the joke that kept on giving. I hadn't admitted that I been involved in the original prank and adopted the role of caring colleague advising him to contact the company as they had obviously sold his details on. The conversation went along the lines of...

"Hello this is Mr Stoneman and you appear to have me on your mailing list. I would like to be taken off please".

"I'm sorry sir but we have no control over who is on that list".

"So you are telling me that I'm going to keep receiving material relating to gay sex and cross dressing events?"

"Yes sir, as I said we have no control on who's on the mailing list".

"What if I was to tell you that I am a serving police officer and you are sending all this stuff to a Police Station?"

"Um, please bear with me a moment...OK sir you have now been removed from our mailing list".

"Thank you".

Nothing more arrived through the post after that and the only mystery still to be solved was who had started the prank in the first place. The News of The World article had been secreted in Hector's crew partner's paperwork drawer where it was hoped that it would be discovered some weeks later as this would cause Hector to retaliate against someone else and I could sit back and watch the fun.

***

Back at the siege Hector was unloading the ballistic shield as a crossbow had been mentioned in the briefing and there was a likelihood we would have to put the door in and storm the house if things got tricky. It was a cumbersome piece of kit to cart about but we wouldn't have time to run back to the car to get the shield if the shit hit the fan. We also added the powerful Dragonlight and our own personal Maglights to the other kit hanging off our belts and TAC vests, dusk was quickly approaching and torches would be necessary if someone made a break from the house.

Having got all our kit together we performed coms checks on the two personal radios we both carried. It was essential that all the ARV crews could communicate with each other on the dedicated and encrypted firearms channel; short sharp updates or instructions were delivered in a clipped and precise manner. The other radio was tuned into the main channel so that we could monitor what was going on outside of our own private little world, enabling us to give the control room inspector situation reports, keeping him and his tactical advisor abreast of what we were doing and planning.

Communications were always the biggest bug bear on any operation and this occasion wasn't going to be any different. I could receive the other team loud and clear in my earpiece and they could hear me but unfortunately Hector's rig wasn't receiving at all. It was the opposite way around when it came to the main channel and I had absolutely nothing going on with my set whereas he could hear clearly. So long as we didn't get split up then we would be able to manage.

"Coms are fucked as usual" I moaned to Hector, "you'll have to update the inspector and I'll relay to and from Tango Charlie Two Five".

"We might have to rely on hand signals" Hector offered gleefully. He loved all the SWAT style gestures but I thought it made him look more TWOT than SWAT.

"Here's one for you to be getting on with Hector" I said giving him the wanker sign.

We stowed all our excess gear with a local patrol officer and moved forward to recce the target building and surroundings. Big Pete's description had been bang on and we soon found a good place to set up our OP. The spot with the best overall view was the rear garden of a little old lady. We had a good view of the area adjacent to the target premises but were still a fair way from the front door should we have to act quickly; there was also a lot of open ground we would have to cover which would leave us exposed and deny us the element of surprise. Our other option was to take cover under a bank of conifers; they were closer but gave us a more restricted overview. We agreed to set up for vision as we knew that the SFG had been called out and should be in a position to take down the building before we would be required to act.

We found some hard cover in the old ladies garden and made ourselves comfortable as these things had a tendency to drag on in a protracted manner once the negotiations phase started.

One of the local officers had asked us if he could come forward to our position to act as a 'gofer' (someone to 'go for' this and 'go for' that). It was always handy having an extra pair of hands on standby and my stomach was already rumbling; I could feel a pizza order coming on. The delivery riders wouldn't be able to get through the outer cordon so we would need someone to fetch the food for us. We might even be able to get him into chatting the old lady up and getting us a couple of hot brews, like I said making oneself comfortable was essential because nobody else was going to look after you. It was also handy having someone watching your back as it wasn't unheard of for a team to be plotted up only to find a householder openly trotting over to them with a couple of bacon butties. At least our additional support would be there to stop the old dear should she feel the need to pop out into the garden. If she felt the urge to knock up a couple of bacon butties then he could bring them out to us. Like I said, the trick was to make yourselves as comfortable as you could.

We thanked the lad and I told him to find himself some hard cover behind our position, in between us and the back door, and he ducked into what had once been a concrete coal bunker. At some point someone had removed the roof and front of the structure and the old lady had been using the area to dump ashes from the fire. He was as keen as he could be to get involved and squatted on his haunches in his concrete box like a coiled spring just happy to have a bit part in what was looking to be a good job. Seeing him cramped up in that position made me chuckle to myself, after twenty minutes his muscles would be screaming for mercy but his enthusiasm was overriding his common sense. Hector and I on the other hand were laid prone on the soft grass of the ladies lawn.

I had the binoculars trained on the ground floor windows hoping to get some indication as to what was going on inside the target premises. The curtains had been drawn and I could just make out a silhouette moving backwards and forwards, it could have been the same person or different subjects I couldn't tell. Hopefully as the evening got darker the indoor light might give us a better insight with more definitive shadows. I passed the bino's to Hector who kept watch while I updated TC25. The other crew were in a lot closer than us and could hear voices but were unable to identify what was being said.

It was certainly shaping up to be a pucker job.

Hector started to make hand signals to me indicating that we should move forward using his fingers in a walking movement before stabbing his hand towards the conifers.

"Hector, I'm fucking lying next to you so there is no need for all the bloody hand signals" I whispered, "anyway I've just got comfortable".

Reluctant to speak but realising that I wasn't going to play charades with him he hissed back, "I think we ought to be in a position to be able to EA".

Hector would have liked nothing more than to rappel in through the window of the maisonette with his hostage release knife clamped between his teeth and MP5 blazing. "If we go forward then we'll never be able to get a pizza" I reasoned.

"Fuck the pizza Scottie, lives are at stake here" he retorted somewhat melodramatically.

"Give it five and let's see if Tango Charlie Two Five can get a better scope on what's happening" I said.

Hector wasn't happy but reluctantly agreed to wait for five minutes. I updated TC25 and Big Pete agreed that there was no need to be hasty at this stage.

I was certain that there wasn't going to be a need to storm the place, it was Norfolk not New York, however if we were going to have to move forward quickly then it would be a good idea if we had a quick route sorted out.

The end of the garden was denoted by a wooden picket fence and I could see there was a wooden gate in the middle of it which had been secured with some cable ties. It wouldn't hurt to cut through them so we had a quick egress out of the garden if the need arose, and I didn't fancy hurdling over the fence with all the extra shit we were carrying. I told Hector that I was going to move forward and cut the cable ties and he agreed by signalling OK with one of his hand signals.

Before I could move I heard mute cursing from our gofer who had broken cover and was performing a strange dance on the old ladies back porch.

"What the fucks up with him?" Hector enquired.

"No bloody idea" I replied, "he needs to shut the fuck up though before everyone in the estate knows we are here".

The lad disappeared sharpish only to return a few minutes later with a rather sheepish look on his face.

"What was all that about? " Hector asked.

"My legs were starting to ache and I was shuffling around to try and get into a comfortable position" he looked embarrassed. "Unfortunately the old girl empties her ashes there and I seemed to have stirred them up" he lifted up the sole of his boot which had become a large squidgy mess, "it's only gone and melted my soles" he moaned.

He hobbled off to change his footwear and with him went my lifeline for a pizza. That made up my mind to move forward, there was no need to be in the old girls garden now so I turned to Hector and signalled that we should move forward.

He responded immediately, obviously pleased that I was getting into the spirit of things. He gestured with a big thumbs up and started to collect up our kit.

"Glad you agree" I said, bursting his bubble on the hand signal only front.

I called up the other team and told them we were moving forward.

Taking the hostage release knife from its sheath on my TAC vest I crawled forward to the gate. Running the blade down between it and the post, I quickly cut through both the cable ties and pushed to make sure it was unobstructed. As I applied the pressure I became aware that the gate itself wasn't moving but the whole length of picket fencing was slowly falling over. Someone had used the stability of the gate to keep the bloody fence in place and it now lay broken on the ground. I looked back at Hector who was pissing himself with laughter and making the wanker sign at me. On this occasion the hand signal was appropriate.

I crawled back. "Fucking garden is just one large booby trap" I complained as I started to gather up my kit.

Taking it in turns to provide cover whilst the other person moved, we leapfrogged our way into the treeline. There wasn't much space under the lower branches of the large leylandi we had chosen as our new vantage point and with us both under the tree along with all our kit gathered around us it was a pretty tight fit. I don't react well to certain types of conifer trees and could already feel the exposed skin on the back of my neck starting to itch. Minutes later I was scratching myself like a flea ridden dog.

Hector looked quizzically at me and mimed "What's up?"

I didn't know the hand signal for my predicament so just pointed to the low branches and a made a clawing action on my skin.

Hector continued to look quizzical.

"Fucking tree's bringing me out in hives" I whispered, "we are going to have to move".

Hector shook his head, "Soak it up Scottie, we've only just got here".

I pulled up the collar of my coveralls and wished that I had brought my balaclava with me but I always felt that it was a bit theatrical and showy as well as being restrictive. The powers to be frowned on their use as the ARV's were a fairly new concept and they didn't want to have gun toting cops running wild on their streets looking like terrorists. It was a view that they had to change over the following months as the professionalism of the crews shone through.

Every time the gentle breeze stirred the trees, branches scraped over the top of my helmet like fingernails on a blackboard. I gave Hector a hateful stare; it had been pleasantly comfortable in the garden and now five minutes later I was being tortured by a sodding leylandi.

"Two Four from Five, we've got movement in the house and a raised voice" Big Pete informed me, "things seem to be hotting up, consider moving forward to EA positions".

I relayed this info to Hector and watched his eyes light up; he was closest to the building so I indicated that he should move first while I provided cover. He crawled forward a couple of metres before signalling that he had encountered an obstacle.

"Two Five from Four we are going to the Form Up Position (FUP) but will take a few seconds to get in place". I informed Big Pete.

"Copy, we'll keep monitoring for as long as we can" he replied.

Hector was trying to climb over a three strand wire fence that was just under a metre high. He reached over and placed his MP5 on the far side and stretched his leg over but it flexed violently with his weight and catapulted him backwards onto his arse. The lower strand of the fence moved forward so violently that it propelled his MP5 into the distance and deep into a bunch of stinging nettles. He looked over to see me miming wanker and he gave me the finger before renegotiating the fence and scrambling through the nettles to find his weapon. His curses were just audible as his unprotected wrists made contact with the acidic leaves. Once he relocated his weapon he motioned that he was going forward. He found cover and I quickly followed, being very careful not to repeat his experience on the wire. The shield had snagged on the trees and there were a couple of branches trapped in the firing notch. From his fall Hector had pieces of bracken stuck to his TAC vest and twigs caught on his helmet strap. Big Pete raised a quizzical eye when we reached the FUP and I just shook my head as if to say "Don't ask".

Hector grabbed the shield from my arm denoting he was volunteering for point duty, typical as I had lugged the bloody thing all the way from the old girls house and across no man's land. Big Pete had the wham ram which was a short snub nosed solid metal tube that would be smashed into the lock on the door to force an entry. He gently pushed against the door to find points of resistance. In his hands the wham ram was lethal and I had never seen anything get the better of him, he was built like a brick shit house and extremely strong. The plastic door confronting us would stand no chance, it already showed signs of having been similarly opened on previous occasions and the large dirty footprint in the middle was potential evidence of the latest attempt earlier that evening.

Satisfied that he had the correct strike point identified he signalled that he was good to go. We took a second just to settle ourselves and started the finger countdown.

"Mum, can I have a biscuit?" The voice of a small child came from the other side of the door. Hector frantically signalled a halt.

"You've had your fucking tea" was the response from a female voice deep in the building. "Stop keep fucking asking for food all the time" she added.

There didn't seem to be any tension within the confines of the premises and that's unusual if someone is threatening your life. Something was wrong and a quick look over my shoulder reassured me that I wasn't the only person thinking that. Hector kept us stacked up but in the hold position.

"When's Dad coming home?" the little girl asked.

"I don't fucking know do I, probably still running scared, cowardly little bastard" the woman replied. "And don't think you'll get any fucking biscuits out of him when he gets back either".

It seemed like the only person who was in any danger at the moment was the child, growing up with the parents she had would be detrimental to anyone's health.

Hector signalled withdraw and we backed up until we were out of sight. Big Pete was on the main channel updating the control inspector with a sit rep. Squawking in his other ear and in those of us who still had working radio rigs was the SFG commander who announced that they were about to arrive on plot and looking for a RVP and safe route in to it. In a quick huddle we decided that Hector and I would go back to the trees and Big Pete would brief the team with the latest developments.

Retreating back into the tree line I murmured, "This is turning into one big cluster fuck".

Hector didn't offer any argument; his wrists were mottled swellings from all the nettle stings and I was rubbing frantically at the raised hives on the back of my neck.

Having been called out and gone through a briefing the SFG decided that they would get into position for a dynamic entry just in case we had wrongly assessed the situation. We had eyeball on the front of the house and sat back to await the next development. Hector had mentally stood down, his chance to crash the building had been untimely interrupted and now he was reduced to a bit player's role. He backed under the bough of the nearest tree and a branch swept over the top of the large powerful Dragonlight he was carrying, it struck the toggle switch and a million candle watts of light illuminated the whole of the raid team giving away both their and our positions. It also wrecked the officer's night sight and the air on the firearms net turned blue.

The mission was heavily compromised and the Bronze Commander decided that the instigator of our little outing be asked to contact his wife to find out exactly what the situation was. She, true to form had told him to "fuck off" in no uncertain terms and had then hung up. He phoned again and after a bit of grovelling she confirmed that the two guys who had broken in had left five minutes after he had and that if he had bothered to call to find out how they were she would have fucking told him so. She was instructed to bring her daughter outside so she could confirm that she wasn't being held against her will to the police officers waiting there. Seeing the armed officer provoked another foul mouthed rant that had put the SFG's earlier tirade at Hector to shame.

We were all stood down and before we left I had to use a set of plastic handcuffs to repair the fence I had inadvertently knocked down.

Some jobs were instantly forgettable and others not, this one falls into the latter category but for all the wrong reasons.

***

Training can often be a ball ache as it takes you away from your normal duties, upsets your routine and is often a complete waste of time and only done so that the job can cover its backside in case of litigation. Some specialist training however can be a lot of fun, nobody ever moaned about TPAC (Tactical Pursuit and Containment) as it involved chasing after one of the driving school instructors in a high performance car in an attempt to box him in or get him to drive over a Stinger unit. Of course the spikes would have all been removed beforehand to prevent any embarrassing accidents as this training is undertaken on public roads.

VIP and 'Category A' prisoner convey driving was also a fun day out and it is one of the few occasions where you are actually trained to ram another vehicle out of the way should it try and infiltrate or attack the convoy. Over the years the Category A prisoner tactics have become a more serene affair, with the onus on keeping the convoy moving at a gentle pace as opposed to the original method of balls out driving and forcing everything else on the road out of your way. It was all noise, flashing lights and high speeds; motorcycle outriders would be flying past the convoy at close quarters in order to get to the next junction so that they could stop the traffic from entering the route we were using. Driving the 'sweep car' was the best position for this type of convoy; you sat at the back of the procession and behind the vehicle transferring the high profile prisoner or VIP.

Your job was to protect the rear of the entourage as well as the flanks of the main vehicle. At junctions the prisoner/VIP vehicle would move to the furthest point away from any potential danger and the sweep car would then manoeuvre so that if anything emerged from that junction it could intercept it, and by intercept I mean ram it. It's actually more difficult than it sounds as we would all spend the majority of our working lives trying to avoid such an incident and then to be suddenly expected to purposefully aim at and smash into another vehicle went against the grain. I can only recall one incident where I had set my car onto a collision course with a vehicle that had ignored the motorcycle outriders signal to wait.

On this particular occasion we were engaged in a royalty protection job; a member of the royal family was undertaking a ribbon cutting ceremony and we were en route from there to a civic reception. The motor cycle escort team were on liveried bikes but the rest of the convoy were in unmarked vehicles with all the protection team dressed in suits. The sweep car in this type of convoy was renamed as the back-up car as it was the vehicle the VIP would be ushered into should their car become unusable for whatever reason. Just in case of this highly unlikely event, it would require the driver of the aforesaid vehicle to spend hours cleaning the damn thing just so that it's distinguished passenger wouldn't be offended by a bit of dust or dirt on the upholstery. The interior of the car had to be immaculate and this included inside the door frames and even covering the door retention bars with strips of cloth so that any grease couldn't possibly find its way onto their clothing. It would be wasted hours of work for a situation that was highly unlikely to happen and I can never recall it ever being necessary.

Sitting in the back-up car with the driver were two additional protection officers who would be out of the vehicle as soon as the convoy started to slow down in order to provide flank protection for the VIP. The additional job of these officers was to act as spotters for the motorcycle escort officers, they would scream out 'bike offside' or 'bike nearside' depending on which side of the vehicle they were going to pass us on. Because the driver is so focused on what is happening ahead it would be quite easy to miss the motorcyclist bearing down upon you at warp factor nine and passing within inches of your wing mirrors. It wasn't unheard of for members of this crazy breed to rap on your window or door as they passed if they didn't think you had given them enough room. Theirs was really the most vulnerable job within the whole convoy, the chances of the VIP being attacked were always very remote but the chances of being knocked off their bikes by either a colleague or member of the public was a real threat.

On this particular job the problem started long before the issue came to a head; one of the motorcycle outriders got held up and this put the whole team out of synchronisation. A junction we were approaching was being held but a larger more complicated one lay ahead, the motorcycle outrider was being asked to get to that junction ASAP as there were problems and this led him to leave the junction he was holding a couple of seconds earlier than he would have liked. All the motorists were seemingly under control, stationary and waiting patiently for further instructions before they resumed their journeys. With the call for him to move on to the next junction ringing in his ears he rode off just as the convoy arrived.

Oblivious to the fact that a convoy of three vehicles were hurtling towards them, one of the civilian drivers moved forward onto the main carriageway into the path of the VIP vehicle. I saw him crossing the Give Way lines at the same time that I noticed the VIP car move quickly over to the nearside, the driver shouting a warning of the possible attack over his PR. I swept up the outside of the VIP's gleaming Jaguar, dropped a gear and prepared to gun the engine. Preferably you would engage another vehicle when it was broadside to you and take it out at its lightest end which is normally the rear for cars where the engines are situated at the front. The vehicle in question was a midsized Toyota saloon with only one visible occupant, it had four doors which could have meant the remaining occupants were lying prone across the seats and out of view ready to fling the doors open just after impact and then leap out of the vehicle with all guns blazing. The doors were still firmly shut which was a good sign. In a collision the ramming vehicles bodywork can buckle and stop the doors from opening which would be a little embarrassing if the intentions of the occupants were to use the element of surprise for their ambush. Having to climb over the seats to exit through another door or a window was hardly very professional; if I was intending to ram a car I would have the doors opened for the last few seconds to give me better egress.

I was shouting to the two back up men in my car to brace for impact and I edged to the side of the VIP vehicle so that the end of my bonnet was just level with its rear passenger door. It's a silly thing but protocol dictates that we never try to scare our dignitary, the motorcycles would throttle back as they passed only to open the bikes back up as soon as they levelled with the driver. I remained in this position until the last possible moment; although the whole manoeuvre only took a split second I felt I had plenty time to assess the situation; the benefit of good training. The back-up team could see that I had every intention of taking on the intruding vehicle and were hastily clipping on their seatbelts.

I observed the driver of the Toyota, who looked to be in his late seventies, a frail looking man who was slowly pulling across the carriageway. With his mouth open he looked totally unaware of what was happening and more significantly he was not aware of what was about to happen. He didn't look like a potential threat but who really knows what one looks like; I wasn't going to take any risks. The distance between the Toyota and Jaguar would mean that I wouldn't have the luxury of taking out the rear of his car, it was going to have to be a front end shunt, a heavy impact that could more than likely result in serious injury or death to the driver. Our airbags and seat belts would give us ample protection and so long as I got my feet clear of the pedals upon impact we should all walk away.

I had been to enough fatal collisions to know that the human body isn't really designed to take large impacts sideways; the neck and spine have a tendency to snap and break the spinal column resulting in death or extremely serious life changing injuries.

We were just at the point of total commitment which would see me break with protocol and overtake the Jaguar and pile straight into the Toyota when the driver looked in my direction, he appeared totally shocked at the scene that was unfolding before him and hitting the brakes he stopped suddenly.

The VIP driver had seen the same as I had and was frantically calling 'abort' over the radio. He moved as far as he could to his nearside to give me room to pass and with my wing mirror centimetres from his bodywork we passed the front end of the stationary Toyota with the same small amount of space. The old boy sat with his mouth open even wider, eyes as big as saucers, no longer totally oblivious to just how close he had come to putting himself in mortal danger. I dropped back into position behind the VIP and the driver moved to the centre of the road and keyed his PR mike, "Well done mate, no dramas in here". The VIP was obviously unaware of the near miss we had just had and sat relaxed in the back of their luxury transport, the only worry of the day for them being just how many glasses of champers they would neck and what the buffet would be like. I looked across at my two passengers and grinned; the pair of them looked pale and shaken, "You heard the man" I said, "he said there were no dramas".

They sat in silence for a second before the guy sitting next to me said: "You lot are fucking mad", a comment I thought strange seeing as the role he was undertaking was commonly referred to as a 'bullet catcher'.

***

Firearm's training was also very enjoyable and could be a real fun day if you were with the right people, I often ended up training with Hector which was always a good source of entertainment. In order to make the tactics as realistic as possible the training team would often use locations that were unfamiliar to us. A large hospital was decommissioned on the North Norfolk coast and this became a favourite place for us to undergo house and room entries as it didn't matter what damage we did. Now telling police officers something like this brings out the worse in them, especially if they have a hooley bar in their hands at the time. The hooley bar is a short solid metal implement that has the sole purpose of breaking things, albeit doors, windows or stud walls; it can wreck anything. It is small enough to be hand held and reasonably light weight, with its spiked end a cross between a medieval mace and a small pick axe. Smashing your way through a glass window is relatively easy and can be done with most implements if the user has the right frame of mind; the danger comes though when you try and gain entry over the broken shards that are inevitably left behind, stuck in the frame like small daggers. The hooley bar was designed to smash the window and then be used to run around the edge of the frame clearing away all the remaining shards. The only realistic way to train with it is to smash lots of windows, lots and lots of them. The spiked portion made short work of a wooden or plastic door, ripping holes through the panels with consummate ease; by levering back on the bar huge rents in the door would soon appear allowing an arm or a gun to be inserted through the shattered section in order to release the lock.

The hospital was the perfect place to try out other tactics and the use of paint rounds added a certain amount of realism to any exercise. Barren, empty wards lent themselves to being a safe environment for this type of round to be discharged. The unfortunate trainer who was playing the 'bad guy' would be dressed in two sets of ballistic body armour and wore a full faced Kevlar helmet with as many leg pads as he could get on. Head shots were severely frowned upon and close quarter shots were to be avoided if at all possible, apart from that it was game on. We would stack up outside the room before commencing the process of room clearance. The most dangerous time for the point man is the actual entry through the door, the advantage is always with the occupant and unlike the SAS we didn't have helicopters to call on to allow us to rappel through windows. The only additional protection provided for him was a metre high Kevlar shield that he could hold in front, at the same time allowing his MP5 to be kept on aim. A small notch cut into the top right hand corner allowed the barrel of the weapon to be rested on it and release the supporting hand in order to support the shield by its two handles that fitted over the forearm. The second person to enter the room has no such luxury and is extremely vulnerable. It's hard work, both physically and mentally as no sooner have you cleared one room than you're tackling the next. If you know that the person you seek is within the building then each cleared room increases your chances of them being in the next.

In our training scenarios we knew that the person we were looking for would only be armed with blanks, he on the other hand knew that we had paint rounds and were not afraid to use them. It was a slightly unfair advantage as often he was unable to move nimbly around the room to seek cover, the sheer weight and bulk of the two sets of body armour left him looking like a sluggish Michelin man and with the pads bulking out his legs it allowed him only to be able to waddle like an incontinent pensioner.

On one particular occasion we were using chalk rounds which left red powder residue at the point of contact. The instructor designated the stooge and he had strapped on as much protection as he could. By the time it came to my turn to be point man he had already been talked into dropping his weapon and not resisting, so I knew that this time he was likely to want to enter into a firefight. The door went in and I stepped into the room using my weight and the shield to follow the natural swing of the door, sweeping the room with my eyes and MP5 as I did so. Hector was hard on my heels and stepped into the room a metre facing the other direction. I felt the door abruptly stop in its tracks and swung around to confront the blockage. It was the bulky form of the instructor who had been knocked onto his arse and was desperately trying to get back up. I screamed at him not to move and to keep his hands where I could see them. He still had a good grip of the 9mm Glock pistol and as gravity took its toll he slowly fell backwards again, lifting his arms to counter balance himself. The Glock started to come up, whether on aim or otherwise it represented a real threat. I double tapped two chalk rounds from my MP5 straight into the instructor's upper body and the impact knocked him fully prone onto the floor clutching at his chest. The chalk rounds had hardly left any residue on the body armour he was wearing, the stock of rounds had been old and had solidified so the impact had been far greater than it should have been. By the time the training session had finished the bruising on his chest was already developing in to purple and blue hues and he was thanking his lucky stars that he had worn two sets of armour. Once he had stopped calling me some choice names he admitted that it had been good tactics and shooting on my behalf. Apparently the bruises lasted well into a second week and this type of exercise was under review.

Other aspects of our tactics training were more cerebral and less dynamic. Reconnaissance played a big part in the role of the ARV; once containment had been established any information we could pass onto the SFG entry teams was very helpful. Working from left to right we were trained to be able to relay what we could see by means of a numbering formula. Apertures were counted and described; white face-1-1-window would equate to first level at the front of the house, the first aperture from the left is a window. White face-1-2-door would obviously be the second opening on that level was a door. By the use of this quick and easy method, the person on the other end of the radio could start building a picture of what the officer was looking at. Once the premises had been mapped out then finer details would be added; double glazed window, wooden door, apertures covered by curtains and so forth. The final details to be added would be where doors were hinged and which way they opened, albeit inwards, outwards or from left or right hung hinges. This method of building up a picture was something that needed a good deal of practice in order to make it second nature to describe in this manner.

One bright sunny and hot afternoon I was training with Hector at the old hospital and instructed that the theme for the day was going to be performing observations and relaying that information back to our partners. We were put in to teams of two before being split up and kept apart; one of us would be the controller and would be expected to reconstruct on paper the building being described by his team mate. Hector was keen to be the observer so I sat in the humid and stuffy room as he received his briefing. All the teams had separate channels to work on and I idly flicked through them to see what the other teams were doing as I had yet to receive any instructions. Hector it seemed was having a bit of trouble getting to the area he had been nominated and was constantly telling me to stand by when I queried his progress. The other teams were well into their outline and I still had nothing drawn on my blank sheet of paper. I flicked back to Hector and he informed me that he was in place but was unable to talk too loudly as the trainers had got someone in the rear garden who kept looking up as if to try and locate his position.

He commenced with his description; he was looking at a detached chalet bungalow and soon began detailing the layout. Suddenly he stopped in mid - sentence and there was a long silence. "Hector come in; are you compromised, over?" I called several times before I got two clicks of static, at least he was receiving me and probably not able to talk due to the presence of the pseudo householder.

After several seconds he was back on the radio. "Fucking hell Scottie, the firearms team have pulled out all the stops here. I have just watched the young lady who is playing the householder strip off her bra and go topless".

"Hector, you're supposed to be passing over details of the fucking bungalow not perving at the bloody staff" I snapped back, annoyed that I was still only halfway through completing my drawings and that he was out in the sunshine watching a strip show. Meanwhile I was sweating my nads off in a small claustrophobic room.

"Ok, ok ready to take the description?" Hector asked.

"Go ahead and send" I retorted.

"Well the left one was pretty pert and had a big nipple, the right one wasn't too far off that either. Both were at least a handful" he chuckled.

Before I could tell him to fuck off, one of the trainers entered the room and told me to recall Hector as the first part of the exercise had finished. We were to regroup, and the scribes would then brief the trainers on the layout of the premises we had just had described to us.

We gathered in the main lecture area, those of us who had been stuck in the classrooms were streaked with sweat and to a man looked totally pissed off at the way things had panned out for us. We waited for Hector as he was the last to return and when he did he was flushed with the effort; either that or he had hung around the garden in the hope that the woman on the sun lounger fancied an all over tan.

It was apparent at an early stage that something was very, very wrong; everyone else had almost perfectly reconstructed the three different faces of one single storey flat roofed building that was completely devoid of furniture, curtains and interest. Nothing at all like the two chimney, pitched roof chalet bungalow I had on my drawing. There was also no mention of any stooges, either in or around their building. Due to his late arrival Hector was totally unaware that something had gone tits up.

"Hector, talk us through your observations" asked the straight faced instructor who was also aware of the error and wanted to get as much mileage out of the situation as he could.

"Well lads, first of all I must say it was a nice touch to have the girl in the garden, I don't think she saw me though", he paused hoping not to be challenged and when he wasn't corrected he continued. "It was really difficult to get around to the face I had been nominated but I managed to climb over a fence and get into a neighbours garden then look through the hedge into the target premises". He looked so pleased with himself, mentally jumping up and down on the prat fall of smugness. "I have to say I didn't expect you to have someone in the garden, she was really good and not at all bashful!"

Before he continued to incriminate himself I pointed to the other team's drawings and he allowed himself a second to compare our efforts with theirs. The penny eventually dropped.

"Oh" was all he could muster.

"Yes Hector, 'Oh' it is. It would seem that you have missed the building you were supposed to observe and have managed to climb over someone poor sods fence before peeking into their neighbours garden and eyeing up the occupant" the head trainer observed.

"Oh shit she was topless" blurted Hector, never any good at keeping quiet at the best of times and digging himself an even deeper hole.

Shaking his head the instructor looked at him "You're a fucking liability Hector; and a peeping tom as well by the sounds of it".

Only Hector could have crawled hundreds of metres through dense shrubbery before coming out the opposite end of the hospital grounds to where he should have been, climb over a high fence, then disappear into a hedgerow in order to intrude on the privacy of the occupant who was innocently trying to catch a few rays of the rare sunshine.

I had nicked people for less.

Sorry Your Majesty

In Norfolk, being a Firearms Officer meant that you were expected to perform Royalty Protection duties at Sandringham, the Queens Country estate. To the uninitiated it must sound like a prestigious posting; hobnobbing with royalty and the 'A list' celebrities who courted them.

If you are wondering just how prestigious this job is then you should stop reading this and go and stand by your front door for half an hour, then wander around to the back door for a similar period and if you are bored out of your skull then you are beginning to get the picture and if it should be late at night and pouring with rain so much the better. Keep repeating this process over the course of the next eight hours and you will start to understand what it feels like to undertake Royalty Protection duties.

For those of you who have just put yourselves through this ordeal I apologise but hope that I have shattered any illusion you may have had about the glamour of such a duty. Get yourself some dry clothes and a warm drink and read on with your new insight.

Despite the fact that I only lived twenty five minutes' drive from the estate I was expected to live in a hotel room in Kings Lynn for the period I was working this duty. We were allowed to travel home only after our week long shift had ended and expected to return once our rest days were concluded. When I challenged this I was informed that this was necessary; the powers to be didn't want us travelling any great distance between our shifts as they were concerned about making us fatigued (by the time I reached the hotel and found a parking space it would have only taken me another five minutes to get home). This was all very caring you might think but I was expected to travel for forty minutes to get to my usual day job and nobody seemed to care too much about me being tired for that.

The idea of having a group of officers languishing at a hotel and theoretically at their disposal was the real reason for their façade of concern. Being told to stay on duty for an additional four hours to cover sickness or court appearances of a colleague was often marginally less boring than sitting in a dingy hotel room listening to the traffic that seemed to be endlessly queuing and honking horns outside my draughty window. The fact that you weren't being paid for the periods you were not working despite being on an informal retainer also helped to make the prospect of an extended tour of duty more bearable. This enforced house arrest originated because one winter the snow was so bad that they couldn't get officers either in or out of the estate for several days. A contingency plan was put in place which was why we were all cooped up in the hotel, just in case heavy snow fell again. The plan was that they would be able to ferry all retained personnel from the hotel either by 4x4 or helicopter, to date this has never been necessary.

Whiling away off duty hours by paying the grotty hotel bar a visit was an option for the desperate. However anyone wanting to have a few beers had to be careful and be sure to declare that fact the following day as we were not supposed to carry a weapon within twenty four hours of drinking alcohol. The odd pint wasn't a problem (unless you had quaffed it for breakfast) so long as you informed the sergeant that you were not suffering any ill effects. Several such declarations would see you in front of the inspector and having to justify why you didn't think you had an alcohol issue.

On Royalty Protection duties officers worked three different shift systems; earlies, lates and nights, each shift consisting of five days working and then two days off. Unlike normal shift work where officers were expected to perform a mixture of the three and juggle their sleep patterns in between, the Sandringham shifts were at least consistent in that you had a full week of each; earlies, or lates or nights.

Each set of shifts brought with them their own respective perks and downsides. Earlies meant that someone (normally me due to my catering experience and unwillingness to catch food poisoning) would cook a full English breakfast in the Police Lodge. This had to be done in two stages as there were always officers out manning the points at any given time. The downside of this duty was the fact you had to get up early and then try and find something to do for the rest of the afternoon once your shift had finished. The sights of Kings Lynn are very few and far between and even if you were able to find the energy to muster up any interest for a visit not one of them required a second viewing. The afternoons were quite often spent lying on your bed trying to shut out the hooting and engine revving from outside.

Late turns gave you the chance to have a lay in and a late brunch before going to work. It also meant that halfway through the shift you would revert to night time posts; these were static positions up close to the house and not the long sprawling areas we covered during daylight hours. Although it doesn't sound like much, this lack of repetitiveness and change of scenery made a big difference. The down side to this shift however was the fact that any evening function at the house made the Front Gate an extremely busy posting as each person had to be checked in with the visitors schedule before informing the house of their imminent arrival. The guest's vehicle would also have to be checked over to make sure nobody had strapped a device (explosive or otherwise) to its underside. We had been informed on numerous occasions that members of the press were trying to breach the security of the Royal Family as it would make a brilliant front page story. They didn't really need to fully succeed, just getting past one check point would be enough for them to create a scandal. There was even one rumour they were going to employ lookalikes, stick them in a green Range Rover and see if we spotted the difference!

Night duties were fine if you were nocturnal by nature; the benefits of this duty were there was very little activity from the household, the down side was there was very little activity per se. I have seen officers standing at their posts fast asleep, the tall box hedge they were leaning against being the only thing preventing them from falling over. Officers would fall asleep on the plastic kitchen chairs in the rest room or just lay on the locker room floor during their half hour breaks. During these times you still had to be available to attend any personal attack button (PAB) activation that might be generated from within the house summoning immediate help, so a constant state of readiness was always required. Finding one of the response officers languishing in the land of nod would always bring out the devil in someone. It was not unusual to find the sleeping persons foot tied to a cord that was tied to a saucepan that was balanced on a cupboard with other saucepans precariously assembled on top. The lights would be extinguished; the PAB test button depressed and the fun would begin. Some startled officers were so disorientated that they actually made it into the back yard still dragging the saucepan after them, others would yelp with shock before trying to play their hysterics down. The old sweats and more experienced officers would raise an eyelid, assess the situation, raise a solitary finger and go back to sleep.

***

Standing on point duty is extremely tiring; keeping your mind and senses sharp in the face of extreme boredom is a challenge in itself. We all had different methods of keeping ourselves amused, some planned out future extensions to their houses, others read or did crossword puzzles. Mobile phones at this time were a rich person's plaything and would have had none of the apps and accessories we now take for granted. One technically advanced officer had a small four inch black and white TV that could randomly pick up a couple of stations. After an hour of viewing the snowy picture, the batteries would die and it became just another bit of kit to lug about. Being a bit dyslexic and pretty bad at spelling I decided to have a go at a crossword book and try to improve the situation. Over a period of two months I have to confess that I managed to complete just one…but boy was I chuffed with myself for doing so.

One of the guys I worked with used to collect cuttings from the shrubs in the grounds, and thrust down the front of his jacket he had a plastic bag full of what he had collected on his rounds. He also kept a pair of secateurs in his pocket to make the task easier. The gardeners didn't mind and would often put bits of bushes to one side for him. One Christmas he decided that he would also collect up some of the large pine cones that the fir trees had shed. He must have carted away tons of them but still felt it necessary to try and get the extra-large ones that hung tantalisingly just out of reach, and in a rash moment of madness attempted to obtain them by knocking them down with his truncheon.

He had limited success before disaster struck and his truncheon snagged in the branches of the tree. He spent the rest of the day in fear of it falling back down to earth and either striking a member of the family or one of their flunkies as they strolled around the grounds. It did eventually fall to earth and was returned to its rightful owner without mishap.

I later swapped the crosswords for books on law and procedure; I had put in for my Sergeants exam and had left it all to the last minute to study. I managed to cram in a year's worth of revision in the short time I had at Sandringham and surprised myself (and probably quite a few others) when I passed.

***

The house and grounds were protected by state of the art alarm systems and a network of camera's all controlled from the police control centre located within the grounds. The Police Lodge (as it was grandly known) had a dedicated operator who handled all the communications, alarms and the CCTV. We all took it in turns to work there for two half hour periods during the day; getting to sit and chat with another human being in this climate controlled environment was a real sanity saver.

By far the worst duty was the front gate, which was in fact the side gate.

The front gate was the portal with the real world and the first avenue of attack for those wishing to enter the grounds. This wasn't necessarily going to be a terrorist (the IRA were still a very active threat at this time), but much more likely to be some disillusioned individual who felt sure that they could brighten up the Queens day by just popping in for a chat. Or of course the press and paparazzi who were constantly trying to get a photograph of the Queen Mother and one of the young princes together. The sum of money this picture was rumoured to have been worth had it existed was quite staggering, but not quite enough to tempt me to set up my Kodak Instamatic on the off chance of a pose.

At the start of each shift we were briefed on who was expected to be arriving during that tour and woe betide anyone who cocked up and let in someone not on the visitors list as you would be returning back to your day job a eunuch, your bollocks left nailed to the gate as a warning to your replacement. We also had a very comprehensive and rather heavy tome that had the mug shots of those people deemed a danger to the Royals, either through threats they had made or through sheer insanity. There were several 'rightful heirs to the throne' as well as distant cousins and forgotten siblings on the less than prestigious list. It just reinforced my theory that there are a lot of strange and unusual people walking amongst us.

***

Foolishly when I first arrived at Sandringham (I notice that some Royal correspondents now insist on adding an additional 'r' in the name in order to make it sound slightly posher as in SaRndringham) I expected the royals to appreciate having officers around the place who were quite literally expected to give their lives for their safety if the shit hit the fan. Finding that we were in fact a necessary evil was a bit of a shock. Now I don't think this had much to do with the royals themselves, the place is infected with jobs worth's who like to speak on behalf of the Queen. Apparently 'the Queen' didn't like to see officers toting guns around the grounds...strange when you think that she has a bloody army of soldiers with rifles on their shoulders marching up and down her front garden at Buck House! Virtually every member of the royal family tote shotguns around the estate, blasting anything with feathers from the sky, so it would be fair to assume that the sight of a firearm isn't an unusual occurrence liable to send her into a hissy fit.

However, someone had decided that officers shouldn't overtly carry their guns (at this time they were the .38 model 10 Smith and Wesson revolvers) and should carry them instead, fully loaded in their trouser pocket. The only uniform deviation that was permitted was a zip sewn into this pocket so the weapon could be secured (I use the term 'secured' in its loosest term). Having a loaded six shot revolver swinging in a pocket next to your own crown jewels is a sobering prospect especially as it doesn't have a safety catch (revolvers just don't, despite what you read in virtually every crime thriller).

A revolver is a very basic mechanical instrument, you pull the trigger back which in turn revolves the chamber (hence the name) and automatically causes the hammer (the bit that hits the bullet and makes it go bang) to be pulled back and then released under pressure of a spring; the weapon fires and if you pull the trigger back again the whole process starts once more. It's not that complicated and that's what make it very reliable. You can of course short cut the system by just pulling back the hammer and letting it fall. Those of you who grew up on the quick draw cowboy films may well recall the erstwhile bad guy cuffing his hand over the top of the gun and producing something akin to a machine gun rate of fire. The pistols we were using were very similar in concept although they did not have the cocking horn on the back of the hammer to aid this process.

The practice of putting the gun in your pocket had been in place for years, the more experienced officers would leave one of the chambers empty in order to create their own safety mechanism thus reducing their firepower to five shots and the need to revolve the chamber manually in order to get the first round off. That is after they had unzipped their pocket and fished about for the damn thing amongst their loose change and car keys. It was a recipe for disaster.

The original Police Lodge was a small, modest affair (unlike its newer, more technically advanced replacement) consisting of a cramped alarms and camera room, a small kitchen come rest room come sergeants office, a small toilet with a 'no solids' note stuck on it and an iron door that accessed the armoury. It was cramped to say the least, especially at shift change over times when all the officers about to go off watch were handing back their weapons and ammunition. It is not a good time to discover that while you are pulling the pistol out of your pocket it has snagged on the lining and cocked itself. The poor soul that had this happen to him now had a pistol that was unstable, half-cocked and with its barrel pointing directly at his right nut. Should the hammer become disengaged the pistol could quite easily fire and that would end his chances of getting any Father's Day cards in the future. Let's face it, it's not the best way to finish a boring shift, and a round discharged in such a confined space is quite likely not to be content with just one victim and will ricochet around the room seeking out others.

The officer managed to get his hand between the hammer and the breach to stop any movement, the gun was safe but still unstable and firmly wedged in his pocket. All remaining officers were now shuffling in a disorderly fashion out into the safety of the rear yard and away from any potential danger, their sympathies with their colleague but glad it wasn't them.

The gun had to be cut from his trousers before the situation could be declared safe and a tragic (and painful) accident was diverted. The next day when we turned up for duty we were issued with a holster and gun belt…apparently 'the Queen' had reviewed the way officers carried their firearms and was now happy to see them.

***

Sandringham is situated near to the Wash, a bleak slate grey section of coastal water that sits between North West Norfolk and Lincolnshire so one cannot be so surprised that with those surroundings it's not the more joyful blue you would get somewhere like the Med. The Royal Estate is in a slightly elevated position which makes it susceptible to some pretty wicked weather fronts and when it's cold its bloody freezing. In the earlier days it was not unusual to see officers looking like Mr Blobby, having put on virtually all the kit they possessed just to keep the bitter cold from penetrating their bones, heaven help anyone who might trip and end up on their back because they would never be able to get up again. Over the years we saw better and warmer kit being issued, state of the art gortex jackets and over-trousers that were actually camouflaged under the infra-red spot lights that bathed the grounds at night. The sentry boxes were eventually wired up so that electric heaters could be used to defrost the occupant as for once the powers-to-be had actually started to think about the officer's comfort, or at least reducing their discomfort.

By far the best thing to be issued to me was about as technically advanced as a house brick. It was the officer's cape, a thick blanket like material that lay over the shoulders and was clasped at the neck by a chain that stretched between two brass ornate lion heads. A series of buttons held the front together and kept out the wind and rain. The design had been around for nearly as long as the police force had been in existence and probably nothing had changed in its design or use.

The beauty of the cape was that when worn the officers hands and arms couldn't be seen, handy for carting a lunchbox or radio out to your sentry box. It also screened any movement made towards the gun. As I mentioned before, if a visitor wasn't on the list then they didn't get in although some people took no to mean maybe. On the odd occasion I had to turn someone away, I could sometimes see in their eyes the temptation to put their foot down and speed past the obstructive soul that was impeding them. To all intense and purpose it looked as though there were no physical barriers between the gate (I should mention that by the time they reached the checkpoint they were already well past the gate entrance) and the front of the house. The cape would allow me to be talking to the occupant of the vehicle and at the same time unclip the retaining strap on my Glock and take hold of the grip. The weapon could now be drawn at lightning speed without the smile ever leaving my face.

Sadly, in the drive for uniformity the cape was no longer deemed fit for purpose and relegated to the locker room. I suppose like most things, it had had its day and it was now time for more hi-tech equipment. I know I wasn't the only person to mourn its passing.

Many other traditional touches went by the wayside under the banner of 'better security', the age old custom of the controller announcing "Purple One, away from the house towards walk one" would have given the person standing in the sentry box a chance to stop picking their nose or scratching their arse and not being surprised by the presence of the Queen standing outside their temporary shelter. It's also handy if when you stop these age old practices you notify the staff on duty…

***

I was making my way around the grounds in the usual thirty minute intervals; I had just left the Lodge and had an hour and a half ahead of me and three separate points to cover. It was a warm day for a change and a pleasure to be out in the open without the usual prevailing wind blowing in from the Wash. The sun was slowly sinking and I knew that once it was gone the remainder of the evening would once again be cold and inhospitable. I followed the estate road past the front of the house; the long drive that swept down to the freshly raked gravel area in front of the ornate portico looked fantastic, flanked as it was by the two long tightly clipped hedges and lawns. In orderly and well-spaced gaps alongside the hedge tall cypress trees stood sentry, swaying slightly either in the breeze or from boredom, I could sympathise with either. I would often plan imaginary attacks on the house, looking to see if I could defeat the security systems and patrols, I don't think I was the only one to try and imagine the prospect. Boredom does funny things to your psyche and it's hard to stop your mind from working. This would be where any frontal attack would be mounted from, the shrubbery and trees giving good cover and a stealthy approach, of course they would have had to breach the alarm systems first and would quite likely meet with a reception committee by the time they got to the front door.

Although invisible to the naked eye I knew exactly where the various alarms started and finished, where the electrical fields reached out to and where they didn't. This wasn't because I was particularly clever or astute; this information came from years of calling into the controller when you were about to set off an alarm or being asked to confirm that it had been you who had just activated it. It was a top of the range piece of kit and in my humble opinion impossible to breach without detection, but that's not to say impregnable. With these thoughts still in my mind I followed the path to the Queen Mothers Gate, a huge, ornate wrought iron structure that was indeed worthy of such an establishment. I checked that the chain and padlock that secured it shut were in place and intact and notified the Lodge, giving the duty sergeant one less thing to worry about. Sandringham was a place where glistening careers could be left in tatters causing some previously sane supervisors to do the most bizarre things in order to make sure that they were not dropped in the shit by the team they were overseeing. One particular sergeant was prone to prowling the grounds at night trying to catch out any officer who might be tempted to grab forty winks on the sly. He would creep up to the sentry boxes or hide in the deep recesses along the terrace and then 'surprise' the officer by suddenly appearing. A fairly foolhardy thing to do I would suggest, startling someone who is armed with a 9mm self-loading pistol, complete with a fifteen round magazine. The bloke wasn't that well liked even before he started his 'ninja' patrols and after a spate of complaints from the officers in his command he was eventually sent back to division before someone ended up shooting him, either by mistake or desire.

***

After I had checked that the gate was locked I headed for the sanctuary of the sentry box, a roughly put together tall thin hut that had a narrow uncomfortable wooden plank inside it for a seat and a front that was open to the elements. I looked at my watch, it had only taken me five minutes to reach this far and I still had another twenty four minutes before moving on towards walk two, the next exciting instalment in my day. The tranquillity was shattered by the bark of a corgi somewhere in the grounds and judging by the volume it was somewhere close to where I was sitting. I stepped out of the box and slipped noiselessly into the foliage behind it. The pages who worked in the household were often tasked with walking the dogs and it was great sport to suddenly emerge from the shrubbery and scare the life out of them.

There was only one problem with doing this...Ranger.

Ranger was the Queens favourite corgi who I am sure acted in a regal manner when in the company of Her Majesty, however when faced with a commoner, especially one dressed in a police uniform he became quite aggressive. I had already had one encounter with him earlier in 'the visit' (the term used to describe the royals being in residence and my life being put on hold) which had resulted in him nipping at my ankles. My gortex boots made a pretty good job of keeping his teeth at bay but I had promised him that his luck would change if he tried it again. We were issued with three-cell Maglite's (a fourteen inch long aluminium torch) before going out on patrol and I now had mine attached to my belt through a metal retaining ring. I am sure that the torch was specifically this length and not the longer version for the very reason that when you swung it there were still a couple of inches between the top of a corgis head and the heavy bulbous lens.

The torch could be used as a formidable weapon; one of the ARV officers had his snatched from him during a scuffle when patrolling the city centre and was hit over the head with it. It knocked him out cold and split his head open, an injury that required several stitches to close it. He returned to work a few days later only to find that some wag had adorned his locker with an image of the seventies comic book figure called 'Torchy the Battery Boy'; sympathy was always in short supply in the job.

***

Standing in the shadow of the box, I could hear footsteps on the path through the shrubs and the heavy panting of a pampered pooch that was obviously out of condition. I slid back into the greenery and waited until I could see my quarry emerge, despite his girth and lack of stamina Ranger was pretty astute and it was obvious that he was aware of my presence. I slid the torch from my belt ring; I figured that if I bent my knees slightly I could compensate for the gap between lens and head if Ranger was looking for a rematch. He sauntered over and sized me up, curling his lips back as he did so, the Maglite swung easily and menacingly in my hand and we had a standoff. He growled at me to indicate his displeasure and I took this as being a declaration of intent…so technically I believe that in the parlance of the playground… *he started it.*

"Come on then Ranger" I purred menacingly, "I told you what would happen if you tried to bite me again".

He growled again and advanced.

"You've had your last go at me, so if I was you I would sod off before you get a nasty clump aside your head". I flexed my knees as I spoke, another metre and he was going to get a short sharp shock.

It was in this position that Her Majesty found her favourite pet and one of her policeman and it was fair to say that both Ranger and I looked quite guilty at the discovery.

She assessed the situation quickly and called out "Come on Ranger, leave the nice policeman alone", and with that they both disappeared off along the track and continued their walk, Ranger briefly looking over his shoulder to indicate that our little tête-à-tête wasn't over.

He had a good point, I guessed that this little encounter wasn't over yet either, the incident quite likely to drop me in the shit; I also guessed that it was going to be very, very deep shit. I couldn't believe that the controller hadn't called up to warn me that the Queen was out of the house and on her way over to where I was. My only consolation was that the cameras couldn't penetrate this particular area of the gardens so it would effectively just be her word against mine…and if that was going to be my only defence then the shit would indeed be very, very deep.

The next hour and twenty three minutes passed extremely slowly, I figured that it would have taken about twenty minutes for the Queen to complete her walk, two minutes to complain to her secretary, one minute for him to contact the Chief Constable to convey Her Majesty's displeasure and a nano second for him to be on the phone to the Lodge demanding my public execution. I crossed onto walk two half expecting a detachment of the Yeomanry of the Guard to be waiting for me, but there were no Beefeaters, just an empty sentry box.

I plonked myself down and looked at the tired walls, old graffiti had once masked them, nothing offensive just the humorous ramblings of some bored officers. Nothing was ever said until one day the Queen Mother brought it up in conversation, mentioning that she thought some of it was quite funny. The scribbling's were immediately removed and a witch hunt started for their authors but because they were so old their originators were never discovered. It was part of our daily duty to check that nobody else had been tempted to add an ode or two to the now pristine wood. I was tempted to scrawl my own epitaph.

In this box I now sit, knowing I am truly in the shit,
When Her Majesty gets back, I'm going to get the fucking sack.
My career's gone down the bog, 'cos I threatened her bleeding dog!

After all, what more could they do to me; at least I would be going out in style.

Had I possessed a pencil then the deed would have been done but a biro seemed a little too permanent and likely to last well beyond my career prospects.

The last point to cover was the terrace before I returned to face the music. This was one of the closest spots to the Lodge and I half expected the sergeant to greet me and demand an explanation. Maybe, just maybe there was a State crisis and in the confusion and turmoil HRH might just have forgotten the small fact that Rangers life had been threatened. I scanned the sky for any tell-tale mushroom clouds that might indicate my redemption; there were none, just heavy black rainclouds similar to the ones gathered in my soul.

When I returned to the Lodge, the sergeant was surprisingly upbeat for someone who might have just had an irate Chief Constable tearing him a new arsehole.

"Sarge, I need to tell you something" I said...honesty being the best policy and all that. "I had a bit of a run in with Ranger". I left the statement hanging; if he knew anything about the incident then I would let him chip in with his account now. You never know, it might not have sounded quite so incriminating after all.

He instinctively looked down to my trouser hems; there had been a spate of requisition for replacement trousers due to Rangers previous handy work. Seeing no obvious damage he asked, "What happened?"

He was totally unaware of the incident and honesty is only the best policy if you think you've been caught, and as far as I could see I hadn't.

"I just told him to get lost..." I said.

"That's hardly a crime, bloody thing ought to be put down... or the very least be muzzled" he generously added.

"I'm glad you think that Sarge because I did have the Maglite in my hand at the time and I wouldn't have wanted anyone to get the wrong idea" I remarked cagily.

He was nobody's fool and knew there was more to this than met the eye, "When you say 'anyone'... specifically who do you mean?" It was a good direct question, straight to the point and no pissing about, he smelt a rat.

"Well actually Her Majesty was with him at the time". I didn't need to go any further and watched as his face went ashen while he imagined his career prospects taking the next fast car out of the estate and disappearing into the distance.

"You threatened the fucking Queen?" he demanded, now apoplectic.

"Not exactly...I just threatened her dog". What more could I say other than adding "the one you just said should be put down".

I could see him wanting to pull out his tongue and stamp on it, the psychotic idiot standing in front of him had not only committed treason he was now trying to implicate him in the plot. "I didn't fucking mean it" he bellowed. Shaking his head he mumbled "I wish you hadn't told me, nobody has said anything and now you've saddled me with this".

"We can always pretend I haven't" I suggested helpfully.

"You can't come to me having just plotted to kill a member of the Royal Household and then ask me to pretend nothing's happened" he raged. "How can I let you go back out there knowing that you'd have no qualms in attacking the monarchy", he wiped some spittle from his lips. "Christ, what if the Duke says something out of turn, would you be planning on putting his lights out with your bloody torch as well?" In order to make sure that I couldn't he snatched the torch from my belt.

He had a fair point; 'the Duke', as the Royal Consort was known was apt to make derogatory remarks to the officers on a regular basis. Should the officer on the gate ever have the audacity to stop him in his vehicle as he entered the estate, the Duke was likely to shout "I bloody live here you fool" before roaring off and leaving them in a cloud of exhaust fumes and gravel dust. On one occasion an officer wearing one of the old fashioned capes had signalled for him to stop only to realise his mistake. He tried to rectify the situation by smartly snapping to attention and throwing up a salute, something you never did when wearing a cape. The long wings of the heavy blanket material followed the contour of the saluting arm, deftly removing the officer's helmet, before settling on top of his head, covering his face. He stood in that position with his helmet at his feet, listening to the Duke's summing up of the situation with the rebuke of…"you bloody cretin" before he roared off leaving the suitably chastised man in the familiar cloud of exhaust fumes and gravel dust.

***

After my 'confession' I was sent out of the sergeant's office and spent the next hour worrying what he was going to do and what my fate or punishment was likely to be. Every time I looked in at him he seemed to be pondering on the same problem as he sat there muttering to himself. Something in my favour was the fact that there had been a change in policy and procedure that day. In the interests of radio security the practice of calling over the air when one of the Royals was out and about in the grounds had been reviewed and deemed unsafe. The radios were supposed to be secure but they had said that the Titanic was unsinkable and look how that worked out. This was an important update in protocol and the sergeant should have mentioned it at briefing before we went out on patrol, he hadn't and now he would have to shoulder some of blame for the predicament I had found myself in.

Poor Sarge, he was clearly caught between a rock and a hard place. If he mentioned the incident to his supervisors it would take but a couple of minutes to find its way all the way up to the Chiefs office, his name would be forever associated with the scandal and he would quite likely be busted for failing to supervise which was a disciplinary offence. On the other hand, if he didn't mention the incident and the Chief got wind of it from another source, it would mean that his name would be forever associated with the scandal and he would quite likely be busted for failing to supervise! A classic catch 22; the scales were clearly loaded and not in his favour. It was a mental wrangle that took him the remainder of the time I was in the Lodge to figure out what to do.

Just before I was due to go out to the front gate he called, "Scottie, get in here". I took it to be a good sign; he was using my first name and not the more officious 'Officer Redington' which normally preceded bad news and never the offer of tea and biscuits. I stepped into his office and closed the door. He was a shadow of the man who had greeted me so cheerfully only an hour earlier.

"Yes Sarge" I said amiably as I wandered over to his desk. I was shocked at just how much he seemed to have aged over the past sixty minutes.

Sliding the Maglite to me across his desk he added "Keep that in its fucking holder and don't you dare take it out unless you are going to shine it at something". It seemed remarkable that throughout this unhappy period he had deemed it fit to remove the torch from me but leave me with my fully loaded 9mm Glock pistol. He obviously had no doubts about my professionalism when it came to possessing a firearm; it was just torches that had him twitching.

I picked up the offending item and slid it into the belt ring; it seemed symbolic, like my sword being returned to me, not having it snapped over his knee and thrown out of the Lodge, the broken end forever disgracing me. *Actually I might just be getting that confused with a 70's Western 'Branded' which starred Chuck Connors.*

"Thanks Sarge" I muttered as I left his office.

Before I closed his door he called out "Not a word, not a fucking word about this ever gets out...do you understand"

"Sure Sarge...not a word" I replied conspiratorially.

Of course I promptly told everyone and I've now put it in this book.

Sorry Sarge.

***

Not content with threatening the Queens dog, I almost blotted my copy book on another occasion as I tried to make up for a tardy start to a late turn. I was five minutes late in leaving for work and didn't have a realistic chance of making up the time; however I didn't let this prospect deter me from driving to Sandringham as fast as I could. I shot through the front gate at warp speed, giving the officer a flash of the headlights and a wave as I shot past. The Police Lodge is situated at the rear of the house and is accessed via a narrow track that leads off from the main driveway. This track dips down next to a small copse of trees that circles what was the old ice house in pre freezer days. A small footpath leads from the house through the trees and continues across the tarmac before disappearing into the shrubbery on the other side of the road.

It was at this point that I noticed a figure wearing a green anorak and headscarf emerging from the trees. There was no time to brake so I had to continue, Her Majesty stepped back abruptly to avoid being run over and I passed within inches of her. Not sure of the protocol in this type of situation I threw up a salute with my right hand and steered with my left. She seemed genuinely bemused, here was the idiot who went around threatening dogs, dressed in civilian clothing, driving like a lunatic and saluting like a maniac. I bet she slept well knowing that I was on the case to protect her!

After my torch incident had caused the sergeant so much consternation I decided that I would do him a favour and not burden him with this information; what he didn't know couldn't hurt him. I quickly parked my car at the far end of the carpark and spent the rest of my tour hoping that affairs of state would occupy her Majesty's thoughts and not the idiot in the black Fiat Panda.

***

The old control room had been a bit antiquated and run down (as had the rest of the Lodge) but a refit and refurbishment had brought the standard up to cutting edge level. The grounds were extremely well monitored day or night and in any weather conditions. Being in the control room was good on several levels; cups of tea on demand, a comfortable environment and a chance to have a good natter and catch up on all the gossip. On one such occasion I was watching the monitor that covered the garage block, a car had just dropped off one of the princes at the front door and was being parked by the chauffeur. I watched in disbelief as the Rover came to a stop behind the estates huge, modified Landrover that had been nicknamed Jumbo due to its size. It had an extended wheel base to accommodate the many guests invited to the shooting parties on the estate, where they could slaughter anything and everything that flew near them. The prince's saloon suddenly shot forward and crashed into the rear of the bulky vehicle, both jolting under the impact. The cameras didn't have sound but you didn't have to be very good at lip reading to see that the chauffeur's day had taken a turn for the worse. He leapt from the stricken car and surveyed the crumpled bonnet and wings. With his head in his hands he mouthed the same expletives over and over before taking a wild swing at the broken car with his foot. By now the control room was packed with officers who were taking breaks or on standby to respond to any PAB activations from within the house. The sergeant pushed his way into the now cramped room, "Fuck off outside unless you're doing something useful" he shouted and the room quickly emptied.

I quickly briefed him on what had happened and the data feed was rewound as we all watched the car crash again and again; each time being as funny as the last. On the 'real time' feed the driver was looking around, obviously looking to see if there had been any witnesses who might contradict whatever story he was concocting in his head to explain the events that had left a royal vehicle with a remodelled front end.

Picking up the phone the sergeant put a call through to the garage bay next to where the collision had just taken place. The driver walked over to the phone and examined it like it was some alien device before he finally lifted it from the cradle. "I saw his lips move on the monitor and heard his voice over the speakerphone, "Garage" he muttered.

"Anything you want to tell us", the sergeant chirped.

"You saw it didn't you?" the chauffer responded dejectedly.

"Oh yes, in fact we have seen it several times...pretty spectacular for what it's worth".

"I'll have to come and watch it sometime" the deflated man replied, "I was looking over my shoulder making sure I didn't reverse into anything".

"Well you got that bit right".

"Fucking automatics" was the only response.

"Any damage to Jumbo?" the Sergeant enquired.

"Not so much as a fucking scratch" was the chauffeur's report.

The sergeant made a quick call to the princes PPO (Personal Protection Officer) and informed him of the incident and once the laughter had stopped HRH was duly updated. Fortunately he saw the funny side of it and the vehicle was quickly replaced by another shiny model, the sponsor quick to ensure that their franchise to provide prestige vehicles for the Royal family was kept intact.

The chauffeur kept his job despite losing his credibility for a short while and as it was Christmas, he received a gift wrapped DVD showing reruns of his unfortunate incident, courtesy of the control room staff .

***

I did a lot of my promotion exam studying at Sandringham, it helped to alleviate the downtime and boredom. It also helped to have a couple of crazy colleagues on shift as it kept everyone on their toes wondering what sort of stunt they would be performing next.

During a particularly cold and snowy January, Hector, for reasons best known to himself decided that he would stamp out a colleagues name in the snow in four foot high letters and announce to the world that the guy was a 'twat'. What he also did was to forget to delete the message before going off shift. It was more luck than judgement that one of the early turn officers noticed the disturbed snow. He hastily stamped out the message and reported the incident to his supervisor only to be told that the Duke had just kicked up merry hell because someone had ruined the pristine snow outside his bedroom window. His whole winter wonderland vista had been ruined by some inconsiderate oik and he wasn't best pleased. I fancy he would have been even less pleased had he popped his head out the window a few minutes earlier to find the message Hector had left. We all arrived for our night duty and walked straight into a shit storm. The inspector wanted to know who the culprit was and Hector owned up immediately before being quickly ushered into a side room. He eventually stepped back out with his ears ringing and the new arsehole he had just been given smarting! Nobody messed up the Dukes snow and got away with it!

***

I used to enjoy the Queen Mothers visits to Sandringham as she would always come and have a chat to the officers as she walked around the grounds. Her knowledge of local matters was phenomenal and she would often seek out the opinion of the officers as they generally had a good take on things. She was alleged to have had a great trick to ensure that she wasn't being given any bullshit by someone toadying up to her. Conversations would start with her bringing up a subject and if the person she was talking to feigned interest she would immediately ask "tell me, what have you heard?" It was a brilliant bullshit trap that gave the recipient no chance to wriggle out and it's a trick I have often used myself in order to get a clear picture on who actually knows something and who clearly doesn't. I've actually seen senior officers go blank and start floundering when their lack of knowledge of an operation or incident is suddenly and 'innocently' exposed by this simple method.

On this particular occasion we were talking about the low water table level of a set of fishing lakes close to where I lived; a disused sandpit had been allowed to flood into them and were then subsequently stocked with fish. She wanted my views on what I thought the impact on the area had been as a result of the new project. I had a natural well in my garden. In the past it had been the water supply for the house but modern plumbing and the development of the village had seen the introduction of a water mains and it had fallen into disuse. Only a few days earlier I had removed the manhole cover and had checked it for any signs of fatigue as we parked our car over it. My fear was that the weight of the vehicle might have weakened it and I didn't want it giving way sending the car plunging into the water below, it was hard enough to start as it was when it was damp. I had been surprised to see just how low the water had dropped since the previous year's inspection.

I had brought the subject up with an old boy whose shotgun licence I had gone to renew, he was in his nineties and had lived in Norfolk all his life apart from a stint in the army during the war where he had lost a leg. Over a cup of tea and a mardle I had mentioned the low level in my well and he had confirmed that his had all but dried up. He just used it to water his vegetable patch and was finding it difficult to get a full bucket any more as it was so low. He blamed the flooding of the sandpits; in fact he showed me a copy of the letter he had sent the Council outlining this very problem. Nobody had taken any notice and the fishing lakes were unveiled as a roaring success on how to return what had been an ugly gravel and sand pit back to nature. It didn't take long before the old boys predictions came back to haunt them. There were several other disused pits in the area and plans had been muted to do something similar with those. In the end they turned them into landfill sites instead.

I had called at the old boy's cottage to renew his shotgun licence and check that his gun cabinet met the latest regulations. It was a bit of a shock when he explained that he didn't have a cabinet as there was no point; the gun was kept in an old railway carriage by the fishing lakes. I had to explain that he couldn't do that, the law had changed a few years back and every shotgun had to be locked away when not in use in an approved steel cabinet. I reluctantly told him that I was going to have to confiscate his shotgun and not renew the licence until he was completely compliant with the law, before driving him the half mile or so to the railway carriage he had mentioned. He wasn't at all stable on his prosthetic limb and the crutch he was using kept sinking into the soft sand as we walked the last few metres from the road to the wooden structure.

The carriage was more dilapidated than he was; the panels pitted with woodworm and dry rot and stained with streaks of rust that had taken a firm hold of all the metal fixtures. He fiddled with the padlock which I was surprised to see was well greased and opened easily and the long side door started to slowly roll back on its tracks. It groaned and squealed as it travelled half the length of the opening before giving up the task and stopping dead. The old boy leant inside and grabbed the shotgun, almost toppling into the carriage before regaining his balance. "Here you go boy" he said as he handed the weapon over to me. It was rusty and riddled with as much woodworm as the carriage, large pieces of the stock were missing, the tell-tale traces of worm burrows evidence of the meal the once veneered wood had provided.

"Not much to look at now I'm afraid" he said as he ran his eyes over the old piece. "Had that since I was a nipper, kicks like a horse but that didn't much bother me even when I lost my leg; always hit what I shot at and was always able to fill the pot so we never went hungry".

"Do you still use it?" I said, having witnessed his unsteady gait on our short journey to and from my car.

"Not so much now, I find it too difficult to get up" he replied.

"Get up?" I queried.

"When I fire, it knocks me over and I have to climb back up. I did tie a piece of rope on the side of the carriage so I could pull myself up but I haven't got the strength anymore".

I had a mental image of this old boy limping all the way down to his lock-up, charging the old gun with a couple of cartridges and waiting for a pheasant or rabbit to pop its head up above the wild grass and weeds of the adjacent meadow. Taking aim and pulling the rusty trigger, the gun bucking violently in his hands and the force knocking him off balance against the side of the carriage or onto the floor. Using the rope to help him stand up he would then limp out into the meadow to claim his dinner. This truly was living off the land like generations before him, country folk doing country things, never taking more than they could eat and respecting the habitat that provided their meals.

I felt awful depriving him of the weapon, especially as it had a sentimental value far beyond the couple of quid scrap value it was currently worth. However in the wrong hands the shotgun represented a real hazard, both to the person it was pointed at and the person doing the pointing. It hadn't been cleaned for years by the look of the barrels and any tension put through the stock was likely to see the wood part company with the metal. Like its owner it had enjoyed better days.

I didn't want to put the gun in the police armoury as the woodworm was likely to still be active and not having too much left to eat on its host would be seeking to find another dinner donor. At the time all the SFG weapons were housed in the armoury along with spare handguns (Smith and Wesson model 10's) for any authorised firearm deployment. Virtually every one of them possessed a walnut grip or stock…a veritable banquet for hungry woodworm.

There was another option, and after half an hour of phoning around we found a relative who had a shotgun licence and a gun safe and he agreed to meet me at the house to take charge of the weapon. It was going to be stored with a relative so I didn't feel quite so bad about removing it. I had no doubt that the old boy would never get a gun safe and therefore never again own a shotgun licence. I figured I was doing him a favour because the next time it was fired it was likely finish them both off.

***

The old boy's reminiscences came back to me as I spoke to the Queen Mother. I told her all about him and she obviously had the same mental picture I had, laughing when I described him falling over after each shot.

We talked for a while until she noticed my replacement hovering in the trees; telling me she didn't want to hold me up from my duties she took her leave and headed off to continue her walk. She truly was a woman who knew how to sound genuinely interested in people even if they were boring the hell out of her.

One of the staff in 'the house' told me that the Queen Mother used to bring up these snippets of local information at the dinner table thereby keeping everyone in touch with the outside world.

Boredom breeds bother

Police officers all complain about being rushed off their feet with no time to write up the last incident before being sent to the next. However whenever there was some down time I found it tended to bring out the worse in some people.

'Zippy' was a well-educated, well-disciplined former marine who had a family history of top ranking police officers to draw from. He was also a bloody nightmare when he got bored and apt to be a liability especially when he was in the company of likeminded individuals.

My first 'questionable' experience with him was on a late turn; we were allocated the unmarked car and this gave us a licence to patrol some of the less desirable areas in the city. The Mondeo we were using looked a little shabby and as a result blended in extremely well with its surroundings. We slunk around the back streets keeping a low profile and an ever watchful eye on whoever was in the neighbourhood. After an hour I noticed a car entering a housing estate; the number plate had featured on the local intelligence sheets as being involved in dealing drugs to the local youngsters. The driver passed us and pulled up next to a group of kids twenty metres ahead, it never ceases to amaze me just how unobservant people can be; especially those caught pedalling drugs who have so much to lose.

Zippy was driving and he slipped the car into a parking space that gave us a clear view of the shonky old Vauxhall our target was driving. It didn't take long before the dealer prompted some interest from the locals. A small group of hooded lads sauntered over to the car and the passenger window was lowered in response. I angled the covert camera and zoomed the lens in close, the evidence being recorded in technicolour on the video player in the boot of our car. Even the CPS (Crown Prosecution Service) would have difficulty in 'NFA'ing' (No Further Action) the damning evidence. I looked over to Zippy and could see the excitement on his face; we wanted to nab some of the lads who were buying the gear as well as the driver of the Vauxhall. The buyers would negate any defence our dealer could come up with once he was interviewed and they would probably get dealt with by way of a caution if it was their first offence (or more likely their first time getting caught). This might give some of them a big enough shock to keep them away from drugs in the future.

In order to get both sets of offenders we would have to be subtle and resist the urge to do a 'Starsky and Hutch'; rip roar up to the Vauxhall in a cloud of spinning tyre smoke and leap over the bonnet to make our bust. Apart from the fact that I probably couldn't leap as high as the bonnet any more, we would stand a good chance of losing either the buyers or the seller, or worse still all of them.

I explained my plan to Zippy who seemed to be taking it all in; his head nodded in acquiescence but God only knew what the hamster inside it was doing. We had disabled our interior courtesy light so as not to spook them when I opened the car door. I slipped the seat belt off my shoulder, opened the door and stepped out of the vehicle. Several things happened at once, and none of them were good. The seat belt snagged on the side handle of my baton and before I could release it Zippy gunned the engine and the Mondeo shot forward like a scolded cat. The net result of these seemingly innocuous incidents was that as the car moved forward the seat belt tightened on the baton, whipping me around like a spinning top and throwing me over the rear of the car, but not before the rear wheel had a chance to crush my foot. Zippy, unaware of the mayhem he had caused, continue to drive away leaving me to pick myself up and hobble over to where he had parked up next to the drug dealer's car door. Surprisingly, the lads who had been buying from him were still standing around open mouthed after our spectacular entrance, seemingly unaware that they should have been running away at this stage. This was all to our advantage and we ended up nicking the lot of them.

It was the source of great amusement when Zippy found that he had captured me on the rear view camera as I slid down the back window before being unceremoniously dumped on my arse in the middle of the road. I am sure that he still has the footage somewhere waiting for an opportune moment to publish it on YouTube.

***

Zippy was also responsible for redecorating our crew room, not that it had needed redecorating as it had been refurbished only weeks beforehand.

In fairness it wasn't totally his fault, however had he not been bored then the situation wouldn't have arisen. We had all just been issued with the extending side handled baton and he fancied himself as a quick draw specialist, able to draw and extend the baton in a split second. He was good, so good that other officers would lob an object at him shouting "Zippy" as they did so, and he would whip out his baton striking the object in mid-air as it reached him. He became so proficient that when a pot of Tipp-Ex was aimed in his direction he struck it with deadly precision. The plastic container split and the crew room was engulfed in an impromptu snow storm and impending shit storm.

The Tipp-Ex had gone everywhere, the walls, carpet, desks and ceiling. Most of the officers present were also affected, firstly by fits of uncontrollable laughter, quickly followed by a case of arse covering which emptied the room quickly as they sought to be elsewhere. The scene they had departed so hastily resembled a winter wonderland...the other wonder being just how deep in the shit Zippy was going to be?

Three of us remained to perform the clean-up operation; Zippy because it was his mess, 'Blurty' because he had been the idiot who had lobbed the Tipp-Ex bottle and me because Blurty was giving me a lift home. We spent an hour scraping the poxy stuff out of the carpet pile and off the walls, it was the proverbial shit and blanket scenario. Whenever we thought we had cleared away the evidence a quick scan of the room would reveal further splats and splashes and we would have to start cleaning up again.

An area next to the waste bin was the worst affected as this had been where the broken container had eventually come to rest. The paint had faded under the onslaught of our frantic scrubbing and in order to explain the damage Zippy scratched out a quick report to the early turn sergeant telling him that he had thrown a Tipp-Ex bottle at the bin and it had hit the wall, split and disgorged its contents over the paintwork.

The following afternoon we turned up for our shift and Zippy was promptly asked to attend the sergeant's office to explain his report. It became apparent that with all our attention being focused on the walls, ceiling and floor the reports that had been on the desktop had gone un-noticed. As Zippy's account was being read out at the morning briefing all eyes fell upon the tell-tale trail of white splats that spread out across the paperwork and lined up perfectly with the damaged paintwork and blotchy carpet.

Faced with this overwhelming and damning evidence Zippy owned up to the incident. The sergeant helped him to recompose his initial report and he had now offered to pay for any damage caused by his error of judgement. Meanwhile all the remaining evidence was hastily cleaned away. Fortunately nothing further came of that particular prank…which probably made Zippy and Blurty's next escapade an all-time classic.

***

The headquarters for the Traffic Department was established in an old warehouse complex on the outskirts of the city. A large hangar attached to the office block housed the patrol cars and the workshops; the place was hot as hell in summer and bitterly cold in winter. The civilian section of the department increased and it soon became apparent that one set of toilets wasn't enough for the female staff members and the small toilet next to the cramped kitchen quickly became the subject of a campaign for re-designation from being unisex into a 'females only' boudoir.

The officers on the upper floor didn't want the riff-raff from downstairs using their pristine porcelain so this resulted in the male officers, who amounted to pretty much all the 'public facing' staff, being told that they could perform their ablutions in the hangar toilets. These were grim at the best of times and damn miserable during the cold months. This caused a bit of an uproar, it was hard enough to find your dick as it was under all the layers of clothing, body armour and reflective clothing, so subjecting your todger to arctic conditions was a recipe for disaster.

The twenty eight male officers showed a united front and we confronted the management to air our concerns. It was all to no avail, the three women who had petitioned for the 'female only toilet' won an undemocratic victory and the men were immediately banished to the outside bogs.

Once victory had been gained, the ladies decided that the existing toilet pan and seat needed to be replaced as it had obviously been soiled by the hairy arses of the male workforce. The sink was also in need of replacement and a mirror set behind it to aid make-up and hair touch ups, the lino also needing to go as did the tiles and door. A larger radiator wouldn't go amiss either as they (and this really did rub salt in the wound) thought that the toilet was a bit chilly! An extractor fan was also an absolute must have just in case one of them discovered that their shit did actually stink.

What should have been a two minute job to print off a laminated sign that declared the toilet was 'Women Only', turned into a several thousand pounds project disrupting the canteen and office for almost two weeks.

Once the refurbishments had been undertaken, and to make sure that their new sanctuary wasn't defiled by some uncouth male, a lock was placed on the door and all the female staff were supplied with a key. The door was religiously kept locked and it became the focus of conspiratorial plans from the male uniformed workers as to what would happen if it was ever found open.

One sunny Sunday morning Zippy noticed that the door hadn't been locked and this haven of femininity was just begging for his attention. He plotted with Blurty for most of the morning, the pair of them seeking to find the perfect way to defile this hallowed space. Later in the day the pair of them canvassed the officers as they returned to base for some change in order to buy chocolate bars from the vending machine. Soon they had a large collection of Snickers and Mars bars on the kitchen worktop. The chocolate was removed from the wrapping and remodelled into what can only be described as the biggest turd known to man. This was then forced into the pristine toilet and lodged halfway around the U-bend. The finishing touch was then added; a dollop of both brown and red sauce poured into the palm of Blurty's hand which he lowered into the bowl before slapping his other hand down on it. The resulting mess was spectacular; it replicated a bowel explosion of a magnificent magnitude and of frightening proportions, an episode that would have most people beating a hasty path to their GP or hospital casualty department for urgent medical attention.

Word of the two protagonists exploits quickly spread and officers travelled miles from the other traffic garages to view 'la turd magnifique'. Speculation as to the reaction to the mess when it was discovered on Monday morning was rife. It was intended that the door would be locked shut after the final viewing and left to be discovered by the first of our ladies to get taken short. The office manager had been the instigator behind the toilet coup and there was much speculation and hope that it would be her.

There was also the question of whether or not the finder would actually say anything or would they quietly beat the beast down the pan and round the bend before flushing away the evidence. Would they then look at their colleagues with a sense of shock or pity as they pontificated on whose arsehole was capable of creating and delivering such a monster?

I could see a couple of problems with the joke; the first being that the office manager was not known for her sense of humour and the second being that the boss was renowned for his strict and draconian approach to discipline. If either of these two became involved then heads would roll, and the world of shit the perpetrators found themselves in would make their constructed turd look like a wet fart.

That evening the nagging worry of what would happen when the toilet door was unlocked the following morning wouldn't go away and I ended up phoning a colleague who was on duty that evening requesting a favour. He was asked to go to the city and flush the monster turd away so that the real shit didn't hit the fan. I knew that one of the girls left her toilet key in her desk drawer; she worked part time and left the office keys for anyone else who 'hot desked' at her work station. I explained all this to my mate and left it in his capable hands.

Monday morning saw quite an array of emotions from the gathered early turn staff. Most had, like me realised that the joke was funny in concept but the reality was likely to have major repercussions. A couple of officers who had not participated, so therefore couldn't be associated with the incident, sat back with the smug assurance that they were fire proof and out of harm's way. However they couldn't wait to see what the fall out was going to be.

Zippy seemed unable to contain his glee at the prospective conclusion to his prank. The skipper and Blurty looked wracked with worry as both knew that their jobs could be on the line, hindsight having been a cruel bedfellow overnight.

I didn't want to be seen as a killjoy so had declined from saying anything about the clean-up operation I had organised. A note from my mate telling me that the deed had been done, or rather undone in this particular case, had been left in my tray so I knew that the coast and the toilet pan were clear.

As fate would dictate in these things it was the office manager who was the first to enter the toilet; she furnished the coveted key with a flourish, her little snipe for feminism. After we heard the toilet flush she reappeared and promptly locked the door behind her, if she noticed the fact that the entire early turn was holding its breath waiting for a response she didn't show it. The anti-climax was palpable and officers quickly collected up their kit and headed off to their patrol cars disappointed in the lack of reaction.

Zippy sat stunned; unable to believe that there had been no shrieks of horror or fainting episode. I suggested that perhaps the finding of a tumultuous turd in the toilet was perhaps something that wasn't so uncommon after all and that maybe one of the staff had a problem she didn't mind sharing with the other girls in the office.

When the room cleared I explained to Blurty and the skipper what I had done; to say that both were relieved would be an understatement, they had both had visions of their careers going down the pan a damn sight quicker that the chocolate turd did once the boss got involved.

Don't get me wrong, I love practical jokes and have performed more than my fair share, but the trick is to be able to control them and get in quickly to abort if things start to go wrong.

Despite Zippy's self-destruct tendencies he continued to manage the balancing act between genius and lunacy on a daily basis. Later, he transferred to a larger police force where I hope that he didn't feel the need to continue playing the joker.

***

There were also occasions during days on the firing range when a bit of competitiveness would bring out the worst in people.

The MP5 was the designated weapon of the Armed Response Unit at that time and was extremely accurate and an absolute pleasure to shoot. On a short 50 metre range it was relatively easy to create a large hole in the target with accurate grouping. Once a large enough hole appeared the fun and games could commence with your neighbours target. The hole meant that the rounds couldn't be accurately counted so you were considered to have scored a perfect fifty unless there were rounds outside the score area which could be counted and then deducted from your tally. If aiming at the target to the side of your own, you could purposefully start peppering it with shots outside the kill zone and lose your colleague points.

It wouldn't be unusual to find though that they wouldn't take this treatment without some form of payback. Often pieces of your weapon would be missing when you came to reassemble it after cleaning and you would have to search high and low to find them or you could find parts had been replaced by dirty components which you then had to clean before rebuilding the weapon.

The guns on the ARV's were scrupulously cleaned every Sunday morning, barring having to attend a firearms call out or a serious or fatal collision. They were immaculate, but that couldn't always be said of the pool firearms used for training. It was potluck with regards to what you picked out of the gun boxes; not knowing if the sights were accurate or had been knocked about in transit. You were never allowed to zero a weapon in when you arrived at the range. The first fifty shots were a classification shoot and you had to score above a minimum percentage to retain your authorisation. Those who failed had one last chance to classify at the end of the session or find themselves suspended from firearms duty until a remedial training day could be arranged.

On one particular day I shot a paltry thirty five out of fifty with the Glock I had drawn from the gun box. All the rounds (those that had hit the target) were down the right hand side of the silhouette. I complained that the gun sights were out but this fell on deaf ears as virtually everyone blames the weapon and not themselves in this type of situation.

During the course of the day my scores started creeping up to an acceptable level but I still complained that the only reason this was happening was because I was 'Kentucky shooting'; a practice of compensating for the sights inaccuracy by adjusting your aim accordingly. I was aiming not at the centre of the target but as far to the left as I could in order to get the round anywhere near the middle and score.

Finally after much bitching and sulking the instructors agreed to check zero my weapon. The trainer went down on one knee and fired; the target remained undamaged. He put two further rounds down the range before conceding that the gun was indeed not shooting true. Its rear sight was eventually adjusted using a special tool supplied by the manufacturers and I was back in the game but still had to shoot at the end of the day to keep my ticket.

***

The instructors were extremely thorough and professional with our training and this has saved lives on more than one occasion; none more so than on an estate one hot and humid summers day. A man who was known to police had gone berserk and his family had called police to sort the domestic situation out. In most places this would not be unusual, but the estate we were being called to had a reputation for sorting things out themselves and never talked to the police about anything. They made the Cosa Nostra sound like blabbermouths they were so tight lipped. Find someone half beaten to death after a good kicking and they would tell you they had tripped up the kerb... five or six times, and nobody else was involved. A few days later there would be another 'clumsy' person falling over the same kerb and again declining to tell us anything.

The estate had been a London overspill development in the sixties and the sleepy little Norfolk town changed overnight as the new inhabitants stamped their presence on the locals (quite literally in some cases). Despite this reputation, the town had a very active industrial area and there was seemingly plenty of work for those who wanted it. As generation after generation grew up in the compartmentalised estates there was still an overwhelming desire to hang on to their London roots and the dulcet tones of 'Mockney' could be heard in the clubs, pubs and bars. Each generation weakened the dialect until it became a cross between Eastenders and Emmerdale ..."I had nowt te do with it, I wuz gathering the harvest, you slag, apples and pears, knees up Muvver Brown". Well maybe not quite that mixed but you get the picture.

On this particular occasion a young gentleman called Rocky Tyne had apparently had problems with his self-medication and in the terms used by his family 'had just fucking gone into one". In order to make the situation clear to the rest of his family he had picked up a meat cleaver and started threatening them with it. One may wonder why the household had such an implement considering they ate almost exclusively from the local take away or out of cereal boxes but this was a rough area and having a meat cleaver with you when out walking your dog or nipping down to the shop is akin to having a Gucci handbag in Kensington. It says something about you and therefore one just didn't leave home without it.

***

I remembered attending a job at the Tyne's house quite a few years previously when I had been a DC, Norfolk by now no longer the quiet little backwater it had been when I first transferred. The crime figures had, like the populace continued growing year on year as more and more houses were devouring the once green belted countryside. Norfolk wasn't the only thing that had changed; I had joined a gym and bulked up a bit so that I no longer looked like the skinny teenager I had been when I had first joined. I had even shaved off the ratty moustache that had adorned my top lip in order to give me some gravitas. I was older, wiser and working in a town that seemingly revelled in its reputation for being one of the most violent places in the county. We were still living in the house that we had bought when I had transferred; our daughter and son had both established themselves in the community with regards to school and friends and I was so glad that I had taken the advice given to me on the day of my interview and had settled down in the middle of Norfolk, a place that still retained some of the country charm it had possessed when we first moved there.

It was just before knocking off time on a Sunday, and as a family we would always try and plan to sit down together for a roast dinner (my shifts willing). It had been a slow day so I had taken the gamble and phoned home to tell my wife to expect me at the usual time. I had a bit of paperwork to do (well actually I had a lot although only a small part of the pile was urgent) but it had been a relatively quiet Sunday so far. That morning we hadn't been greeted with an overflowing cellblock and a cupboard full of exhibits for a change, so it was a good chance to get stuck into the backlog of crime sheets that littered my desk. Most cases were going nowhere and after a rudimentary investigation I would contact the victim and let them know. Sunday was a good day for this, not because it was a day of rest, a family or religious day but because most of the population didn't start to emerge from their pits until around lunch time having slept off the skin full they had consumed the night before.

People who I didn't like would have me thumping on their doors at 9am and after a good few minutes of knocking they would eventually drag themselves to their front doors to sort out the git who was making so much noise. How things had changed since my early days in Norfolk and far from being welcomed by a jolly farmer with a cup of tea and bacon butty, I was now most likely to be greeted with the front door being opened a crack and a sullen groan of "What the fuck do you want?" It was just like being back in London.

Most of the 'victims' were also offenders in other cases and by the nature of checks and balances they would win some, lose some. "Good morning young man, I have just come to inform you that we haven't been able to identify the person who used your head as a football last week. However there is some good news, the person whose teeth you knocked out the previous week in a street fight claims that they fell over a kerb and caused the injury themselves". I always tried to smile; I had stopped fretting over the karma of it all months before. If people wanted to live in a place where nobody 'grassed' then why should I lose sleep over it? It was their community, so as far as I was concerned they could play by their own rules. The only times I got annoyed was when innocent parties were involved and these were the cases I put all my energies into investigating. I had lost count of the court cases that had folded because a witness had retracted their statement at the last minute.

On one occasion I went to see a fairly active young criminal who had taken a rather nasty beating from another fairly active young criminal from another estate. It happened in the middle of a packed pub where there were dozens of witnesses and when the assailant was nicked he was covered in his victim's blood. When it came to getting statements you could have been forgiven for thinking that the pub had been visited by St Dunston's school for the blind as nobody had seen a thing.

"So you'se are telling me fuck all's gonna happen and that the fuckers just walking away scot free?" the 'victim' shouted indignantly in a thick Mockney accent, "He was bang to rights and you'se lot know it".

"That's right, no further action, the CPS have said there is insufficient evidence to prosecute" I told him for the umpteenth time, hoping that some of it would be retained if I said it slow and loud enough.

"How the fuck did he git off wiv it?" he demanded.

Oh good I thought, a thread of understanding has reached the bit between his ears sometimes referred to as a brain

"He had your solicitor representing him in interview" I told him with relish.

"Well yeah, he's fucking good aint he?" he replied with begrudging respect.

***

I had made a couple of similar type visits that day and was just putting the final touches to a crime file where someone had actually made a witness statement and the CPS were looking at giving the case a run at court. I kidded myself that I could now see the top of my desk, a rare sight that hadn't been witnessed since the bloody thing had been brought into the office several years previously. It was the desk used by the CID aide, a dubious title that meant different things to different people. To the officer sitting there it meant a potential gateway onto the department; to everyone else it meant that the officer was a general dogsbody who they could heap their crap on to.

This Sunday was going to be no different... Half an hour before I was due off the DS sauntered over to me.

"Cleared a corner I see" he said, pointing to the melamine birch veneer that was starting to appear on the far corner of the desk.

"Yeah, had a good day Sarge, squared away a fair bit of crap today" I said quite smugly.

"That's good; you've got room for this file then" he smirked as the melamine birch veneer disappeared under a bulky file. "Nice easy little nick for you, this one" he said as if he was doing me the biggest favour in the world. As he started to walk away he turned back, "needs to be sorted before you go off shift" he added with an even bigger grin.

"I'm off at four, Sarge" I pleaded.

"Well don't hang around bleating about it then, get your arse into gear". The other officers in the office looked up with sympathetic smiles, at some point they had all staffed this desk and the memories still haunted them.

I saw the name at the top of the file 'Rocky Tyne'.

"It's Rocky Tyne" I blurted out.

"We'll make a detective out of you yet Scottie" he laughed. "I don't know what the problem is, just nip round his house, nick Rocky and pick up the stolen stereo, easy job". He turned tail and collected his jacket from the coat rack.

"Are you coming with me?" I asked. Rocky could be a real handful and it never hurt to go there in numbers.

"Fuck off, it's Sunday. I'm off for a pint before I go home, missus will have a roast on the table and I don't want to spoil that". With that he walked straight out the office and left the nick.

It was looking like my dinner was definitely going to get spoilt as my chances of getting away in time were getting slimmer by the minute.

There had been a fight at the local pub a couple of nights before and Rocky had been implicated. The fight had allegedly been over the theft of a car stereo which had previously been stolen on so many other occasions I knew the serial number off by heart. This unit was normally sold to a gullible punter and then removed from the new owner's vehicle a few days later to be sold again. The activation code etched into the side of the machine was known to most of the inhabitants of the estate as they had all 'owned' it at some point.

Rocky was a bit of a wheeler dealer thief when he wasn't being a smack head; he was a right shitbag when he was on the gear and a complete arsehole when he wasn't. In either guise he was a nasty, unpredictable violent fucker with loads of form for assaults on both the public and the police. The altercation in the pub had taken place because Rocky, who was 'off his face' according to eyewitnesses, tried to sell the stereo to a lad he had only sold it to a few days earlier. The item had been retrieved from the dash of the new owner's vehicle sometime in the night and Rocky's calling card, the half brick that had been used to smash the side window in order to gain access had been left on the driver's seat.

The theft hadn't been reported to the police because the lad with the damaged window knew that the stereo was nicked when he bought it. He also knew that grassing up the likely suspect would get him ostracised by the community and quite likely a bloody good hiding from Rocky and his family.

Everything had gone wrong when Rocky sauntered over to a table in the pub and knocked some drinks onto the floor, by way of apology he offered the occupants of the table a deal and produced the stereo from his bag. Sitting at that same table was Rocky's latest victim who identified the stereo as being the one he'd had nicked the night before. The lad's family and friends decided that they would intervene and Rocky, realising his mistake tried to rectify the situation by head butting the nearest person squarely across the bridge of his nose. There was then some retaliation and a large fight took place , causing a couple of tables to collapse, a few glasses to get broken and a quantity of blood needing to be mopped up off the floor and walls.

Surprisingly, the injuries were not particularly serious, this quite likely being due to the fact that a police patrol was passing and stopped when they saw a lad rushing across the road towards the pub holding a snooker cue. When they asked him what he had the cue for he told them it was pool night in the pub and he was late for a game. The fact that the pub hadn't had a snooker or pool table for many years gave the game away and he would have been nicked then and there had the sound of breaking glass and knuckles not been heard emanating from the lounge bar. On entering the pub the officers had been met by the landlord, a shifty horrible man called Rosie on account of his surname being Rose. Rosie had halitosis that would be considered a Weapon of Mass Destruction by anyone who had the misfortune to get within a couple of metres of him; he appeared to have worn the same clothes for the last two months and his BO could stop bullets.

He had claimed that there wasn't any problem and stalled the officers long enough so the wounded could be evacuated out the back of the pub and an attempt made to clear away the debris they had left behind. Claiming that the blood and splintered table were the result of an unfortunate accident the officers asked to view the CCTV tape from the bar camera. Rosie had sauntered over to the machine and hit the eject button; when the expected tape failed to emerge he shrugged his shoulders and mournfully announced that he must have forgotten to put one in, much to the amusement of his clientele. The officers left the bar to the roars from the jubilant crowd.

A report had been made about the incident and yet another letter was sent to the brewery complaining about the incumbent landlord. It would make no difference, on the occasions they had sacked a manager or landlord they had replaced them with an equally despicable and incompetent person of a similar nature. The pub was the seediest place in the seediest part of the town with the seediest customers, if it was going to be improved in any way it didn't need a new landlord it needed an air strike from the local air force preferably when the place was full.

The reason I had been dragged into this sorry affair was due to the fact that the DS had a couple of informants in the pub that night who had witnessed the events and they let him know what had happened. The fact that our favourite stereo was back on the market led him to believe that he could nab Rocky in possession of the goods and hopefully get him put away for a bit. It was a pipe dream to say the least, for a start off Mystic Meg provided better information than his network of snouts. The two particular informants he had been speaking to were the scum of the earth who would feed us tit bits in order to get themselves a few bob. I wouldn't have trusted them to tell me the time of day let alone set up any form of operation on the strength of their say so.

Armed with these dubious snippets of information it took me five minutes to arrive and knock on Rocky's front door, a door that had previously been 'knocked' on by several police raiding parties armed with a battering ram and a warrant. The glass in the upper pane had long ago been replaced by an MDF substitute, the local housing authority reluctant to replace the glass as it never lasted more than a week. Either the police or disgruntled neighbours took turns in smashing it, us to gain lawful entry them to settle a score with the family. The MDF did however give me the advantage of an element of surprise as they couldn't see who was at the door before they opened it.

"Hello detective, who are you after this time?" Rocky's mother asked in her

Mockney accent.

"I've come to see Rocky, Mrs Tyne" I said as I invited my foot over the threshold.

"Well he's done fuck all so's you're wasting your time". She spat back as she wedged the door firmly between her buxom bosoms.

There was no way I was going to be able to move the door with that sort of weight behind it so I ventured, "Can I come in?"

She smiled. "Got a fucking warrant?"

"Who's at the door mum? Tell em to fuck off if they want me" Rocky's voice boomed out from somewhere upstairs in the house.

I smiled back at Mrs Tyne, "Don't need one luv, I'm here to nick him and he's inside so I get to come in one way or the other".

She stepped back, "He's as thick as shit that boy, can't keep his fucking mouth shut".

I entered the house and into a potential health hazard, the smell of stale sweat, dog urine, a years-worth of take-away's and a thousand smoked fags rushed down the hallway and straight up my nose. Find a way of putting that odour into a spray can and there would be no need for CS; it was a fact that on some occasions you could actually tell whose house an officer had visited that day by the residual smell that had leached into their uniform. Avoiding a pile of dog shit that had crusted over I stepped through into the lounge. Mrs Tyne invited her son down to converse with me.

"Rocky, get your fucking arse down here, the old bill are here to nick ya" she called out at the top her voice.

I stood with one foot in the hallway in case Rocky tried to do a runner. If he decided to go out the bedroom window there was every chance he would break his neck on the assortment of fridge freezers and an old three piece that were biodegrading back to their composite elements in the front garden. Rocky falling and breaking his neck would in all honesty be a right result, our crime figures would go down overnight, the town would be a better place and I might still make it home in time for my dinner.

My daydream was broken by the sound of heavy footprints on the stair treads and Rocky came into view. That is, a naked pair of legs sporting what had once been a white pair of Y-fronts but were now grey and stained appeared. The rest of this excuse for humanity called Rocky Tyne quickly filled the hallway.

"What the fuck ya want this time?" he growled.

I smiled, his body looked more emaciated than ever and it could only be a matter of time before his drug habit killed him. It would be a sad day for the local dealers but everyone else would be having a fucking street party. "Not interrupting you from doing anything important I hope"? I ventured as he removed his hand from down the front of his disgusting pants. "Excuse my manners but I don't particularly want to shake hands".

"You got a warrant?" he asked.

"No Rocky, just a power of arrest and the powers to search the place once I've said the magic words" I responded.

"What magic words?" he looked perplexed and sought reassurance from his mother.

"You're nicked for screwing cars and selling the stereos".

His mother tossed her head "I told you he was fucking stupid didn't I...what magic words he asked...reckon you were the one I dropped on their head when you was a baby".

"Do you want the caution Rocky?" I asked. He was entitled to it every time he was arrested and I thought that he had heard it more times than I had.

"Nah, give us a break…you know I ain't gonna say fuck all anyway" he replied with a smirk.

"Well that ain't going to stop me asking you some questions down the nick though is it" I replied, wincing as my grammar started reflecting my present company.

Time was ticking on and my dinner was going to be heading back to the depths of the oven. Without any evidence i.e. the stereo, a witness statement and some facts I was going nowhere with this and neither was Rocky. I hadn't got anything substantial to nick him for but the word of two unreliable scroats who would never put pen to paper and give a witness statement. "Tell you what Rocky, to save everyone's time I am prepared to do you a deal. If I don't find the stereo I won't nick you. How's that?"

The cogs in his head started to turn, his mind slowly shovelling coal into the furnace to create enough steam to start the thought process. "You ain't gonna to find it here, I wasn't anywhere near that car when it got done and there's loads of bricks lying about just waiting for anyone to pick em up and smash a window with".

"Interesting Rocky, I didn't even mention which stereo I was talking about and you have already told me how the vehicle got broken into. You're interviewing yourself without your brief being present". I wouldn't be able to use anything he said as he would deny it and traipse half the family into court to back up his story. "So how are we doing regarding my generous offer? Or were you about to admit to anything else?"

He looked to his mother who was scowling at him for being so stupid, his slack jaw hanging open as more steam was required so he could work both his mouth and a couple of brain cells at the same time. Fortunately Mrs Tyne stepped in before any steam emerged from his ears due to the strain. "Is he going to find the stereo here Rocky?"

Rocky, glad for the mental assistance turned to his mother, "Course not, I'm not stupid enough to bring the fucking thing home am I?" sadly confirming that he was at least that stupid.

"What you meant is you didn't thieve it in the first place so it can't be here can it!" she corrected him.

I couldn't believe that Darwin's elusive missing link was now standing before me and was a virtual one man crime wave, yet he struggled to perform on the most basic level. It wasn't that we couldn't nick him; that was a regular occurrence. He would come in, get a brief and say fuck all and then be put out on bail; the witnesses would then be queuing up to withdraw their statements or claim they had mistakenly identified the wrong person.

We had even caught him hanging out of a broken car window with a stereo half out of the dash. The owner had come in later that day with a cut lip and black eye to tell us that he had told Rocky he could have the stereo as he didn't use it anymore, it was all above board and he didn't want to make a complaint. Fear is a powerful weapon and I couldn't blame the owner for wanting to forget the whole episode; the Tyne family had long memories and a very nasty streak.

It was Rocky's mum who broke the deadlock. "Search the fucking place and then fuck off" she offered.

This did put me in a bit of a spot as my powers to search only extended to post Rocky's arrest and if I wasn't going to nick him then I hadn't got the grounds to search. "Ok Rocky you heard your mum; this is how it's going to work. I will de-arrest you; you or your mum will then sign a 'consent to search' form and I will look for the nicked gear, then as your mum so eloquently put it, fuck off if I can't find anything".

With both Mum and Rocky nodding their heads in unison I whipped out the relevant forms and got mums scrawl in the correct places. "Right Rocky let's start with your bedroom and work our way around the rest of your estate shall we"

"Hurry up" prompted mum, "his dad will be back with our tea soon and I don't want that getting cold".

"Don't worry Mrs Tyne, I've got a roast dinner waiting for me at home that I don't want to get ruined either". I replied amiably.

"Oh 'ark at him with his fucking roast dinner…must be paying you more than you're worth if you can afford a roast fucking dinner. Can't remember the last time we could afford one of them" Mrs Tyne mocked. "Fish and fucking chips is all we can afford…alright for some 'eh?"

Rocky chipped in "It's all our tax money paying their fucking wages, that's why they get to eat posh".

"We are quite lucky" I explained "Our chef is really quite talented when it comes to knocking up some posh grub" I retorted. None of their family had ever worked as far as I knew, I'm sure it was one of their ancestors who informed Noah that he couldn't cut any wood for the ark because he had ADHD and that if he didn't get a lift on the boat that would be discrimination and his brief would sue him.

"Funny fucker…ain't he?" replied Mrs Tyne who was turning into a proper little wordsmith.

This was the problem with the country as far as I could see it. Contrary to the belief of the two people facing me, we didn't have pots of money; my wife had taken a part time job in order to pay for the extra fuel it was costing me to travel to this shit hole of a town. We couldn't afford to have take-away's or buy fish and chips for the whole family as it cost an arm and a leg. A chicken and some vegetables hardly fell into the category of haute cuisine and wasn't anywhere near as expensive as a trip to the chippy. The family barely drew a breath without it being laden with the toxic fumes of a nearby fag, the floor was strewn with empty cigarette packets that had been generally thrown in the direction of the overflowing bin and had either failed to hit the target or had toppled from the existing pile onto what had once been a carpet but was now a collection of bare threads and filth.

This family took all the government had to offer and then went out and stole off their own kind; they made no effort to contribute to anything other than making other people's lives a misery. They were the first people to mock anyone who bettered themselves and the first people to despise anyone who had more than they did regardless of the effort and hours that person had sacrificed in order to afford them.

Their three bedroom council house backed onto woodland and a water meadow, a prime location for a home. The garden was a tip of their own making, there was a recycling service that would come and collect old white goods for free but they were too lazy to phone them. The only effort they made was to collect their benefits every month and walk to the pub and chippy. The lounge wall was dominated by a huge flat screen TV about the size of my dining room table; the latest DVD's and computer games laying next to their relevant players. In the back of my mind I just couldn't help but think who was the mug, them or me.

Rocky's bedroom reflected the state of his underwear, rank, manky and covered in dubious stains. I hadn't brought any latex gloves with me but guessed that they would have rotted away as soon as I put my hands anywhere near his bedding. If it was ever going to be removed from the bed they would need a disc cutter and a blow torch. The sheets looked like they could survive a full on assault of disinfectant and penicillin, the bacteria laughing in their faces. NASA was spending billions sending probes into space to find new organisms and the Tyne's were growing millions of the fuckers in their bedrooms...funny old world when you look at it like that.

As predicted by Rocky I found 'fuck all' and as predicted by Mrs Tyne I 'fucked off' without her son or any evidence in tow. I wouldn't say I came away empty handed however, as within the hour nasty red blotches started to appear on my calves where fleas had bitten me...don't suppose I should complain, at least something in their household was willing to put a bit of effort into getting a meal.

I made it home in time for a family dinner; I even managed to get a shower and a change of clothing before we sat down to eat.

The following day the sergeant wasn't happy that I hadn't brought Rocky in for questioning, but soon showed some begrudging respect when I showed him the consent to search form and explained that I had at least turned the place over regardless of not finding anything. I think he was surprised that I had managed to worm my way into the household without being given a good kicking, he was equally surprised that someone in the Tyne household could actually sign their name.

***

Shaking off the memories of that Sunday afternoon I focused on the briefing the chief inspector was giving the two crews of the ARV. We had arrived at the police station in a flurry of blue lights and sirens only to be left kicking our heels in the rear yard while the management decided whether or not we were going to be needed. We were on a 'Zebra Zero Two' status which meant that we were authorised to arm ourselves with the Glocks and MP5's from the vehicles safe.

There we were, standing around in full body armour overalls and burdened down with kit, while someone upstairs procrastinated as to the need to unleash us on the public; it was bloody annoying as we trained and trained to make sure that we were as professional as could be. We never went into black and white situations and often had to adapt to ever changing scenarios that would test our capabilities and skills to the limit. We were bloody good at what we did but despite being invited to come to our training sessions to observe these skills some of our governors just saw us as cowboys who would ride into their town, shoot the place up then ride off into the sunset with all the fair young maidens. Now I'm not saying that there were not those on the team who wouldn't hesitate to disappear with a fair young maiden given half the chance but the rest of the perception was grossly unfair.

Besides, in this particular town all the fair young maidens didn't tend to get past their fifteenth birthdays before getting banged senseless by the local scroats. Nobody seemed to have heard of contraception, which kept the local pre natal and STD clinics very busy. Over half the jobs that officers had to attend here related to someone being called a slut or a slag due to their promiscuous behaviour. Having read some of the stuff that had been posted on social media sites you couldn't help but agree that the comments were often a harsh but fair summarisation. Father's day in this town was the definition of confusion.

While we waited we performed quick radio checks, linking our coms to the secure network the teams worked on and taping our ear pieces in place. We tuned the other radio we carried into the local channel. Slowly we began to piece the information together; Rocky Tyne had or was having a psychotic incident and had run amok in the family house brandishing a meat cleaver, smashing the place up and threatening anyone who didn't get out of his way. He had been dispossessed of the aforesaid cleaver when his eldest sister had punched him out and disarmed him.

Before she could inflict any further injury on his person he had grabbed a twelve inch carving knife from the kitchen worktop and bolted out of the house into the estate. Police officers were now trying to follow, protect the public and get him to drop the knife, all without getting stabbed themselves.

Within a few minutes the officers were calling for urgent assistance and I gate crashed the boss's cosy pow-wow. "Guv, Tyne is now attacking police officers and they are calling for urgent assistance, we are kitted up and ready to roll". It was a statement of fact and not something I would consider him having to ponder on for more than a millisecond. His unarmed officers were now running away from a knife wielding psychotic nut job who was off his tits on god knows what and he was just sitting there deep in thought like I had asked him if he wanted a doughnut with his coffee.

After what seemed like an eternity and to the backdrop of the radio hysteria of colleagues trying to locate the officers being attacked and get a sit rep, the boss said reluctantly "I suppose I am going to have to deploy you lot". The fact that he should have deployed 'us lot' a good ten minutes earlier was something that would have to wait until the debrief. People needed our help and wasting time arguing wasn't going to help them.

"Sir, are you deploying us?" I asked. Officially we came under the command of the control room inspector who would deploy and brief us as he generally had the best overview of a situation. Somehow there had been a pissing contest between the chief inspector and the control room inspector and I wanted clarification as to who had control.

The chief inspector looked up, "Yes Zero whatever Two. But be careful, I don't want you shooting anyone".

I ran from his office transmitting on both radios "Zero Two authorised by the chief inspector, CCR inspector please confirm our status and confirm that you now have deployment control".

The response was quick and professional and within seconds we were screaming out of the nick towards the last location Tyne had been seen in. For some reason I was being partnered by 'Gregs' as KP was off for the day, it wasn't a problem as we trained as mixed crews and often guested with another team. Knowing the area from my days on CID I directed Gregs and the other car followed us. During our initial briefing it had been mentioned that

Rocky had threatened a member of the public with being shot but no weapon had been seen. Feedback from the officers who had initially tried to apprehend him suggested he had made the same threat to them.

In view of this intel I had grabbed the short ballistic shield from the boot and thrown it onto the back seat. It normally lived under all the paraphernalia we used for our traffic role; the collapsible cones and road signs which were used far more frequently. Going into the estate was a nightmare as all the houses were in small closes and walkways; the numerical system used to identify address's had been undertaken either by a halfwit or a dyslexic buffoon as they didn't correlate with any known system in the western hemisphere.

The two officers who had originally been chased by Rocky had now turned the tables and started pursuing him. They had been able to deploy their side handled batons and had bravely fronted him up before he disappeared again. The baton is a good piece of kit, it extends with a thwack that shows you mean business, it's tough and sturdy and more than up to the task of turning an assailants smile upside down. Trying to locate a fast moving target who was running through alleys and walkways was both frustrating and virtually impossible when you yourselves were in a car.

"Fuck this" Gregs decided, "Let's deploy on foot and see if we can get to the centre of this maze and let him come to us".

It was as good a plan as any, both ARV's pulled over and we were out on foot. Our Kevlar helmets lay in the rear foot well of the car as you couldn't sit in the vehicle wearing them without seriously reducing your mobility and vision. I reached in and slid the shield off the seat but before I could grab my headgear Rocky ran out of the estate and spotted us. There was no time to grope about and don our helmets and we set off in hot pursuit. I had kept hold of the shield and it seriously restricted my movements, at over a metre high and two thirds of a metre wide it was unwieldy to say the least. It was also fucking heavy and with all the other gear I was carrying it didn't take long before I was breathing out my arse.

Rocky disappeared from the alley we had pursued him down at the point it merged with four other similar walkways. He had gone to ground somewhere and was hiding in one of the back gardens that backed onto the narrow footpaths. Both teams stopped and started to test the back gates; as this was a high crime area residents would have at least two or three padlocks securing the rear of their properties which helped us quickly disregard potential hiding places. It was 'Hoops' from the other team who found the insecure gate.

I signalled I would cover him and he pulled his MP5 tight into his shoulder waiting for me to do a finger countdown before he would thrust the gate open. I had got to two when the gate burst open and Rocky emerged, he hadn't anticipated the combined reception committee of four MP5's pointing in his general direction and he jumped like a startled rabbit. On the other hand we hadn't been expecting him to come to us either and Hoops had jumped out of the way in self-preservation mode which impeded his partners aim.

I on the other hand had a grandstand view but the speed of the incident and the lack of 'immediate threat' restricted my actions. Rocky had the knife down by his side for all to see but he wasn't directly threatening anyone with it. He took off like the devil was behind him and the chase continued. By now I was completely fucked off with carrying the shield but didn't dare dump it, the estate was inhabited by a den of thieves and some unscrupulous bastard would nick it for a trophy. It was well known that if you fell asleep here with your mouth open someone would nick your fillings and sell them for scrap.

I don't know what Rocky had been taking that day but I knew I could have done with a snort. He had been running around the alleys and walkways for nearly half an hour and didn't look the least bit out of breath. This was a man who had never done a day's exercise or work in his life, abused his body with alcohol, tobacco and some seriously heavy drugs. I on the other hand went to the gym every other day, ran miles on the treadmill and put in hours on the cross trainer and was absolutely fucked after ten minutes.

It took a few more minutes of frantic pursuit before Rocky's energy levels gave up. He suddenly slowed and I was only a few metres away. Turning he brandished the knife, "I'll fucking do you" he hollered.

"You come any closer Rocky and it will be me doing you mate" I replied. We had both started breathing heavily while trying to regain our composure. To emphasise my point I whipped the shield in front of me and slotted my MP5 into the support notch. This allowed me to keep hold of the shield and keep my weapon on aim. With my ragged breathing however it wasn't that simple a task. The ring sight at the front of the weapon rose and fell with every breath; it certainly wasn't going to be the most stable shot I had ever made should I have to take it. Rocky's eyes were dancing all over the place, spittle dribbled from his lips and he held the knife out in front of him, the pointy end facing me.

"Drop the knife Rocky" I commanded.

"Fuck off" came the predictable response. "You gonna fucking shoot me if I don't?" he asked.

"Put it down Rocky, don't make me shoot".

Rocky had been slowly shuffling forwards and I had been easing backwards as I didn't want him getting too close. If he got within a couple of metres he would be able to stick me before I could drop him. I had though got to a point where going back was no longer an option as the ground was uneven and liable to trip me over. He was pumped up and I could see the veins standing out on his arms and his neck, he was clenching his muscles and pulling his lips tight over his teeth working himself up into a frenzy and I started looking at my options.

I figured in his present state of mind Rocky was going to take more than a couple of rounds to the body and one to the head before he fell. In my mind I settled on two in the chest and then the rest in his head until he went down, I had a fifteen round magazine and was prepared to use the lot and then beat him to death with the empty gun if I had to.

It was at this point he stopped coming forwards and ripped open his T shirt, "Two in the chest and one in the head" he screamed, "that's what they teach you isn't it".

I held my ground; it was the first time I had 'the target' coaching me on my grouping. I had done talking to him, it was his move and if it was a silly one he was going to be pavement pizza.

He raised his knife and I took up the pressure on the trigger with the tip of my finger. Looking past Rocky I could see a garage block which would act as a good back stop if any of my rounds went through him, I didn't anticipate any were going to miss; not from this distance.

To my astonishment he drew the knife across his chest and cut a cross in his skin, the blood slowly filling the cuts and running down his bare torso. Arresting someone at gunpoint isn't just a case of point and they instantly become compliant, a lot of training time is invested in tactical communications where you use verbal commands and reasoning to bring the situation to a peaceful and nonviolent conclusion. This does however rely upon the other person being able to see reason and understand the folly in continuing to pose a threat. Cutting in to your chest with a twelve inch carving knife in order to give the guy pointing a gun at you a better target didn't bode well in the sanity and reasoning stakes.

We were in a standoff, I wasn't going backwards anymore and if he took a step forwards he was getting as many rounds as it took to drop him. He was already closer than I was comfortable with, but if I fired I was going to have to justify why I had shot him to Uncle Tom Cobley and all. It's not like the cop shows where you just heave the body into the back of an ambulance before returning to the nick for tea and medals. The minute I fired I would be in a world of stress from all angles, the family, the police professional standards department, the coroner, CPS and let's not forget the media who would be all over me and my family like a rash.

I had a shield and great play would be made of the fact that I should have defended myself with it rather than shoot an unarmed man, the kitchen knife would be deemed a low tech weapon compared to my MP5. It was suddenly a lonely place being on point and having total control of the situation.

***

There was also something else nagging in the back of my mind, the last armed job I had been on had turned into a proper cluster fuck. We had been called to a residential caravan site where a falling out had taken place between two men late one night, resulting in the resident of the caravan pointing a bloody big handgun at his mate (now ex-mate) and threatening to blow his head off. The guy had been scared enough to run out of the caravan and through the blokes back gate; quite literally right though it like something from a cartoon. The ARV's had been called and deployed to the scene to contain the area in case 'Billy Big Gun' went on the rampage.

Caravan sieges are a nightmare, especially vastly populated ones like the site we arrived at. The flimsy aluminium side walls of a caravan aren't designed to stop a 9mm round and the bullet will continue on its merry travels until it hits something substantial, and that could be an innocent person. The local Superintendent arrived just a couple of minutes after us which led me to believe that the incident was a lot older than we had been told. An officer of this rank doesn't tend to be burning the midnight oil and wearing full uniform. He had 'scrambled egg' all over the peak of his pristine cap and as we were to find out later, plenty of the same between his ears.

What we needed was a hot briefing and not the 'let's sit down and do a power point presentation' type of affair I could see him leading up to. The crew of the other vehicle immediately went to the caravan in question and put on a containment…something that had been neglected so far. The superintendent started banging his gums about us going and knocking on the caravan door and talking Billy Big Gun out, retrieving the weapon and then going back to the local nick for pats on the back. I tried to explain that we were not trained to undertake a caravan clearance unless the situation was such that lives were in danger. This was a Special Firearms Group job, he would have to call out the team and we would provide cover and containment until they were briefed and could take over. It was basically a case of if (and a bloody big if after this length of time) the guy was still sitting in his caravan we would stop him from coming out, unless it was to be arrested. If he came out blasting or went on a walk about with the weapon then we would be there to stop him.

In situations like this, most of the high ranking bosses listen when you tell them what you can and can't do and then take that under advisement. This one didn't.

"Do you know how much it would cost to get the SFG here?" he asked.

I didn't so I kept quiet.

"You're here and you've got weapons and body armour, something my men haven't. So I am ordering you to go and knock on the door". He spat out.

"Sorry sir, that's not a lawful order so I won't be doing it" I said holding his gaze.

KP was standing next to me and he reinforced my statement by adding "With respect sir neither will I. It's not something we are trained to do".

I had never told a boss that his orders were unlawful before and I don't think he had ever been challenged either. He went puce and his mouth hung open as he tried to absorb the information. Before he could say anything further I reiterated what our role could provide for him but I could see he wasn't listening.

After a few minutes he turned and said "Well you lot might as well bugger off then and I will get my lads, my *unarmed* lads to go and knock on the door". With that he turned on his heels and marched away. I thought I heard him muttering 'this won't be the end of this' as he went.

KP and I went and joined the other team who were also adamant they would not be carrying out the unlawful order. Big Pete from the other crew decided that he would put a call into the control room inspector despite the fact that the superintendent had assumed the role of Silver and Bronze Command and had taken responsibility for the whole incident. Big Pete's call would do two things; it would give the control room a heads up if the shit hit the fan and also get down our objections on the call log. The inspector's landline was recorded so the conversation would be taped.

Big Pete spoke to the inspector who thanked him for the update and then hung up. A couple of minutes later Big Pete's mobile vibrated and he answered it, the inspector had left the control room and found an unmonitored landline where he could vent his spleen safe in the knowledge that it wasn't being recorded.

Meanwhile the superintendent had managed to get one of his unarmed lads to volunteer to knock on the door of the caravan. To say I felt guilty would be an understatement, what if the guy was in there just waiting for his first victim to step up to the door before blasting away. There is no safe place to hide outside a caravan; the bullets will pass through the fragile walls and into whoever happens to be standing there. Not only would they get a bullet in them, there would be a fair amount of shrapnel caused by the aluminium and chipboard that would cause secondary injuries.

I tried to talk the volunteer out of such a foolhardy mission but he was old school and kept saying "this is how we would do it in the old days". Well that might have been so but it was no longer 'the good old days' and policies and procedures had been updated to reflect that fact. I handed over the ballistic shield I was holding, removed my Kevlar helmet and gave them to him, giving him some quick instructions to ensure that he kept the shield between himself and the side of the van at all times. If he kept his head down the helmet would also stop or slow down anything heading for it. I think it was at this point that he finally realised there was a higher risk than he had at first anticipated. We didn't carry a spare set of ballistic body armour so he was going to have to rely on the fact that the shield was his only protection if it all went tits up.

The superintendent sauntered over to deliver his final gambit before subjecting his volunteer to chance. "Decided to stay have you, going to watch your colleague here put himself at risk because you won't?"

It was a scathing attack on our morality and courage and I could see Big Pete starting to bristle but that would only end up causing more trouble and this job already had trouble written all over it in capital letters.

"We have kitted him out with as much kit as we can spare sir, and we are standing by to assist if things go badly". With that I outlined what our immediate plans were going to be and what our 'emergency action' would entail if the guy started opening fire. He didn't even bother to hear me out, turning on his heels and nodding to his officer to approach the caravan as he walked away.

"Pompous prick" Big Pete remarked easily loud enough for the boss to hear.

Both ARV teams quickly scurried into positions close enough to the van that we could react quickly if needed. We were in far too close for comfort but it seemed as if the rule book was out of the window on this job.

The knock on the door was loud and distinct as was the command of "Fuck off" that came from within. I willed the officer to withdraw. The guy (or at least some guy) was at home and not willing to come out so now was the perfect chance for him to withdraw to safety, for the SFG to be called out and a negotiator drafted in to bore the pants off him until he lost the will to live and surrendered.

Explaining that it was the police he knocked once more and a voice from inside reiterated his reluctance to leave the confines of the caravan. Reaching up our man tried the door handle which surprisingly opened and a man fitting Billy Big Gun's description filled the void. The next few seconds were a blur, officer and protagonist merged into one as they both began rolling around on the ground in front of the caravan. We had no way of knowing if he had the gun or was the only occupant, we also didn't know who had hold of whom as the men wrestled on the floor.

We moved forwards, guns up ready, KP and I secured the doorway of the van and the other team quickly assessed the status of the bad guy. It's not good practice to get up close and personal when you are armed, you are less efficient and most certainly vulnerable with a very good chance of losing your main weapon or sidearm. However a couple of well-placed boots pinned the angry man down and allowed the unarmed officer to get his cuffs on him. They performed a quick search for the gun and Big Pete shook his head to notify us that he hadn't got it with him. The unarmed officer also intimated that there may well have been someone else in the caravan as he thought he had heard a couple of different voices.

Bollocks; we were going to have to clear the sodding caravan despite all our attempts to avoid it.

Stealth was no longer an option as the shouting and screaming from the scuffle had woken other residents who were now crowded at their windows to watch the excitement.

"Armed Police, stand exactly where you are with your hands where we can see them" I shouted at the top of my voice. KP was on my heels as we quickly went through the kitchen and into the lounge area. We spun around and moved forward into the bedrooms and bathroom and it was at this point something caught my eye emerging from the far doorway. I tracked the shadow with the ring sight on the gun, the safety was off and I was ready to rock and roll if they were a threat. "Armed police, stand still, show me your hands" I screamed at the top of my voice.

Hoops suddenly emerged into the light and I moved quickly off aim, "Bit fucking jumpy Scottie" he jibed.

"You fucking twat Hoops, I could have fucking slotted you then, creeping about like a fucking burglar. You knew we were in here clearing the place". My heart was thumping in my chest and I was fucking angry. Angry at Hoops for wandering in to a zone we were clearing, angry at the superintendent who had orchestrated this cluster fuck and angry at the officer who had marched up to the door and set all this emergency action into practice.

With the caravan clear, I stomped outside and made my way back to the car to de-kit. The voice behind me pulled me up short.

"Looks like you made yourselves useful after all and it confirms that we didn't need the SFG like I told you" the Superintendent sneered.

I wanted to shoot the twat and KP knew that as he took my arm and hustled me to the rear of the ARV. "He's not worth it Scottie" he said, "the shit is going to hit the fan over this so let's just make sure our arses are covered". It was good advice but I still wanted to shoot the prick.

We unloaded our weapons and placed them back in the onboard gun safe, removed the heavy ballistic armour and TAC vest and stowed all our kit including the helmet and shield I had lent out earlier.

The superintendent was still strutting about so I approached him, "Are you holding a debrief sir?" I enquired.

"What for" he replied.

"We always debrief sir that way we can discuss what went right on a job and what didn't".

"Well the guy has been arrested by my man so in my book it all went right". He stood there staring at me, "Good night officer, I shall be sure to mention your er... input to your boss".

I didn't know if that was some sort of threat or not. "Thank you sir, we always complete a debrief report ourselves at the end of every deployment and he will get a copy, but it's good of you to offer to speak to him personally; I am sure he will appreciate that". I smiled and returned to the ARV, "Get us the fuck out of here" I said to KP.

As predicted the shit did hit the fan, bloody great big steaming piles. It took a couple of days before we got a call from the Firearms Training Department telling us to get there as quickly as possible. KP and I were ushered into one of the classrooms by the two leading instructors where they set about telling us how we had exceeded our training by entering the caravan and that it should have been the SFG doing the job not us. Thinking ahead, I had brought a copy of the debriefing report we had made that night and I had also made a full report in my pocket book. I had recalled all the conversations as best I could and it was a damning document if you were a 'shit for brains superintendent'.

I handed the reports across the desk and the two trainers started to read them, pausing only to tell us to go and get a cup of tea while they read through the documents. I informed them that there was also a recording on the control room inspector's phone line which may also help them to clarify the situation.

We had just started our second brew when the other ARV crew pulled into the carpark, they looked as apprehensive as we had when we arrived. I explained what we had told the trainers and what documentation I had brought. They gleefully informed me that they had just heard that the superintendent from the operation had been involved in a slanging match with our boss who had apparently reported the whole thing to the chief constables office.

When the four of us were called back into the classroom I was surprised to see the trainers had been joined by our superintendent who was red faced and mad as hell. Fortunately it wasn't with us, his beef was with his colleague and he wasn't going to be happy until there was blood on the chief's wall.

"For what it's worth I think you did extremely well under the circumstances, you acted professionally and didn't bow down to pressure from a ranking officer". Both the instructors were nodding in unison which bode well for us. "As you might be aware I have referred this to the very top and I know that the chief will take a very dim view of what happened, especially when he reads this report". He waved my report when he spoke, before thanking us and leaving the room.

"Right you glory hunters, which one of you prats went into the caravan when it was being cleared?" demanded one of the instructors.

It seemed that we hadn't been completely vindicated…

***

Back on the estate the caravan job had whizzed through my brain, there hadn't been any further mention of the incident but the recent training had included room clearances and it was clear to everyone that it was due to the cock up Hoops had made. I didn't want a reputation of being gung-ho, rushing into situations without exercising the right amount of caution. In view of this I had let Rocky get slightly closer than I would have liked and I had cut him some slack with regards to his waving the knife around. Had it been a training scenario I would have probably shot him already.

Blood was running freely from Rocky's disfigured chest and soaking into the waistband of his trousers. He stood there knife poised waiting for me to shoot him…death by cop, that's what the Americans call it; someone not able to take their own lives pushes law enforcement officers into doing it for them. The shield was making the muscles in my left arm scream in pain, they were supporting the full weight of the shield and the front end of my MP5. The ring sight was starting to waver under the stress; I wasn't unduly worried, at a range of two metres it wasn't going to make a lot of difference if I pulled the trigger. Rocky was going to be a target that would be hard to miss.

Rocky broke the deadlock; "You chicken shit; shoot me you fuck" was all he said before turning tail and running off towards the garage blocks that serviced the estate. The chase was back on.

It might seem strange to members of the public that he wasn't shot 'when we had the opportunity to do so'. But our rules of engagement as such are that we only shoot when life is in immediate danger or might be if we didn't. Immediate is the relevant word here, the person you fire upon must be practically about to do the deed or be preparing to do so. Rocky, at the moment was just a prick running around with a carving knife with a self-inflicted wound carved into his chest. Of course, should he go on and stab someone after we had cornered him there would be hell to pay for not shooting...a case of damned if you do and damned if you don't.

As we pursued him back into the estate I chucked the shield to an unarmed officer who was standing in the wings. "Cheers" he said, not realising that within ten minutes he would be cursing my generosity. Without the ballistic shield to impede my progress I felt a lot better and soon made up the ground on Rocky who was starting to lurch from side to side in a laboured gait. He ducked into the corner of a car parking area and hid behind one of the wrecked vehicles that had been abandoned there.

We quickly covered his exits and were relieved to hear the barking of a police dog as it and his handler joined us. After a quick briefing Rocky was given the option of coming out or having the hound set on him. I was hoping it would be the hound as Rocky had really spoilt my afternoon.

I was in luck; a few curses and threats from Rocky indicated that his preferred option was going to be the dog. I settled back and waited for the fun; the collar was slipped and the beast shot between the wall and the car straight to where Rocky was lying. There were a few growls, followed by a couple of yelps and then the animal high tailed it out from behind the car straight back to his handler where it was feared he had been stabbed. The dog was not long out of training and had taken a kicking only a short while before; Rocky had just plain scared the shit out of it. He had obviously decided he would much rather be lying on a nice warm hearth licking his balls than facing the mental case hiding behind the car.

Rocky was laughing his nuts off and stood up to show the world just how tough he was. "Fucking thing is soft as shit" he slurred.

He wasn't getting any argument from me on that score.

"Is that the best you can do?" he asked. Raising the knife he started to wave it about and all the non-armed personnel quickly blended back into the shadows.

"Rocky, put the fucking knife down. You've had your fun, scared the dog, now let's all just go home". I was on one knee and four metres from where he was standing and he looked as though he was suffering even more effects from the copious amounts of pills he had popped shortly before going on the rampage.

"Hey chicken shit" he called to me, "you gonna shoot me or not"? The knife was now above his head and he made as if to throw it.

"Put it down" I screamed, I hadn't got my helmet on and I could just see this bastard throwing the knife and sticking it in my head. He lowered it to his chest and started carving; a second scarlet cross appeared next to the first. As he looked at his handiwork, he raised the knife to his forehead and a further series of slashes left another bloody cross in the middle of his head.

"Two in the body, one in the head, I've marked the target so why don't you shoot?" He sounded desperate and disorientated and kept reaching for the bodywork of the car for support.

Rocky's clock was ticking down and I guessed that it was only a matter of time before the mainspring gave out and he collapsed. However, just when it seemed like his body was starting to fail he quickly rallied and jumped onto the boot of the car, climbed onto its roof and then up onto the high wall that surrounded the car park. You would have to be either high as a kite or out of your tree to try and balance all the way along the precarious four inch wide coping...as Rocky was both he managed to complete the balancing act until he reached the flat roofs of the garage block.

He couldn't escape and was in fact in a better position for all to see him, there was no way out. Rocky assessed his situation, wiped the blood from his eyes and fumbled for his belt before turning and dropping his jeans and pants to his knees. He mooned at me before turning back to waggle his genitals in my direction, doing a little jig whilst singing a song denouncing me for being a chicken shit, much to the amusement of the locals who were lining windows and standing out on the street. Some to see Rocky mocking their mutual enemy...us... and others watching in the hope of seeing him get shot. I am sure there wouldn't have been any tears shed had the latter happened.

Rocky held out for a further thirty minutes or so before he finally collapsed and was bundled into an ambulance. At first the hospital thought it would be touch and go if he survived but within a couple of hours his system had rebooted itself and he was sitting up in bed wondering what the fuck had happened. To give him credit he pleaded guilty at Crown Court despite not recalling any of the events that had placed him there. He had been bestowed local hero status and revelled in the antics that had been attributed to him.

***

I met up with him years later when he was brought into my custody office to be processed. He had tried to turn his life around; was relatively clean of drugs, had stopped drinking and had undertaken anger management training. Although he had been caught shoplifting he came into custody as meek as could be and was the model prisoner, polite and compliant and very honest regarding the stolen items.

He was refused bail and was being kept in custody overnight for transferal to court the following day and as I was on a twelve hour shift I would be in charge of his wellbeing until the morning. I checked up on him in the early hours and he was wide awake. The years of substance abuse had left his body clock completely broken and permanently damaged. At that time prisoners were not allowed to smoke in the cells but were allowed to have a ciggy in the exercise yard and I arranged for a smoke and sorted him out a cup of coffee and a few biscuits as he was hungry.

As it was quiet I sat in the yard with him and we both supped our drinks and dunked biscuits. He kept looking at me, trying to plumb the depths of his mind to remember where he knew my face from. After a while I said to him, "You can't place why you know me can you?"

He shook his head. I traced an imaginary cross on my forehead and he put his hand to the faint scar his still bore.

"I'm the guy who was pointing the gun at you when you did that" I told him.

We spent the next hour reminiscing, he had forgotten most of what had happened and had been fed a load of bullshit by friends who had claimed to have been there. When I prompted him he also remembered me as the detective who had called at his house that Sunday afternoon. Laughing he told me that his mother had been sitting on the stereo throughout the search, certain that I wasn't going to be probing there. He told me that he had stolen and sold the same stereo over a dozen times before 'some thieving git' nicked it before it was retrieved.

Rocky would come and go through my custody suite on an infrequent basis, a bit of shoplifting when he was hungry and the occasional unpaid fine. It was a strange kind of relationship between us, he knew that I was responsible for him still being here and I felt a kind of responsibility that he was. I was always able to find him a fag or two and some biscuits for his tea or coffee and he never gave me a moment of trouble. Quite the contrary in fact, as one day I had some prisoners to get ready for collection by Group Four who took all our remands to the relevant courts. One cocky young lad had been playing up all night and figured to make himself a handful when I turned him out of his cell and locked him in the shower for his ablutions.

Rocky was waiting to go to Norwich Magistrates Court for an unpaid fine and he asked if he could be let out to clean his teeth and have a quick wash. I knew that he would behave and having both prisoners out at the same time would ensure that I could get them ready for the early morning transfer in good time. Master A R Sole was still in the shower shouting his mouth off and I saw Rocky sidle over to the door and start speaking in low tones to the lad on the other side.

The taunting and shouting stopped immediately, the lad suddenly conforming and keeping his head down. I loaded our trappy friend onto the transport wagon first and he apologised for his behaviour before the Group Four officers handcuffed him. As they were placing him in the wagon Rocky was sitting on the bench smiling.

"Ok Rocky what did you say"? I finally asked.

He laughed, "I told him that I owe you big time and that I wasn't very happy with the way he was treating you...no fucking respect".

I loaded him onto the wagon and smiled to myself; there went a man who waggled his cock in my face and bared his arse at me talking about respect.

It was the last time I saw Rocky. He died a year or so later, the ravages of his misspent youth finally catching up with him just as he had started to get his life together.

The things they say

Over thirty years I have heard some pretty good put downs and jibes, mostly from the public directed at officers but sometimes the other way around when they finally reach breaking point. The best time to catch an officer at this low ebb is to pull up next to them when they are stuck on a detour at a road closure. It will be even better if the weather is either roasting hot or pissing down with rain, and especially good if they have been there for several hours, have a full bladder, missed their meal break and are parched with thirst. All you will need to do is stop and bring the traffic behind you to a halt, wind down your window and say any of the following to get a response…

Motorist - "Is the road blocked?"
Officer's likely response - "No sir, every so often we like to just stand in the road all day and see how many people we can send on a detour".

Motorist - "Can I get through please?"
Officer's likely response - "Well that depends doesn't it. When you bought the car did you get the vertical take-off option? No…then I'm afraid not".

Motorist - "You can't close this road; it's the only way I know".
Officer's likely response - "Well you'll know another one then by the time you get home".

Motorist - "Have you got a map?"
Officer's likely response - "No, I know where I am".

Motorist - "You know you've made me an hour late".
Officer's likely response - "Yes sir, I said this morning when I got of bed, I bet I can make that guy in the flash Porsche an hour late this morning if I cause an accident and close the road".

Motorist - "This has ruined my day".
Officer's likely response - "The two dead teenagers mangled in the car wreck

down the road aren't having much fun either".

None of the above remarks are professional; a few are quite funny and some are downright rude but in vindication I would say that most people bring it upon themselves. If you don't want a snidey reply don't make a snide comment; sure you're having a shit day, nobody enjoys endless queues and being shunted off into the unknown. Buy a map or a satnav if you don't know your way around, take some responsibility for your own life and don't expect someone else to wipe your backside for you. I have lost count of the number of complaints I have had to deal with from angry motorists who were turned off a main road and promptly got lost because they blindly followed someone else who was equally as lost. When a major road is blocked all available officers are either at the scene of the holdup or trying to stop other motorists adding to the carnage by running into it.

The routes the diversions follow are designated so that Heavy Good Vehicles and buses can also safely negotiate them without getting jammed up in the middle of small villages because the narrow lanes can't cope with their bulk. The police don't carry diversion signs as it is not their responsibility to place them; that comes under the remit of the highways department and their agents. It's not that we are unsympathetic or uncaring to the motorists plight because let's face it as soon as the road is re-opened the officer can go and get a toilet break and deal with all the other calls that are stacking up waiting for them. With a bit of luck they might even get to have a meal break although no one in their right mind expects one of those anymore.

***

Now I can understand a driver not being too happy when they are pulled over for a motoring offence as it's often going to be a costly experience. A good way to ensure your day is going to get worse is to develop some attitude and get out of the vehicle ranting. You can use phrases like...

"Haven't you got anything better to do?"

"I bet your mother's proud of you".

"This is how the Nazi's started, picking on the working class".

"I hope you're pleased with yourself, you've just cost me my job".

The list is long, endless and tedious. I am sure on a few occasions some unlucky motorists have been caught out in a speed limit they have missed or when they have genuinely forgotten to put their seat belt on. However, you certainly don't forget that you have a mobile phone in your hand while you are driving one handed, or that you were travelling at almost twice the speed limit overtaking fellow road users who have responded with headlights flashing and horns blaring. In those circumstances you are making a lifestyle choice, you know the risks you are running and must therefore take responsibility for your actions and accept the consequences. So if you get caught it's your own fault, better luck next time, jog on.

***

Friday and Saturday nights are always guaranteed to result in some smart arse trying to show off in front of his mates guaranteeing some brilliant put downs.

Idiot - "Who's shagging your missus tonight?"
Officer - "Probably your dad and if I ever find out his name I'll let you know what it is".

Idiot - "Let's try your hat on".
Officer - "I wouldn't if I were you; you'll end up with all sorts of drunken twats coming up to you asking to wear it".

Idiot - "Sonny, does your mummy know you're out this late?
Officer - "Yeah she told me to pop down the High Street to see if I could find a couple of tossers...looks like I can go home now".

Idiot - "I know your chief constable".
Officer - "I'll be sure to pass on my condolences".

Idiot - "You can't talk to me like that".
Officer - "Sorry, am I using too many big words?"

Idiot - "I want your number".

Officer - "If I give it to you will you promise to call me?"

Idiot - "Who are you looking at?"
Officer - "My next arrest".

Idiot - "I don't know how you sleep at night".
Officer - "I lie in bed thinking about your prospects in life, and when I've stopped laughing I'm so tired I go straight to sleep".

Idiot - "If you weren't wearing that uniform I'd have you".
Officer - "Whilst that is very flattering I have to tell you that I'm not gay, but thanks for the offer".

Again, another long and tedious list. Maybe, instead of sending the weekend night club arrests to the court, we should sit them down and play them eight hours' worth of the verbal shite they subject other people to. Sit them in a room that stinks of piss and blast shots of halitosis, stale beer, rancid kebab and vomit into their faces, let them feel what it's like to police the streets of England.

***

Over the years I have heard some great excuses from the public for their misdemeanours…

A motorcycle traffic officer who worked the Western area of Norfolk was performing radar along one of the fen roads when a car shot past, well in excess of the speed limit. The officer put the radar gun he was using into the side pannier of his bike and rode after the vehicle. It took the driver several miles before he checked his rear view mirrors and noticed that they were full of police bike with blue lights flashing. In a belated attempt to reduce his speed back down to the 60 mph limit he anchored up and the vehicle violently reduced speed sending puffs of smoke from the abused tyres. After a couple of minutes he was able to respond to the flashing blue lights and pulled over.

The driver wound down his window, smiled and said patronisingly "Officer I'm so glad you are here, I desperately need the toilet and can't find one. That's why I was driving so fast".

The officer, who was not known for his tact or diplomacy skills replied, "Well sir it's your lucky day, I'm the biggest shit house in the county".

The driver got a ticket for his speed and the officer gained a reputation for giving the best one liner.

***

Whilst on patrol in the wilds of North Norfolk, I was crewed with KP on the ARV. It had been a long and wet Sunday and we were returning to base to write up the reports and speeding tickets we had issued. The area in which we had been working had a particularly active parish council who constantly complained about drivers using excessive speed through their village. The problem was that this was one of the main coastal access roads and a rat run in the summer and early autumn. Despite the rain there seemed to be quite a bit of traffic on the roads and the small seaside town had been bustling when we had visited it earlier for a couple of bags of chips.

Parked up on the quay and tucking into lunch is a great way to spend twenty minutes, just watching the world go by in the dry and climate controlled interior of our car. The public would glare through the windows as if we had no right to be sitting at the seaside munching on a bag of chips...surely it's no different from what normal people might do during their meal break.

We had caught quite a few offending drivers when we had used the speed gun. Our policy was that we would rather give someone a bollocking if their speed wasn't over the limit by more than twelve miles per hour even though the guidelines were that it should only be four miles, but ultimately it was left to our discretion. There were more than enough people who were taking the piss with excessive speed to keep us gainfully employed.

We had an hour left before we went off shift which would give us the chance to take a leisurely drive back to base, write up the tickets and reports and hand the car over to the late turn. We would also have a chance to give the interior a good sanitising to rid it of the chip aroma.

As we negotiated the narrow coastal road we caught up with an old Mondeo being driven by an elderly lady. The rain had eased off but there were still large puddles on the road surface. We followed the car for some time as the road wasn't suitable to overtake and we noticed the driver in front was fairly erratic with their road positioning. Every now and then the Mondeo would suddenly veer onto the other side of the road, to the extent that the driver negotiated tight bends by driving on to the opposing carriageway.

We followed for some way until it became evident that if we didn't stop the vehicle soon there was every likelihood of being an accident. When it eventually pulled over I approached the driver to speak to her. KP was busy inside the ARV doing checks on the registered keeper and firing up the breath test kit as the driving had indicated that a drop or two of giggle juice may have been consumed.

The lady was in her seventies and extremely polite as I explained what I had seen regarding her erratic driving.

"Well you had better speak to my passenger about that" she offered and pointed to the even older man sitting next to her. A husk of a man, his small frame was easily enveloped in the Mondeos passenger seat. He had a white mop of unruly hair that seemed to be trying to escape from his head and his fringe hung over the blacked out glasses which dominated the rest of his face. Clutched in his hand was a white cane and it was blatantly obvious (even to a traffic officer) that the guy was blind.

"Tell the officer why I have to drive like that...go on you can do the explaining" the lady driver chided her passenger.

Fearing the onset of a domestic I stepped in, "Perhaps seeing as you're the driver you would like to explain?" I asked.

She glared over at the man, who was totally oblivious to the scowl she was making. "Well as you can see he's blind" she started, "so every time I go through a puddle he shouts out in a panic 'what was that?'"

The old boys head started nodding, "It's very frightening when you can't see anything" he informed me.

"Well I got so fed up with his constant fidgeting and jumping about every time we drove over a puddle I thought that I would try and avoid them".

I explained the folly of her strategy and allowed her to continue her journey.

Back in the ARV KP was sitting in silence waiting for an explanation; as I turned off the breath test machine I relayed the story. We waited until the Mondeo was out of sight before both of us collapsed in fits of laughter.

***

Years later and late one evening I had parked my traffic patrol car next to the main arterial road running through the county. I had several 'fatal collision files' back on my desk in the office but had decided that they could wait another couple of hours before I brought them up to date.

These types of files were complex and thorough and were given the same meticulous attention to detail that a murder case would have had. Every job that was carried out in connection with the file had to be 'actioned' by the Senior Investigating Officer (SIO) and I was the SIO for eight of the fifteen active files we had in our office.

My two fellow supervisory colleagues were also snowed under with their own workload but for some reason I had collected the lion's share of the work. It had got so bad that my shift were begging me not to attend the scene if they had a collision, as no sooner would I turn up than seemingly uninjured people would drop down dead. Some even joked that I should replace my siren for the death march theme.

The types of collisions that required this type of intense investigation came in phases and some months you wouldn't attend anything that resulted in you being the SIO. Other months they would come in one after the other until you felt yourself going under and drowning in paperwork. Despite this our section had an excellent track record with regards to bringing our serious or fatal investigations to successful prosecutions at court. In my time on the department as an SIO we never lost a prosecution and only had one fail to stop collision that we never located the driver for. However getting out of the office for a short period of patrol work was a must if you valued your sanity.

We didn't have enough roads policing supervisors to cover all the shifts so we would take it in turns to be on call for the night duty period. This effectively meant that you would work your eight hour shift on a late turn and then be on call out from home between midnight and 4am; the guy who was on the early turn would then be the next person to be called out for the next four hours until he started his shift. This provided cover for the whole county and not just our area. You didn't get paid for this service unless you got a phone call and then the overtime clock started ticking.

Quite often I would book off duty but remain in the office for a couple hours, catching up on reports and files, as it was a quiet time and I found I could get far more done without being disturbed with the day to day crap that infested the job. I didn't get paid but at least I slept better knowing that I didn't have a pile of shit to contend with on my desk the next day.

On this particular occasion I was sitting in the supervisors patrol car with the air conditioning on full blast (a luxury we didn't have in the office) and I was updating my time and motion study card. The Government had decreed that we should account for every fifteen minutes of our day on a time sheet for a three week period. Virtually everything you did had to be cross linked to something else such as: 'working in the office' 'paperwork' 'fatal RTC enquiries', the card looked like a bloody pools coupon by the end of the day. Just how this was making us more efficient I did not know.

They took ages to complete and then every card had to be checked by some poor sod for accuracy (for our department this was me) before they could be submitted to the divisional administrator. Due to the complexities of the card, officers were making mistakes and at the end of the three week period they would have to be sifted through again to make sure they all met an acceptable standard. All because some bright spark (obviously not someone who had ever had to complete one or check the bloody things) had decided that they would set a 90% accuracy standard.

This put all the divisional commanders into a panic and the whole process became a pissing contest between these high ranking officers who should have known better. It was all about one-upmanship and getting themselves noticed for having the best returns.

I had a personal interest in all this as I was going to be the poor sod doing the second lot of checking and would end up spending days acting like a human scanning machine, running my eyes over the cards looking for obvious mistakes. We were doing this three or four times a year and I can't recall any useful action ever being taken by the Government to redress some of the more obvious activities that were eating into officers' time.

Paperwork accounted for a huge chunk of activity and as most of it had to be completed on the IT system officers were desk bound. Another huge problem I noticed was that officers were not taking meal breaks and were forced to eat their lunch or meal on the hoof. This meant that in real terms they had no down time at all during their shift. The amount of unpaid hours being worked was also phenomenal and it didn't take Einstein to work out that the job was running on the good will of the workers.

However when all these facts were spewed out by the computer the Government conveniently chose to ignore them.

***

With one eye on the dark ribbon of road close to where I was parked and the other on the time cards I was checking I was slowly making headway through the last few days' worth of activities. I hated this job but even I had to admit that I was extremely good at it. Having done it so many times over the past couple of years my mind had become a barcode reader and I was surprised that I didn't go beep every time I completed a scan.

I was disturbed from my work by the sound of a high revving engine approaching. It wasn't the tone of an engine designed to work hard, some thoroughbred horsepower harnessed for the track or the autobahn. As the strangled engine note grew louder a white Citroen van came hammering past the junction I was sitting beside at full tilt; the driver clearly wringing the nuts off the old engine. This could be fun I thought as I slipped out of the junction and followed the oily black vapour trail the vehicle was leaving. I picked up my speed and caught up to a distance where I was close enough to be able to conduct an accurate follow check.

Using the Vascar equipment in the car I ran several checks which confirmed what I had already reasoned...the driver was in a fucking big hurry to get somewhere. My intention was to make sure that it wasn't the morgue. The driver was getting a staggering amount of speed out of his vehicle bearing in mind the make and model and the smoke was billowing out behind it like a Red Arrows flyby. I could smell the burnt oil as it was sucked through my vehicles air vents.

When I eventually stopped the van the driver tried to kill the ignition but the engine continued to overrun for several minutes; wheezing like a knackered racehorse as it coughed and spluttered to a standstill. He stood next to his vehicle, the heat being generated from under the bonnet making it uncomfortable for him to stand too close.

The driver was quite pragmatic, "I'm glad in a way that you've stopped me; I would probably have ended up killing myself".

His car was still coughing and a trickle of water was pooling underneath the radiator, "Well it sounds like you've probably killed your van" I said nodding at the wet tarmac.

The young man thrust his hands in his pockets "What was I doing?" he asked.

"About three miles to a pint of oil I should think judging by the plume of smoke you were trailing" I replied. I was still making up my mind as to what to do with him so I didn't want to start discussing numbers in relation to his speed. Up to twenty five miles per hour over the limit and I could issue a Fixed Penalty Notice, beyond that it was a case of reporting the lad for summons.

He clarified his question, "Don't you have to tell me what my speed was?"

I gave myself a couple of extra moments to weigh up the circumstances and what action I was going to take. "This isn't Top Gear, I'm not Jeremy Clarkson, you're not the Stig and there's no leader board". Despite some of the speed checks putting him in the 'report for summons' category, there were also a couple that would be suitable for a FPN.

He laughed at my joke and shrugged, "Well whatever it is you've got me fair and square, I don't know what the speedo was saying as I didn't dare look down".

"I should think it was saying 'for fuck sake slow down'!" I ventured. The lad had taken it in good part and thrown his hands up so I decided that I would make things a bit easier for him and go for the Fixed Penalty Notice. He was going to get points and a fine but it would be a lot less punishment than if he had to go to court. His driving hadn't been dangerous, the roads had been empty and I felt sure that the ticket would be enough of a reminder for him to watch his speed in the future.

"I suppose technically this is all my girlfriends fault" he said, resigned to the fact that he was in trouble.

I rechecked the vehicle and he was the only occupant. "How is this your girlfriends fault?"

The lad withdrew his hand from his pocket and showed me his mobile phone, "She sent me this". He turned the screen so I could see the image of a young ladies naked nether region with the caption *'If you want some of this you'd better get here now. I'm wet and horny'*.

It was the first time anyone had shown me a picture of their naked girlfriend to get them off a speeding ticket. I have had plenty of women try undoing their blouse buttons or hoisting up their skirts, but never anything quite as graphic as this before. "Where the hell was your girlfriend when she sent this?" I asked.

"She's in a club in Norwich".

"Where were you when you received the message?"

"Kings Lynn".

I checked the time of the message and did some mental arithmetic; the speed of the Citroen had been excessive throughout the entire journey. "If I was you I would give her a call and tell her the only thing that's getting fucked tonight is your engine".

The lad listened balefully to the ticking of his engine as it spewed out the remaining coolant "Yeah I think you're probably right".

I can definitely confirm that he got a FPN but I can't vouch for him having got his leg over that night. Especially if he told her that he had generously shared her text with the sergeant who had stopped him.

Authors' Note

I would normally put the author's dedication at the front of the book but I thought that I would take advantage of the fact that if you have read this far you would probably be prepared to give me the benefit of the doubt for another couple of minutes.

This book is dedicated to those officers who went to work and never came home.

To those who went to work and never came home the same.

And to those who see their loved ones off to work every day wondering if they will come back home safe.

For those of you out there doing it...remember; don't treat the joke as a job!

I would also personally like to thank the charity 'Care of Police Survivors' (COPS) for all the work they do for the 'police family' behind the scenes. Supporting the families of police officers who lost their lives on duty.

Anyone wishing to learn more about the charity can visit them at www.ukcops.org

Also by this author

The Wrong Conclusions

Hilarious tale of what can happen when everyone jumps to the wrong conclusion...and then just keeps on jumping. Her public row with her ex-boss and lover, Tony Tagger MP has left Jasmine angry and worried. Somewhere during the argument there had been some confusion over a document that she had been mistakenly given. Tagger had threatened her with an MI5 investigation as he thought she had taken a copy.
Whilst having a quiet beer in the pub, Gerald 'Slimy' Copeman overhears this conversation and he believes that he can take advantage of the situation. The out of work and unscrupulous private investigator contacts the shady boss of a national newspaper with his suspicions and a covert (and deniable) investigation is launched.
Jake is a young and naïve reporter assigned the task of working with Slimy on the investigation, unaware that he has been chosen because he is expendable.
Jasmine has started to fear that she is being watched by MI5 and given the chance to get away from it all she is persuaded to drive her grandfather's motorhome to Spain, unaware of the reporter and investigator who are now following her.

Printed in Germany
by Amazon Distribution
GmbH, Leipzig